The Conquistador
with His Pants Down

Other Books by David Ramsay Steele

The Mystery of Fascism: David Ramsay Steele's Greatest Hits (2019)

Orwell Your Orwell: A Worldview on the Slab (2017)

Therapy Breakthrough: Why Some Psychotherapies Work Better than Others
(with Michael R. Edelstein and Richard K. Kujoth, 2013)

Atheism Explained: From Folly to Philosophy (2008)

Three Minute Therapy: Change Your Thinking, Change Your Life
(with Michael R. Edelstein, 1997; second edition 2019)

*From Marx to Mises: Post-Capitalist Society
and the Challenge of Economic Calculation* (1992)

The Conquistador with His Pants Down

David Ramsay Steele's
Legendary Lost Lectures

DAVID RAMSAY STEELE

ST. AUGUSTINE'S PRESS
South Bend, Indiana

Manufactured in the United States of America.

1 2 3 4 5 6   29 28 27 26 25 24

Library of Congress Control Number: 2023945739

Paperback ISBN: 978-1-58731-141-3
Ebook ISBN: 978-1-58731-142-0

∞ The paper used in this publication meets the minimum
requirements of the American National Standard for Information Sciences –
Permanence of Paper for Printed Materials, ANSI Z39.48-1984.

St. Augustine's Press
www.staugustine.net

In loving memory of David McDonagh. If I'd suspected I might outlive him, I would have exploited his mind more ruthlessly.

Cet animal est très méchant. Quand on l'attaque, il se défend.

CONTENTS

PREFACE

Most of these pieces have never been published before and some of them have been published only in obscure places; nearly all of them had their origins in talks I have given, usually several times with modifications, often to tiny groups of libertarians, sometimes to slightly bigger and more diverse audiences.

As a writer, I have always been concerned about explaining the most technical points as clearly as possible. The order of the chapters here is only very loosely chronological. I have departed from a chronological presentation, mostly to make it so that the level of challenge rises with each chapter, thus the earlier chapters should generally be the more comfortable to slip into.

Don't get me wrong. Every chapter is a barrel of laughs. But if you happen to be a cognitively challenged six-year-old or ninety-six-year-old, your best bet is to begin at the beginning and proceed straightforwardly to the end. (If you're the ninety-six year old, you might keep on forgetting how far you've read and repeatedly start at the beginning again. This is what we call eternal bliss.)

I owe big thanks to Benjamin Fingerhut of St. Augustine's Press for taking an interest in this collection, as a sequel to *The Mystery of Fascism: David Ramsay Steele's Greatest Hits* (2019), even though that didn't make him or me a billionaire. Perhaps this one will do the trick, or maybe markets aren't really as efficient as Eugene Fama claimed.

I also express my thanks to those who have given their criticisms of parts of this volume: David Gordon, Ray Scott Percival, Barry Smith, and Sandra Woien.

1

THE CONQUISTADOR WITH HIS PANTS DOWN

> I am not really a man of science, not an observer, not an experimenter, and not a thinker. I am by temperament nothing but a conquistador—an adventurer, if you want to translate the word—with the curiosity, the boldness, and the tenacity that belongs to that type of being.
>
> —Sigmund Freud to Wilhelm Fliess

For almost a century after Freud first announced his theories to the world, even his harshest critics accepted that he was honest, responsible, and at least fairly scrupulous by the standards of his day. But since the 1970s, several scholars have closely scrutinized Freud's work and a very different picture has emerged.

We now know that Freud was habitually untruthful: his accounts of his cases are routinely distorted and in large part fabricated, and so are his reports on how he developed his theories. Where the accounts are not demonstrably false, they are often cunningly worded to give a misleading impression. Freud also sometimes behaved in an ungentlemanly manner and caused needless suffering to his clients in order to further his own ambitions.

The Case of the Anguished Addict (1880–1882)

"Anna O." was treated by Breuer, not Freud, and Freud broke with Breuer before inventing psychoanalysis. Yet Freud always referred to Anna O. as the key case which led to the founding of psychoanalysis. It supposedly showed that people with emotional problems are "suffering from reminiscences." Their suffering is due to buried memories of past events, and can be dispelled by recovering those memories and reliving them.

Why should we accept this theory? Because (says Freud) it works. And how do we know it works? Why, because of a whole string of cases where the "patients" were speedily "cured" by recovering those lost memories. And the first of these is the case of Anna O., whose symptoms, Breuer tells us, were quickly and completely eliminated once she had recalled and relived the traumatic event which started it all.

We now know that the story of Anna O., as originally reported by Breuer and as elaborated by Freud and later psychoanalysts, is a tissue of falsehoods. The patient had serious problems for years after the date of the supposed complete cure, and was committed to a sanatorium for treatment.

Anna O.'s problems were varied, bizarre, and complex. They included (on different occasions in the period 1880–82) being unable to speak her native tongue (German) and only able to communicate in a foreign language (English), being unable to drink water, even though tortured by thirst, having episodes of "*absence*" (pronounced the French way), as though unconscious. The evidence suggests that some of these symptoms were deliberate play-acting. But Anna O. did have real problems, including addiction to the morphine and side-effects of the chloral hydrate both prescribed by Dr. Breuer. This drug dependency, along with other relevant facts, was never mentioned in Breuer's and Freud's subsequent accounts of the case.

Some years later, Anna O., whose actual name was Bertha Pappenheim, became a prominent advocate for social work and feminism. She was hostile to psychoanalysis. Freud would be aware that he could count on the fact that she had no incentive to blow the whistle on the myth of Anna O., because this would expose intimate details of her private life to public scrutiny and probably destroy her career.[1]

The Case of the Bleeding Virgin (1892–1895)

The early case of Emma Eckstein is worth mentioning even though it predates the invention of psychoanalysis in its classical form. At this time, Freud (having fallen out with Breuer) was very much under the influence of his friend Wilhelm Fliess, who believed that abdominal

1   Borch-Jacobsen 1996; Webster 1995, pp. 105–135.

diseases in women are related to the nose. Women's diseases could therefore be cured by treating the patient's nose, either by surgically removing part of it or by applying the miraculous new tonic, cocaine, to the inside of the nose.

Application of cocaine to the nasal passage will indeed ameliorate pains such as menstrual cramps and stomach aches, but this is now known to be due to the direct effect of cocaine upon the brain and can be achieved equally well by injecting cocaine into a vein in an arm or a leg. There is some connection between the nose and the genitals but Fliess misconceived and exaggerated it.

Emma Eckstein's symptoms included both menstrual and gastric pains. Under Fliess's influence, Freud viewed her as a case of "nasal reflex neurosis," and arranged for Fliess to operate on her nose. As a result of this operation, she suffered several severe bouts of bleeding, coming close to death on two occasions. In these emergencies, Freud had to call in consultants, one of whom found that the incompetent Fliess had left a half-meter of gauze in her nose. A second operation had to be performed to remedy the life-threatening effects of the first.

Following this fiasco, Freud continued to treat Fraülein Eckstein, in conformity with Fliess's theories, for another two years. He then wrote to his friend Fliess to communicate his remarkable discovery: Fliess had been right all along. Her symptoms were hysterical, and were caused by her love for Fliess. "She bled out of *longing*," Freud informed Fliess.[2] Subsequently Emma's love for Fliess became transferred to Freud, or so Freud believed. Her hemorrhages, Freud decided, were caused by her wishes, specifically the wish to be loved by her doctor.

Despite being left permanently disfigured and in continual ill-health by Fliess's surgeries, Eckstein became a convert to psychoanalysis and a practicing analyst herself. This early case illustrates a number of Freudian themes. Freud was an enthusiastic proponent of the use of cocaine, the new wonder drug, for himself, his fiancée, and his patients. Some commentators have attributed his worsening delusions and dishonesty to the after-effects of this drug habit. Freud was already assuming that symptoms must have symbolic meanings, and that these meanings must nearly

2   Masson 1984, p. 186.

always be sexual. He saw symptoms as symbolic wishes, and he saw the wishes as unconscious sexual urges arising in infancy. Freud was already ignoring facts that appeared to go against his theories and manufacturing bogus "clinical facts" which confirmed them. He was already exhibiting callousness and lack of compassion toward his patients, seeing them as mere fodder for his own theories and his own career. He was already convinced that all his female patients were unconsciously in love with him.

The Child Seduction Episodes (1896–1897)

In 1896, Freud announced to the world that he had made a great discovery. All "neuroses" (emotional problems) are caused by sexual encounters in childhood. Freud referred to these experiences as "seduction." He claimed that every one of his own neurotic patients had had such experiences. In 1897, Freud abandoned this theory and replaced it with the new theory that the supposed sexual experiences in childhood had not really happened, but represented the children's phantasies,[3] the fulfillment of their unconscious wishes. This change in Freud's theory led to the creation of psychoanalysis. According to the once-standard historical narrative, relying on Freud's own later accounts, Freud listened to stories of childhood seduction, recalled by his adult patients, and at first believed them; later he came to see that these lurid and shocking tales had to be false.

> ... almost all my women patients told me that they had been seduced by their father. I was driven to recognise in the end that these reports were untrue ... (Freud 1958, Volume XXII, p. 10)

And so, Freud implied, he had developed the basic concepts of psychoanalysis in order to explain why his clients would unconsciously invent these stories and come to believe them.

3   The spelling "phantasies" refers to unconscious processes, while "fantasies" are conscious thought processes, though this psychoanalytic terminology was not always consistently adhered to.

Eighty-seven years later, in 1984, Jeffrey Masson gratified feminists and annoyed Freudians by publishing *The Assault on Truth*. Here Masson argued that the stories of seduction told to Freud by his clients were true, and that by originating the theory that these stories were wishful phantasies, Freud had taken part in suppression of the truth that there was and is widespread sexual molestation of children.

Masson's interpretation was eagerly taken up by many feminists, and this helped to prepare the climate of opinion for the appalling "recovered memories" witch-hunt of entirely innocent people in the 1980s and 1990s.

Close study of the records, however, demonstrates that Masson and his feminist followers are just as hopelessly wrong as the Freudians. The simple fact is that *there never were any stories of molestation in childhood, or of any other sexual experiences in childhood,* reported to Freud by his patients.

Freud himself made up these accounts. They were Freud's surmises as to what lay behind his patients' symptoms. Having informed his patients that these scenes had occurred, Freud then worked hard to convince them of this. Just how often he succeeded in convincing them is unclear. What is not unclear is that every one of them at first strongly and sincerely denied that anything like this had happened to them.

The Manufacture of Reminiscences

How do we know this? We can compare what Freud wrote about these patients at the time, or shortly afterwards, with what he wrote about the same patients later. In the earlier references, Freud repeatedly states that the "primal scenes" of infant sex are inferred or constructed by the analyst and that the patient remembers nothing of them. The analyst then tries forcefully to convince the patient, who "resists" this information because her unconscious knows that it's true. Even when the analyst succeeds in getting the patient to acknowledge that the sexual scene "must" have occurred, the patient fails to recall it.

As the years passed, Freud gradually changed the words he used to refer to these cases, so that it appeared as though the patients had actually remembered these scenes and recounted them to the astonished doctor.

A further twist is that in the earlier versions of these case histories, Freud states that the other individuals involved in these early sexual experiences are siblings, playmates, teachers, strangers, governesses, or other servants. Parents are not mentioned, not once. It was only later, when Freud had come up with his theory of the universal Oedipus Complex, that these siblings, playmates, teachers, strangers, or servants were retrospectively transformed into fathers.[4]

Actually, any person of normal common sense, uninfluenced by the hoopla about Freud the "great discoverer," would wonder why at a certain stage in Freud's career, every single one of his clients told him stories of infant sex with parents, whereas subsequently in Freud's career, and in the clinical experience of therapists ever since, such stories are not at all common.[5] The story that Freud's patients had told him they had been seduced by their fathers was useful for his fable about the invention of psychoanalysis, but having performed this service, it was forgotten.

And there's something else, staring us in the face all the time, like the blatant contradictions in the *Bible* and the *Quran*. If Freud's patients had indeed spontaneously volunteered stories of molestation in infancy, as his later accounts implied, then the patients could not have repressed these memories, and so, according to Freud's own theory, these memories could not possibly have had anything to do with the patients' emotional problems as adults. For these patients' cases to have any relevance for Freud's theory, it just has to be the case that the patients could not recall anything of the experiences, and would sincerely protest that they had never happened. And that is precisely what Freud reports in his *earliest* accounts of these cases.

4   For details see Esterson 1993, pp. 11–31.
5   I refer to spontaneous recollections of molestation in the first few years of life. "Recollections" conjured up after much coaching, or genuine recollections of sexual encounters later in childhood, are not so rare. Freud saw memories of seduction in later childhood as "screen memories," created by the unconscious to disguise the true source of disturbance, which must always lie in the first six years. Masson would have had a point if he had simply claimed that occasionally a real case of child abuse is neglected because of the Freudian prejudice that the child's recollection must be merely a screen memory.

It does not necessarily follow that Freud was nothing more than a cold-blooded liar. If we observe that twelve-year-old Tommy always blushes when he meets Mary, we might say that by his blushes, Tommy is "telling us" that he is in love with Mary. If we observe our opponent across the poker table making a big raise before the flop, we might say he is "telling us" he has a pair of aces. This usage of the verb "tell" is metaphorical. To be strictly literal, neither Tommy nor the poker player are telling us anything. In the strictly literal sense, Freud's clients never told him they had been seduced in infancy by their parents or anyone else. Freud's inferences were characteristically far-fetched, and yet he had such confidence in them that he might have thought of them as information his patients were figuratively "telling" him.

Similarly, when Freud at first reported that his patients had told him they had been seduced by siblings, playmates, teachers, strangers, and servants—but never fathers—and then later reported that the same patients had told him that these same seductions had all been perpetrated by their fathers, he was not necessarily engaging in willful fabrication.

What the patients had "told" Freud was never what they literally said, but the interpretation he had put on their "symptoms." First he had a theory that things said by patients that had nothing to do with early sexual experiences were unintentionally "telling" him they had had sexual relations with persons other than parents, then later he had a theory that the very same things said by the same patients were unintentionally "telling" him they had had sex with their parents.

But didn't Freud's patients actually relive the seductions? Didn't they recall them and re-experience them with much display of emotion? Actually, although this was the announced goal of Freud's treatment, it isn't clear how many of them did, or whether any of them did. We know that Freud not only reported cures where there was no cure, but also reported cases as completed when they were still going on. But those, if any, of Freud's early patients who did relive their infantile sexual experiences were "reliving" what Freud had energetically persuaded them had occurred—and this was quite different from the phantasies he imputed to them years later.

So it's not simply that Freud thought that something had occurred and later thought that this same thing had been imagined to occur. The very essence of what had supposedly occurred or been imagined changed completely. Many of the supposed early experiences recalled in the seduction theory period were with other children. Freud's theory in 1896 is that most people do not experience premature sexual arousal, but in those few who do, it can cause neuroses in later life. Sexual arousal in infancy—nothing to do with the children's fathers—caused adult neuroses.

His later theory, developed over several years beginning in 1897, is that everyone without exception has early phantasies of sex with their mothers (which in girls switches to fathers around the age of five, when girls unconsciously realize that they have been castrated). Most people somehow work through these phantasies, but sometimes something goes wrong, and these people become neurotic. The culprit in causing adult emotional problems is no longer premature sexual arousal, but incest guilt, something Freud hadn't thought of at the time of the seduction theory.

Dishonesty or Delusion?

When Freud abandoned the seduction theory in 1897 (though he kept quiet about this change of mind for several years), he continued to maintain that sexual upsets in childhood were at the root of all neuroses, but now he concluded that the seduction episodes *he had surmised* were not real events but products of his patient's wishful phantasies. The patients had not really been seduced, but had phantasized their seduction because of their own sexual desires. And since these episodes were constructed by Freud according to his theoretical convictions, he was free to change them retrospectively.

Thus, what Freud thought in 1900 that his 1896 patients had "told" him was quite different from what he thought in 1896 that they had "told" him, and was somewhat different from what he thought in the 1920s they had "told" him in 1896.

Freud's standard procedure in 1895–96 was that he would tell his patients they should recall a picture or an idea. When they told Freud what they were thinking, Freud would tell them that this referred to their being seduced in infancy.

Freud would watch their facial expressions, and any signs of alarm or disbelief would be greeted as proof that Freud's surmise (always the same surmise) was accurate. From the beginning, the stories of sexual experiences in childhood were composed by Freud, who then worked hard to convince the patients that these things had happened to them.

Instead of being simply a liar and con artist, Freud may have also been both seriously deluded and prone to a loose metaphorical way of talking.[6] At the same time, Freud must have known that some of his statements were factually misleading. His line of misrepresentation may be similar to that of the spirit medium who sincerely believes that she can channel spirits, but is also prepared to fake spirit manifestations in the good cause of convincing skeptics.

The fact that Freud's patients did not literally tell him that they had been seduced in childhood puts in a somewhat different light one of Freud's characteristic rhetorical tricks. Freud is a highly adroit persuasive writer. One of his effective ploys is to denigrate himself in a way that adds to his credibility and gains the reader's sympathy. In recounting the fable of the origin of psychoanalysis, Freud draws attention to his simple innocence in believing what his patients had "told" him:

> If the reader feels inclined to shake his head at my credulity,
> I cannot altogether blame him.

This works upon the reader's mind quite skillfully: it suggests that Freud is a direct, straightforward sort of fellow, inclined to take people at their word. It also suggests that he is humble, in that he is ready to admit past faults and that he is open to changing his theory if the facts dictate it. These suggestions are the very opposite of the truth. However, more than anything else, this device diverts attention from the remarkable claim that all of Freud's early patients had told him they had been seduced in infancy, causing the reader to overlook the possibility that these seductions had been made up by Freud, who then endeavored to browbeat his patients into accepting that these products of his own imagination were real.

Why did Freud abandon the seduction theory? As Cioffi shows, Freud gave several different reasons for its abandonment, reasons which

6   On the issue of the extent to which Freud was consciously dishonest, see Cioffi 1999, pp. 199–204. Cioffi attributes much of Freud's misrepresentations to his unusually fallible memory.

both contradict each other and contradict the evidence.[7] The simplest explanation is that no one believed the seduction theory, so advocacy of this theory was not helping his career prospects. When he abandoned the seduction theory, Freud also abandoned much else. During the period 1896–1899, Freud's theories were transformed, leading to psychoanalysis as we know it. The main aspects of this transformation were:

1. From an approach of fiercely browbeating the patient to an approach of free association, apparently allowing the patient's thoughts to roam, though actually guiding them in a predetermined direction.
2. From the claim that all adult neurotics have been prematurely sexually awakened in early childhood (but most people haven't) to the claim that everyone is always sexually awakened in early childhood.
3. From the claim that decisive early sexual experiences are real to the claim that they are unconscious phantasies.
4. From the claim that early sexual experiences have nothing necessarily to do with parents to the claim that the phantasized experiences are always about parents.
5. From no mention of dreams to the reliance on dream interpretation, and the interpretation of everything else in the patient's life in terms of dream symbols.

What remains constant is Freud's unswerving determination to find the origin of all neuroses in early childhood sex. He's convinced that this is the great breakthrough which will bring him fame and fortune. He's casting around for a convincing story to present this finding, and for a theory which will be immune to any possible objection from the ranks of unbelievers.

The Case of the Deep-Throat Daughter (1901)

The case of "Dora" is the first of the most famous landmark cases in Freud's career. We now know the patient's real name: Ida Bauer.

7   Cioffi, pp. 240–48.

The "Dora" case has been hashed over interminably in numerous works on psychoanalysis, and Freud's own narrative[8] is considered one of his masterworks. We do not need to give a complete account here. But some aspects of this case are useful to illustrate Freud's method.[9]

The eighteen-year-old Ida was sent to Freud by her father. She had physical symptoms, including shortness of breath and a persistent cough, all of which were assumed to be "hysterical." She was also found to be depressed and suffering from "hysterical unsociability."

Ida explained to Freud that she felt uncomfortable because her father was having an affair with "Frau K.," the wife of a close family friend, "Herr K." Herr K. had made sexual advances to Ida since she was fourteen, and was now pressing his attentions on her again. Ida explained that she felt that her father, Herr Bauer, found this convenient, since it preoccupied Herr K. and left Herr Bauer a free hand to pursue his affair with Frau K. Ida had complained to her father about Herr K.'s attentions, so he sent her to Freud to be analyzed and thus disciplined.

Freud brushed aside Ida's assertions about the motives of her father who was, after all, paying Freud's fee. Freud saw Ida's rejection of Herr K. as a neurotic symptom, and throughout his exchanges with Ida, Freud tried to convince her that she was really in love with Herr K. and was duty-bound to yield him sexual favors. Any hesitation in so doing could only be a symptom of her "illness." Freud explained her symptoms in his usual facile and farfetched way. His explanation for Ida's cough, for example, was that she harbored the unconscious desire to give Herr K. oral sex.

By analyzing one of Ida's dreams, Freud inferred that she had wet the bed at an unusually late age, and that this was because she had masturbated in early childhood. Ida denied this, but Freud later observed that she was playing with a small purse[10] which she wore at her waist. This purse, says Freud was nothing but a representation of the genitals,

8 Freud 1958, Volume VII, pp. 1–122.
9 More detailed analyses of all the cases we describe in this chapter are given in Esterson.
10 The word used for this purse is "reticule," a word which is now somewhat obsolete and unfamiliar to many people.

and her playing with it, her opening it and putting her finger in it, "was an entirely unembarrassed yet unmistakable pantomimic announcement of what she would like to do with them—namely to masturbate."[11]

He described this behavior of toying with her purse as Ida's "admission" of the masturbation and bed-wetting, an example of Freud's misleading use of language to suggest that his patients had literally asserted something when in fact they had done nothing of the kind. In any case, bed-wetting has nothing to do with masturbation. Freud knew less about sex than any farmer's wife. And fiddling with things has nothing to do with masturbation. Poker players, for example, often play with their chips. This does not represent masturbation. Ida's sessions with Freud lasted eighteen months, after which she broke off the treatment. Freud regretted that he had not been able to persuade her to give in to Herr K.

Why could Freud never convince Ida of any of his theories, and why did she break off the analysis? To account for this, Freud applied his theory of "transference," by which psychoanalyzed patients would transfer their feelings onto the analyst, in this case Freud himself. The patient's irritation with the analyst could be explained as an expression of the patient's unconscious love for the analyst. If the patient developed a crush on the analyst, this too would prove that the patient loved the analyst. See?

Freud maintained that Ida was in love with Herr K., an emotion which stemmed from her repressed desire to have sex with her father. In Freud's judgment Ida's love for Herr K. eventually became transformed into a love for Freud. When Ida had a dream about smoke, Freud concluded that this proved that Ida was unconsciously hankering for a kiss from Freud himself, who habitually smoked cigars.

The Case of the Obsessive Officer (1907)

In this brief chapter we do not mention all of Freud's famous cases, though they all provide evidence of factual misrepresentation.

The case of the Rat Man (1907) is particularly revealing. Freud nearly always destroyed his original case notes; factual discrepancies in

11   Freud 1958, Volume VII, pp. 76–77.

his reports of his cases are usually found by comparing his first written-up account of a case with its later embellishments. In the case of the Rat Man, however, part of the original case notes somehow survived. Not surprisingly, in view of Freud's habitual flexibility with facts, there are distortions even in his first account of the case, when compared with the original notes.

The Rat Man, whose name was Ernst Lanzer,[12] came to Freud complaining of obsessive fears and compulsive influences. Lanzer had heard from a fellow army officer a vivid story of a Chinese torture, in which a hungry rat was induced to eat its way into the rectum of the torture victim (the other torture victim, if you count the poor rat). Among Lanzer's obsessive thoughts was repeatedly imagining his father and his fiancée subjected to this form of torture (even though the father had been dead for some years).

Lanzer free-associated on the word *Ratten* (German for "rats"), and came up with *Raten* ("installments"), and *Spielratte* ("gaming rat"), a slang term for a habitual or reckless gambler. Lanzer also talked of marrying (in German, *heiraten*) his girl-friend. Lanzer's father had indeed been a gambler. Freud also elicited that in his childhood Lanzer had once been punished for biting someone.

Putting this all together in his predictable way, and bringing in Freud's notion that children think of intercourse as occurring through the anus, Freud concluded that Lanzer unconsciously identified himself as a rat, having anal intercourse with his father and his girl-friend. This supposed phantasy of Lanzer's, dreamed up by Freud, stemmed from Lanzer's aggression against his father which arose, as we have by now come to expect, from the father having threatened Lanzer with castration.

In his study of this case,[13] Patrick Mahony, himself a psychoanalyst and admirer of Freud, found numerous inaccuracies and misleading omissions. Freud claimed he had treated Lanzer for over eleven months, which Mahony shows to be impossible. Freud manipulated the order of events to make a better story. For instance, Lanzer reported to Freud

---

12 Some writers say it was Paul Lorenz. Anyway, it's the same case we're talking about.

13 Mahony 1986.

that he would open the door of his apartment after midnight, apparently so that his father's ghost could enter, and then stare at Lanzer's penis. (Yes, there's no dispute that Lanzer was a tad eccentric.) When Freud wrote up the case, he stated that he had deduced from this information that Lanzer had once been punished by his father for masturbation. Freud's original notes show, however, that Freud came up with this theory about punishment for masturbation before he had heard the report of Lanzer's unusual nocturnal habit. In another example, Freud reported that Lanzer had begun to masturbate compulsively, shortly after his father's death—cause and effect in Freud's opinion. The notes show that Lanzer reported his commencement of masturbation as occurring two years after the father's death, and did not say that there was anything compulsive about it.

In this case, Freud made his usual mendacious claim of the patient's total recovery, when in fact a letter to Jung penned after his written version of the case history described Lanzer as still having problems.[14]

The Case of the Bewildered Boy (1909)

After seeing a horse fall down in the street, a little boy named Hans developed a fear of horses, and a fear of going out into the street (at this time, horses were as common in city streets as cars are today). Hans was analyzed by his father, who corresponded with Freud. The father was a convert to Freud's ideas and eager to find them instantiated in his son's behavior.

The analysis of Hans showed Hans's father that the boy's fear of horses arose from his sexual desire for his mother and murderous feelings towards his father. When Hans said on one occasion that he was frightened at those times when his father was not there, both the father and Freud interpreted this as the sure sign of a repressed wish for the father's death.

After being taken to the zoo, Hans showed fear of the big animals, especially the giraffes. Later he had a dream about two giraffes, a big one and a crumpled one. The interpretation composed by Hans's father was

---

14   Freud 1958, Volume IX, p. 155. See Mahony 1986 and the discussion in Esterson, pp. 62–67.

that the big giraffe was the father's penis and the crumpled giraffe was Hans's mother's vulva. Believe it or not, Freud applauded this interpretation as "penetrating"!

It's almost unnecessary to add that children may inherit a genetic predisposition to fear large animals, that Hans had witnessed a violent and disturbing accident involving a horse, and that any search for the origins of such a fear in his sexual desires is extraordinarily silly.

The Case of the Retentive Russian (1910–1914)

The case of the Wolf Man has often been hailed as one of the most brilliant, if not the most brilliant, of Freud's therapeutic achievements. It became Freud's most famous case, and was acclaimed by psychoanalysts as a showcase of the Freudian method. Unfortunately for psychoanalysis, the Wolf Man long outlived Freud, wrote his memoirs, and was later interviewed at length.

Sergei Pankeev[15] was treated by Freud for four and a half years, beginning in 1910. Central to Freud's analysis of Pankeev was his interpretation of a dream Pankeev recalled having had at the age of four. In the dream, Pankeev saw through the open window of his bedroom six or seven white dogs with big bushy tails, sitting on a large tree and facing the window. Pankeev screamed and woke up.

The following is Freud's interpretation. The dogs, which Freud chose to describe as wolves (why not?), represent Pankeev's parents: the number of the dogs being six or seven, instead of two, because Pankeev's unconscious is working hard to disguise the meaning of the dream. The fact that the dogs are perfectly still represents the opposite of stillness: violent motion, and therefore (wait for it . . .) sexual intercourse. The dogs' whiteness indicates bed linens. On the principle that objects often symbolize the opposite of what they seem to represent, the dogs' big tails refer to castration. That the dogs were staring at Pankeev indicates that Pankeev was staring at his parents.

15 Pankeev was Russian. His name is pronounced "Pan-kay-yeff." In some discussions of the Wolf Man case, his name is spelled according to the German transliteration, "Pankejeff."

From this, Freud deduced the following: at age one, Pankeev had watched his father and mother copulating doggy style, three times in succession, while Pankeev was so horrified to see this that he soiled himself. The little boy was able to see from this that his mother lacked a penis, and therefore concluded that she had lost it due to castration.

Freud was never able to convince Pankeev that this episode had occurred, and the sleeping arrangements in Pankeev's fairly wealthy household would not have permitted it. For a small child watching a copulating couple to be able to make the discovery that the woman has no penis is an observational feat that "would defy the ingenious staging of any pornographic film producer."[16] Pankeev later called Freud's interpretation "terribly far-fetched."[17] However this "primal scene" was the centerpiece of Freud's analysis. (Freud's own peculiar personal preoccupations recur in these cases: he had convinced himself late in life that he had seen his own parents copulating doggy-style, for example.)

When Freud planned to publish his account of the Wolf Man case (publication was delayed by the First World War), the psychoanalytic movement had to deal with criticisms from Alfred Adler and Carl Jung, both of whom had parted from Freud's movement and begun to recruit their own independent followings, and both of whom denied that sex was at the bottom[18] of all neuroses. It was essential to defend Freudism by "demonstrating" that the cause of all neuroses lies in early childhood sex. The Wolf Man case was therefore seen as a fine propaganda weapon against these deviationists.

Freud claimed in his 1918 case history that Sergei Pankeev had been completely cured. This was quite the opposite of the truth. Freud repeatedly claimed success in cases where it has been shown the facts were otherwise, and there is no proof that Freud ever had a real "success."

Pankeev outlived Freud by forty years, and remained prone to depression and obsessions for the rest of his life. His physical problems, which Freud pronounced to be hysterical and announced had been cured as the result of psychoanalysis, were actually genuine bodily ailments and

16   Mahony, p. 52.
17   Obholzer 1982, p. 35.
18   Sorry.

were never cured. Owing to mistreatment by a village doctor early in life, Pankeev could not empty his bowels normally, and always had to use enemas. This condition was diagnosed by Freud as due to repressed homosexuality, and Freud declared it had been cured. In fact it persisted until the end of Pankeev's life.[19]

Pankeev was made the prize exhibit of psychoanalysis, but he became an embarrassment because of his continuing physical and emotional problems. The head of organized psychoanalysis, Kurt Eissler, through the Freud Archives, sent Pankeev regular sums of money to enable him to pay off a former lady friend who was blackmailing him. At the same time, Eissler dissuaded Pankeev from emigrating to America, with its amber waves of well-to-do neurotics, where he might spill the beans about his dealings with psychoanalysis and his continuing problems. Eissler also tried to dissuade Pankeev from talking to Karin Obholzer, who eventually produced the book of interviews with him. She was able to secure Pankeev's agreement by promising him the interviews would not appear until after his death. In short, the facts about Pankeev were an embarrassment to psychoanalysis, so he was paid off to keep him quiet, but he rebelled somewhat against being silenced and communicated his real feelings to Obholzer for posterity. As Pankeev summarized it:

> In reality the whole thing looks like a catastrophe. I am in the same state as when I first came to Freud, and Freud is no more. (Obholzer 1982, pp. 171–72)

The Case of the Uncured Analyst (1921–1924)

Horace Frink, a handsome man who looked a bit like Frank Sinatra, was a well known figure in the American psychoanalytic movement, having published a popular book on psychoanalysis, *Morbid Fears and Compul-*

---

19 Pankeev wrote his memoirs (Gardiner 1971) and was interviewed at length (Obholzer 1982). His recollections often contradict Freud's account, and in the few cases where it's possible to settle the matter, Pankeev is accurate and Freud inaccurate. There are also occasions where Freud gives different details at different times, the earlier ones being closer to Pankeev's account.

sions, in 1918. A practicing psychoanalyst, Frink had an affair for several years with one of his patients, the rich bank heiress and married woman Angelika Bijur. Freud became involved in February 1921, when Frink went to Vienna to undergo a training analysis with Freud. Frink idolized Freud and was eager to follow any of his suggestions.

Freud exhorted Frink to divorce his wife, and urged Bijur, who also became his patient, to divorce her husband. Freud even gave Bijur a signed photograph of himself with an inscription beginning "To Angie Frink," taking her future marriage to Frink for granted. Freud never met Bijur's husband or Frink's wife. It is clear from all the facts[20] that one of Freud's motives was to secure Angelika's financial fortune for the psychoanalytic movement.

Frink suffered from depression and hallucinations. Freud told Angelika Bijur that Frink was a latent homosexual who would turn into an outright homosexual and become seriously "ill" if she ended the affair. Frink himself "resisted" Freud's diagnosis of homosexuality, and expressed doubts about a long-term future with Angelika, who sometimes struck him as unattractive. Freud wrote to Frink in November 1921:

> May I still suggest to you that your idea Mrs. B had lost part of her beauty may be turned into her having lost part of her money.... Your complaint that you cannot grasp your homosexuality implies that you are not yet aware of your phantasy of making me a rich man. If matters turn out all right let us change this imaginary gift into a real contribution to the Psychoanalytic Funds. (Edmunds 1988, p. 45. Reprinted in Crews 1998, p. 270.)

The divorces and the marriage did occur as recommended by Freud. Freud pronounced Frink cured. While on his honeymoon, Frink, known to be Freud's protégé, was elected president of the New York Psychoanalytic Society. Both Bijur's husband and Frink's former wife were devastated, and both died shortly afterwards. Bijur's husband wrote an accusatory open letter to Freud which he planned to publish as an ad in

20 Edmunds 1988.

the New York newspapers, but fortunately for Freud, he died before he could carry out this intention.

Frink's emotional disturbances grew worse, and his new marriage quickly turned sour. In May 1924, Frink committed himself to the Phipps Psychiatric Clinic under the care of his former teacher, Adolf Meyer, the most eminent American psychiatrist at the time, who found Freud's involvement in the case "nauseating." Meyer had had some sympathies for psychoanalysis, but from now on became more firmly committed to the "biological" approach to psychiatry. (Nothing like Cognitive-Behavioral Therapy had yet come into existence.)

Angelika Bijur divorced Horace Frink, who became severely depressed and made repeated suicide attempts. He later expressed the view that he should never have left his first wife and that Freud had made serious mistakes. Frink resumed practicing as a psychoanalyst when his own mental problems had abated sufficiently.

Individuals who do foolish things because they rely on a persuasive and charismatic advisor must retain some responsibility for their own choice of that advisor. Still, four people's lives were made more wretched by Freud's self-promoting and self-serving intervention. And because Freud was also invariably obtuse and inept about the most elementary human interactions, his intervention was a botched job, even from his own egoistical and mercenary point of view.

Looking on the bright side, Angelika Bijur's fees made up the bulk of Dr. Freud's income for a couple of years, and a scandal which might have discredited psychoanalysis and thus imperiled Freud's subsequent income was narrowly averted. The evidence of Freud's bad behavior in the Frink case was successfully tidied away for seventy years.

References

Borch-Jacobsen, Mikkel. 1996. *Remembering Anna O.: A Century of Mystification. Routledge*.

Cioffi, Frank. 1999. *Freud and the Question of Pseudoscience*. Open Court.

Crews, Frederick, ed. 1998. *Unauthorized Freud: Doubters Confront a Legend*. Penguin.

Esterson, Allen. 1993. *Seductive Mirage: An Exploration of the Work of Sigmund Freud*. Open Court.

Freud, Sigmund. 1958 [1953]. *The Standard Edition of the Complete Psychological Works of Sigmund Freud*. 24 volumes. Hogarth.

Gardiner, Muriel, ed. 1971. *The Wolf Man and Sigmund Freud*. Basic Books.

Mahony, Patrick J. 1986. *Freud as a Writer*. International Universities Press.

Masson, Jeffrey Moussaieff. 1984. *The Assault on Truth: Freud's Suppression of the Seduction Theory*. Farrar, Straus, and Giroux.

Obholzer, Karin. 1982. *The Wolf-Man Sixty Years Later: Conversations with Freud's Controversial Patient*. Routledge.

Webster, Richard. 1995. *Why Freud Was Wrong: Sin, Science, and Psychoanalysis*. HarperCollins.

2

AN INCONCEIVABLY HUMBLE DEFENSE OF
THE INCONCEIVABLY HOLY BOOK

Excerpt from an address by the
Inconceivably Reverend Dr. Inigo Morningstar

Recovered and restored by the Inconceivably Wise
and Wonderfully Pious Dr. David Ramsay Steele

We have come a long way from the times when unbelievers and blas-
phemers were subjected to excruciating tortures, followed, after an adequate interval to aid in the process of self-examination, by death. I for
one do not want to return to those days, which are a blot upon the record
of the One True Faith, even though most of those excessively punished
richly deserved their severe treatment.

Yet occasionally, as a scholar with many hundreds of peer-reviewed
publications in respectable journals, I cannot help being exasperated almost beyond measure by the ignorance and sloppiness of our ultra-mod-
ern, excessively up-to-date, so-called skeptics.

The skeptical attack upon the Sacred Scripture began with seemingly
quite reasonable criticisms. It was difficult for broad-minded and com-
passionate persons to ignore these criticisms—even though some of
them were rather far-fetched, fanciful, and presumptuous in their claims
to privileged insight.

Let me begin by reviewing what is established fact, accepted by everyone except a few disturbed individuals who, whether they acknowledge
it or not, require the most pro-active kind of psychiatric help. The Sacred
Scripture was composed shortly before the Great Chill, which destroyed
an ancient civilization of which the Sacred Scripture was the final flower.

Traditionally, we have accepted the view—promulgated by many worthy authorities and substantiated by very solid Church traditions—that the Great Chill, a Divine punishment for unbelief and depravity, lasted for ten thousand years. Recently, some cocky young scholars have informed us that the Great Chill actually prevailed for more than one hundred thousand years!

Just how they can be so sure of that is a mystery to me. Were they there, during those one hundred thousand years? Were they writing down on parchment, every day for one hundred thousand years, "It is very cold and there is almost everywhere an ice sheet many miles deep"? I don't think so! These people call themselves skeptics and free inquirers, but they appear to be quite ready to swallow the most outlandish tales because they can make them agree with what they arrogantly call their "data." They scoff at faith but they want us to take a whole lot of their "science" on faith!

However, far be it from me to pick quarrels with leading voices in any scholarly discipline, however deluded by their own impious arrogance they may be. Let us therefore accept, for the sake of argument, the reckless and controversial hypothesis that the Great Chill prevailed for one hundred thousand years. What does it matter, after all? We are not giving up any essential item of our Holy Faith if we entertain this admittedly outlandish supposition.

These early critics of the Scripture started from the acknowledged fact that the Sacred Scripture was originally set down in the ancient language known as English. Some say it was American English, or the American dialect of English, though exactly what this means is impossible to fathom, since all the English writings that have come down to us appear to be in this so-called "American" dialect. Obviously, there are difficulties in re-animating this dead tongue, but those of us who are guided by faith willingly accept that the translation by Saint Fezzik of Keeto is divinely inspired and therefore authoritative. Keeto, a city on the Equator, and therefore never crushed under the ice, has been repeatedly conquered and reconquered over the past ten thousand years (or, if you are determined to be fancifully "modern," one hundred thousand years), and yet various copies of the authorized translation of the original have most providentially been preserved.

Scriptural criticism began with attempts to reconstruct the original text. Though it appears that the ancient speakers of the inconceivably strange tongue known as "English" had developed the art of printing, only rediscovered many centuries after the Great Melt, the versions of the Sacred Scripture that have come down to us are all copied by hand, some in English and some in now-obsolete dialects of languages still living. Since there were variants in the manuscripts, choices had to be made by our Holy Mother Church, and it was at first agreed that these choices should be made according to spiritual inspiration. Gradually, however, the point of view prevailed that, while inspiration and a general sense of decency and fitness should be the overriding considerations, there were cases where it could be demonstrated that quite arbitrary constructions had been incorporated because of innovations by comparatively recent scribes.

It was argued that if the Sacred Scriptures are to be respected and followed, it must be because of their original form and not because of recent improvisations or mistakes. So the argument for finding the earliest and most authentic versions was eventually accepted. Some holy scholars persisted in maintaining for many years that even accidental or incompetent changes by scribes were guided by the omnipotent Divine power, and I still think this thesis might have had much to recommend it, but it gradually lost influence and was eventually condemned by the Church, so that in all humility and obedience I must reject it without reservation.

The Insidious Corruption Spreads

No sooner had this principle won the day, than there appeared something called the Higher Criticism. The Higher Critics argued that in order to restore the original and perfect text, it was necessary not only to compare one manuscript with another but also to look for obscurities, improbabilities, and even discrepancies within the meaning of the text.

Dr. Swinkel, in *The Quest of the Historical Man in Black*, looked closely at the scriptural report of the appearance in Florin of the Man in Black. Dr. Swinkel decided, purely as an exercise in hypothetical reasoning, as he claimed at the time, to approach various episodes in the Divine Text as though they were ordinary historical sources.

Dr. Swinkel argued that wearing a mask would not make the wearer inconspicuous but rather quite unusually conspicuous, and therefore an object of suspicion. So here, he claimed, is something perplexing in the narrative, if it be treated (merely as a heuristic exercise and without disrespect) as an ordinary historical source. He also concluded that there would be little point in wearing a mask unless someone would recognize the wearer's features. Yet who could have done so?

Taking the scriptural report at its word, the Masked Man is the current incumbent of the role of the Dread Pirate Roberts who, the Inconceivably Holy Text informs us, took no prisoners and whose name was passed on to a different individual from time to time—a procedure which relied for its effectiveness on the fact that no one would recognize the face of the Dread Pirate Roberts. Therefore, no one alive could possibly have recollected the features of the Man in Black, and therefore there could have been no possible reason to disguise those features. So here is something else quite puzzling for the reader of argumentative proclivity but little faith.

The truly devout did not trouble themselves with such morbidly pedantic reflections, because they knew that the Man in Black had a hidden purpose—to become a prisoner of Humperdinck and Rugen, so that he would undergo his Passion in the Zoo of Death, and thus pay the penalty for the sins of all believers. Ordinary calculations of immediate expediency would therefore never occur to the Divine Westley, his mind set implacably on his sacred mission.

Many other replies were offered to Dr. Swinkel's argument. Dr. Morgen made a strong case that the wearing of masks was quite common in Florin at the time, and would have aroused no suspicion. With breathtaking audacity, Dr. Swinkel countered that all the immense collected lore of Florin is a late development, compiled since the Great Melt under the influence of the Sacred Scripture, and although indisputably of intensely real spiritual meaning, has little direct connection with any historical information about the actual Florin in the days before the Great Chill.

But how could Dr. Swinkel be so sure that no genuine tradition from the actual Florin survived to influence the composition of the *Collected Florinese Lore*? Here, as always, it seems to me, the so-called skeptics do not apply their skepticism to their own pet theories which are, after all, merely their all-too-human inventions, and not comparable in weight of evidence to the mighty testimony of the Sacred Scripture, and the other sacred texts, hallowed over the centuries by the prayerful adherents of the One True Church!

Dr. Morgen pointed out that today we have numberless sacred festivals in which the faithful wear masks, in imitation of the Divine Westley, and reasoned that the influence of this contemporary practice, attended as it is by much sacred emotion, could be expected to exert an influence back through the millennia and thus condition the expectations of the Florinese in the scriptural period. But Dr. Swinkel's defenders artfully raised the ingenious objection that this argument would imply a closed time loop of a kind already condemned as heretical by the Church.

At any rate, Dr. Swinkel came back with the clever point that the Scripture itself indicates that some people found the wearing of a mask curious, and therefore plainly unusual.

The most disturbing novelty of Dr. Swinkel's approach was his account of the motives of the Man in Black. Dr. Swinkel did not, of course, dispute that the Man in Black came to Florin to undergo his passion in the Zoo of Death and thereby save all of suitably compliant humankind. But, Dr. Swinkel claimed, the Man in Black was under a spell of amnesia so that he did not know this was his mission, and had to rediscover it for himself. And what was his conscious motive for returning to Florin and seeking to liberate Princess Buttercup from the clutches of the vile Vizzini? Why, the purely fleshly motive of securing Princess Buttercup for one of his mating partners!

Freedom is all very well, but what if some degenerate individuals abuse freedom? Does not this turn freedom into slavery? And must we not therefore decline to tolerate those who abuse freedom? I would, with all tender love and solicitous compassion, advise Dr. Swinkel's disciples to watch their step!

Dr. Kwels took the wretched argument of Dr. Swinkel a miserable step farther. Dr. Kwels argued that although there could have been no point in disguising the features of the Dread Pirate Roberts (since no one alive in Florin could have recognized him), it was necessary for the Man in Black to wear a mask so that the Inconceivably Divine Buttercup would fail to recognize him. But this means, in the regrettably disrespectful terms of Dr. Kwels, that the reason for the mask was to make the story work, not because it really did happen. But in that case, the wearing of the mask might possibly have to be viewed as a fictional addition to the historical record.

Dr. Morgen, with his customary acuity, pointed out the obvious flaw in this reasoning. Although the Dread Pirate Roberts took no prisoners, this was merely his standard operating procedure. It is entirely possible that one of his prisoners managed to escape and that this escaped prisoner was Florinese. The Man in Black would have known this and would therefore have known that he might be recognized in Florin.

Dr. Earwing made the shrewd, and to my mind unanswerable, point that anything in the Sacred Scripture which appeared to be discreditable to the Divine Westley would never have been fabricated, because there could have been no motive for such a fabrication, which would embarrass the Church. Therefore anything in the scriptural account which is hard for faithless minds to grasp, because it seems to show Westley in an unfavorable light, has a high likelihood (by the standard methods of historiography) of being true. Consequently, anything seriously dubious about the Sacred Scripture proves it to be authentic.

Thus Dr. Earwing arrived at the deservedly famous Earwing Theorem, a masterpiece of the new science of Logic: Whatever is credible in the Holy Book must be true because it is credible. Whatever is incredible in the Holy Book must be true because the writers could have no conceivable motive for making it up. Therefore, everything in the Holy Book is true. Dr. Earing was quite deservedly awarded the Miracle Max Memorial Prize, which brings with it mating rights with one thousand females, for this masterly application of advanced Logic.

Set Pieces

After Swinkel and Kwels came the Form Critics. The Form Critics did not show the same ferocious disrespect as the egotistical and shamelessly ambitious Swinkel or the evidently unbalanced Kwels. They looked at the literary structure of the Sacred Scripture for clues as to the ways the accounts originated.

They held that the Sacred Scripture can naturally be broken down into various "set pieces." One set piece follows another. According to Form Criticism, the Sacred Scripture itself was compiled from pre-existing fragments, which represent the early Church's liturgical practices.

We can illustrate the method of the Form Critics by their analysis of the so-called "sword fight" between the Man in Black and the "Spaniard" (a word of obscure meaning) Inigo Montoya. The Form Critics asked whether polite conversation of the kind reported would be likely to occur between two men fighting to the death. If these were ordinary men rather than Divine beings, then of course the answer is: certainly not. The Form Critics, with their superficial cleverness and deficiency of faith, insisted on taking the combatants for more or less ordinary men, instead of the archangels we know them to be.

According to Form Criticism, the best explanation of the sword fight is that it originated as a customary ritual of response in the churches shortly after the beginning of the Great Melt.

An exchange like this:

> You are the simulacrum of human decency, O Divine Being.
> I would not wish to see you come to the end of your life.

> You in your own way are a simulacrum of spiritual rectitude,
> O Virtuous Being. Neither would I wish you to see me come
> to the end of my life.

This exchange is hardly rough banter between ruffians (or persons posing as ruffians) fighting to the death. But, the Form Critics argued, it makes sense as a liturgical response dialogue in which the priest, embodying the Divine Westley, converses with the Head Deacon, representing the congregation of Believers. Some Form Critics hypothesized that it had once had a musical accompaniment, and some went so far as to reconstruct this accompaniment and organize performances of it.

The Insane Audacity of Evil

I turn now to one of the most scurrilous, the most mischievous, and the most blatantly sacrilegious of these so-called scholars, the notorious Dr.

(if he really is a doctor!) Portier. He began to perpetrate his outrageous theories in his book, *What Did the Early Believers Believe?* An innocent question, even a highly relevant question, you might suppose! But then he moved through more than a dozen books on the Sacred Scripture to the position he now holds, or perhaps, for the most mischievous of motives, pretends to hold: that the Sacred Scripture was originally a work of what he calls "pure entertainment," that in all probability it originally bore the title, translated from ancient American English as "The Royal Betrothed," that although it depicts events in the only kind of political organization ever known to humankind (thank the Divine Power)—the divinely anointed monarchy—it was actually a highly ironic reference to such a political order viewed from within an utterly different political system, which Dr. Portier styles "a liberal democracy."

Let us see where this stupefying farrago leads. Portier actually maintains that the Kingdom of Florin did not exist! He brushes aside the eloquent and inconceivably moving *Testimony of the Twenty-Seven Florinese Eyewitnesses* as "a puerile concoction fabricated over one hundred thousand years after the alleged events described." You will notice that Portier is not lacking in self-confidence! He has plenty of faith in his own faithless brain! Here are some samples of his superficially "clever" reasoning.

He theorizes that the two kingdoms of Florin and Guilder were entirely fictitious entities, so named because these were originally the names of two coins of different origin yet equal value, thus signifying that the two kingdoms were morally on a par, or as Dr. Portier puts it (since he flatters himself with the conceit that he can recapture American English locutions), "There isn't a dime's worth of difference between them." The dime, he maintains, was a small coin, roughly equivalent to our kaching. The florin and the guilder were each equivalent in purchasing power to two or three dimes, roughly equivalent to our kwadros! I am not making this up; this is what the pathologically unbalanced Portier contends! I am reminded of the saying of the Inconceivably Blessed Dr. Chestyman, that those who turn their backs on the One True Faith do not believe nothing, but rather they believe anything and everything!

Portier also contends that the author of the Sacred Scripture was satirizing the war-mongering tendencies existing within so-called "liberal democracy," as when he grievously mutilates the holy text "The greatest of all transgressions is to make war upon the Archangels" and rewrites it as "The greatest blunder is to get involved in a land war in Asia." Dr. Portier, you see, holds to the truly bizarre theory that the liberal democracy in which American English was spoken, unwisely committed troops to a war against the old-fashioned monarchies in "Asia"—a reference of doubtful meaning, which pseudo-Dr. Portier quite fantastically equates with "the world's biggest land mass." The absurdity of this hypothesis should be evident—and notice the elementary contradiction, for Florin itself was part of the world's biggest land mass, and a Florinese would therefore hardly refer to "a land war in the world's biggest land mass." In reply, Portier has countered that the smaller western part of the world's biggest land mass was customarily given a different name from the bigger eastern part—you see what shameless special pleading these inconceivably clever yet inconceivably silly infidels are reduced to!

It is doubtful whether anything remotely resembling a "liberal democracy" could ever exist, but if it did, lacking a divinely anointed monarch, it would certainly never engage in far-flung military adventures, but would be a community of wretched cowards, huddling together in fear for lack of a divinely anointed protector. Unless we have completely taken leave of our senses, so much is obvious and indisputable.

Furthermore, if there really could exist any such entity as a "liberal democracy," how could it produce a tale called "The Royal Betrothed"? In this febrile fabrication of "a liberal democracy" people obviously would not know of any such persons as royalty, and if they had heard of them, would hardly commemorate them in entertaining yarns! But Dr. Portier responds that the liberal democracies might have evolved out of earlier monarchies, and harbored some residual popular respect for kings, queens, princes, and princesses. Can anyone credit this pitiful trash? See what a tangled web the deplorable Portier feels compelled to weave! It is not surprising that according to some reliable sources, the doctoral diploma of the supposed Dr. Portier is a forgery, or that he has been credibly accused of several sexual improprieties. That would account for a lot!

And let me put to him this question. If liberal democracies were preceded by monarchies, how is it even conceivable that the subjects of those monarchies, being palpably aware of the unmatched benefits of monarchical rule, could allow themselves to "evolve" into manifestly dysfunctional liberal democracies? I do not believe that Dr. Portier will dare to give an answer to that question. He will no doubt keep in mind that although heresy is no longer punishable by torture and death, the same does not apply to treason!

I can hardly begin to convey to you the repulsive interpretations which the wretched Portier puts upon some of the best-loved and most highly revered of scriptural passages. Here are a few samples.

The sublime text, "We derive holy satisfaction from any assault upon the evil ways of the uninformed," the miserable Portier re-translates as "Have fun storming the castle!" Don't think I am making this up! This is what the pretended Dr. Portier seriously maintains. His argument, if you can call it that, is that the Sacred Scripture is a satirical debunking of a traditional kind of adventure story, and that the juxtaposition of "having fun" and "storming a castle" is entirely deliberate, a comical effect depending upon incongruity! I would caution "Dr." Portier that with such arguments he comes close to denying the literal historical existence of the Man in Black, and as he well knows, that still carries the death penalty.

Or again, the sacred text, "Demanding that holy men justify their activities will lead to a deficiency of divinity in our lives," the filthy rodent Portier translates, or rather rewrites, as "Rush the miracle worker, and you'll get rotten miracles." This, he maintains, was intended as a jest. Well, I can only conclude that those shadowy figures, the ancient speakers of American English, had a fatally perverse sense of humor, if they could attribute such uncouth expressions to the Archangel Max, and then consider this a rich piece of comedy!

The disgusting reprobate Portier even goes so far as to dispute the existence of the original author of the Holy Book, Simon Morgenstern. Portier speculates that Morgenstern was a pure invention of the real author, employed as a comical literary device! Listening to such demented ravings, we have that creepy feeling of hearing the outpourings of a seriously disturbed mental apparatus. We get the feeling that Portier has sadly descended into the very depths of insanity.

I think I have said enough to show that in their tendency these dangerous new ideas constitute a subversive threat to the continued existence of the One True Faith. We all know that if the masses lose their steadfast belief in the divine mission of Westley, then murder, robbery, sex with lizards, and even the public eating of cabbage will become commonplace, and the kingdoms will collapse into well-deserved anarchy, bringing about the return of the great ice sheets for another ten thousand (or for those who prefer it, one hundred thousand) years.

Remember the Holy War!

Why did we wage war upon the Ozians, and eventually extinguish all three hundred and fifty million of them, man, woman, and child, because they persisted in their idolatrous devotion to the demon "Dorothy" and her three hideous demon companions? After all that we have won by burning out the Ozians, root and branch, by devoutly picking up their superficially cute yet inwardly corrupted babies by the ankles and, with purity of heart, piously smashing their skulls against the Cliffs of Insanity, are we to tolerate equally foul ideas emanating from within the Holy Motherland of the True Faith?

Is it even possible that the vermin of unusual size, Swinkel, Kwels, Portier, and the others of their deplorable ilk, are Ozianizers, undercover agents of Ozianism, craftily using the pretext of excavating the meaning of the Sacred Scripture, to prepare the world for a return of the poisonous foulness of Dorothy-worship? Then all our glorious labors in piously tearing apart the bodies of the Ozians, "limb from limb, eye from skull, and liver from spleen," must have been in vain!

In these disturbing, dispiriting days of uncertainty and the looming dark clouds of brazenly insolent skepticism, let us take solace from the inspiring words of the Inconceivably Divine Westley: "I am no one to be trifled with!"

3
Dexter the Busy Bee (2011)

Be brutal. Tell the truth. Would you rather live in Miami with Dexter than without him?

I think we'd all have to agree. Miami with Dexter would be a safer and healthier place than Miami without Dexter. To know that someone is unobtrusively and efficiently disposing of really, really bad guys—especially really, really bad guys whom the official law enforcers can't or won't touch—can only be reassuring. The fact that this highly conscientious executioner is somewhat more painstaking than the police in refraining from hurting us good guys is an additional comfort.

It's part of Dexter's M.O. that we wouldn't know this was going on. Dexter's discreet way of working loses the tremendous social advantage of deterrence: if everyone knew what Dexter was doing, that would cause some of the bad guys to become less bad, or at least to behave less badly. Murders would be prevented by discouraging the murderers, not just by eliminating them before they could murder again. Once you're on Dexter's table, you don't get to call your lawyer, so deterrence wouldn't be pissed away by the uncertainty of retribution. Unfortunately, that very salutary deterrence has to be given up, for the sake of Dexter's secrecy (the first rule of Harry's Code: Don't Get Caught).

Killing Killers, Saving Lives

Despite the absence of deterrence, the elimination of the really, really bad guys can only be judged really, really good. Just think about it. If each of the bad guys dismembered by Dexter would have killed one more person, then Dexter's actions would save just as many lives as he deleted. And if each of the bad guys would have killed two more persons, then each of Dexter's disposal operations would save one net life.

Given the quality of Dexter's targets, that we've been able to see, that would be a very conservative estimate. Let's suppose that the average Dexter target, but for Dexter's timely intervention, would have gone on to kill six more people, which seems about right. Say Dexter kills twenty of these bad guys a year, which also appears to be in line with what we've been shown. That means Dexter saves one hundred net lives a year! Can any Miami fireman or heart surgeon say as much?

And that's counting the lives Dexter terminates as equal with the lives saved. But we all know perfectly well that the lives of Dexter's targets are not worth the same as the lives of the people Dexter rescues from death. The targets deserve to die, whereas the targets' prospective victims deserve to live. Can you deny that Dexter's a public benefactor? If so, just what kind of a twisted monster are you?

Back in the 1930s when Ronald "Dutch" Reagan was a teenager in Dixon, Illinois, and everyone still pronounced his name "Reegan," he worked as a lifeguard on the Rock River and was credited with saving seventy-seven lives in seven years—eleven lives per year. That's a suspiciously high figure, and it's been suggested that local damsels contrived to put themselves in a position to be saved by this dishy hunk, which may have somewhat inflated Dutch's life-saving, umm, score. But making all due allowances, it was highly creditable. Obviously, that boy would go far. But it couldn't begin to approach the magnitude of the public benefit conferred by Dexter Morgan. Maybe this boy will go farther.

Without deceiving himself about his motives, Dexter clearly understands his contribution to human welfare. After Special Agent Lundy has commented that there's but one justification for killing, "to save an innocent life," Dexter observes (not to Lundy, of course, but to us):

> How many bodies would there have been if I had not got to those killers? I didn't want to save lives, but save lives I did. Motivation aside, I think Harry and Lundy would agree on this one. ("An Inconvenient Lie," Season Two)

Wait, wait. Is Dexter an unmitigated social benefit? He doesn't respect habeas corpus or the Miranda rule. We need habeas corpus, the Miranda rule, trial by jury, and a slew of other checks on the powers of the official enforcers because we need to be protected against the official enforcers becoming bad guys themselves. We need the official enforcers to stop bad guys attacking us, and we need the Bill of Rights to stop the official enforcers attacking us. (That's the theory. Some of us anarchists are not completely sold on the theory, but it does have its points. And, like it or not, it is the theory.)

But don't we need protection against Dexter? No, no, no! Dexter is driven by an irresistible force, a passion as remorseless and unreasoning as a tornado, to kill the guilty and save (or at least, avoid killing) the innocent. Oh sure, Dexter makes mistakes. Who doesn't? But he tries as hard as he can, and a lot harder than any government employee on a pension plan ever would, not to screw up. As Dexter tells Doakes:

> My Code requires a higher standard of proof than your city's laws, at zero cost to the taxpayer. If you ask me, I'm a bargain. ("There's Something about Harry," Season Two)

But wouldn't we need protection against a real-life Dexter? Yes, of course. But Dexter isn't real-life, silly. He's all made up. That's why he's so marvelous. A real-life Dexter might become a bad guy. A real-life Dexter might start slicing and dicing folks according to their race, their religion, their sexual preferences, their astrological signs, or their musical tastes. (Musical tastes? Hey, wait a minute . . .) A real-life Dexter might go after children or cats or, like the Unabomber, after exceptionally talented and productive people.

Even more ominously and more probably, a real-life Dexter might become a Miguel Prado, classifying as guilty people like defense attorneys who sometimes help to get the guilty off. But we and Dexter understand what the late Miguel didn't: that occasionally getting the guilty off is the price we pay for not convicting the innocent. And we all know what happened to Miguel. Dexter got to him and administered the *coup de grâce*. "This isn't over," says Miguel. "It is for you," says Dexter, swiftly garroting him. Did I mention that our Dex is witty?

The Thrill of the Kill

But one thing might still worry us about Dexter Morgan. And this is the element that makes Dexter such an astounding innovation in the history of fiction and drama. Dexter's fundamental motivation, so we're repeatedly told, is arbitrary, amoral, inhuman, inherently malign, fearsome, and revolting. It's an addictive imperative. Dexter has an urge to ritualistically kill warm-blooded creatures. As a child, he begins with non-human animals, but he soon graduates to those opposable-thumbed naked apes who flow so expendably through the streets of Miami.

This urge, this drive, this hunger owes nothing to a sense of justice or any other kind of disinterested intention. Dexter does not kill to fulfill a mission. He kills because of his addiction to the thrill of killing. Usually it has to be killing by sharp steel implements. Shooting, poisoning, strangling, rigged auto accidents, we feel, just don't (pardon me!) cut it. Miguel Prado is dispatched by garroting—but that's only because it has to look as if the Skinner (a serial killer without a Code) has done it.

But then there's something else: Harry's Code. Harry's Code controls and restricts Dexter's howling appetite for blood. Harry's Code doesn't modify the primal urge to butcher people for the sheer joyous gratification of butchering them. It doesn't change that motivation to one of justice or benevolence or concern for public safety. Fundamentally and intrinsically, Dexter doesn't give a rap about these notions, one way or the other, though as an intelligent observer keeping tabs on that wondrous beast, *Homo sapiens non-serial-killerensis*, they do mildly interest him as worthy of his urbane and amused comments.

What Harry's Code does is to impose a rigid pattern, like a superstition or an obsessive compulsion, on top of the naked urge. Harry's Code takes a terrifying, mindless, brutal force and channels it into a solid benefit for humankind.

The exact relation between Dexter's hunger to kill and Harry's Code has yet to be (if you'll excuse the expression) fully fleshed out. Maria Montessori was an educational theorist who believed that there's a point in time when a child is just ready to learn some particular type of thing. Maybe Harry Morgan, Dexter's step-father, caught Dexter at just the right Montessori moment where the Code would "take" with Dexter. Maybe Dexter would go to pieces without the Code. As Dexter says, "I know I'm a monster."

His wistful, secret, impossible dream is to be normal, fully cured, with normal headaches and normal heartaches, just like all those millions of non-serial-killers out there. Although this doesn't bother him enough to put him off his knife stroke, it does seem possible that complying with Harry's Code makes it easier for Dexter to live with himself. And so the two parts of Dexter's make-up, the basic instinct to chop up humans and Harry's Code, may support and sustain each other. But maybe not; we don't really know.

In the novels, Dexter is a sadist who has fun torturing his subjects before he recycles them. In the TV show, Dexter only tortures them mentally, for a minute or two, by reminding them of their horrendous crimes. The physical process is not protracted. Though both Dexters have their engaging side, the TV Dexter is more thoroughly likeable, more charming, and more of a wag than the Dexter of the books. We feel that any gratuitous inflicting of pain would be entirely foreign to the TV Dexter.

Not that he's a softy. He's capable of acting with impressive ruth-lessness, as when he frames Rita's husband for breach of parole to get him sent back to jail. Come to think of it though, this may be more a matter of opportunity than motivation: as a highly trained ambusher, abductor, and eraser of forensic clues, at the top of his game, Dexter can easily get away with exploits that just wouldn't be practicable for those of us who maintain our upper-body strength mainly by pushing the but-tons on the remote.

But Dexter lacks even normal spitefulness, just as, we're repeatedly informed, he lacks much of normal sentimentality and human warmth (though he sincerely regrets his lack of these). This can lead him to send the wrong signals, as when he responds to Quinn's overtures with pro-found indifference, after Quinn knows that Dexter has seen him steal money from a crime scene. Quinn just doesn't get it: Dexter simply doesn't care the teeniest bit about Quinn, except that Quinn should leave him alone. (Oh dear, Quinn, me boyo, do I see hefty bags and duct tape in your future? Just try not to murder anyone, there's a good police officer, or you'll become a legitimate target under the provisions of Harry's Code.) The vengeful payback motive, among many conventional emo-tional responses, seems pointless and barely intelligible to Dexter.

The uniqueness of Dexter as a character in drama is that he totally does the right thing for totally the wrong reason. (Shut up, all you

ADHD cases. We've established it's the right thing, remember? Just get used to it.) He's a good guy, a hero, whose primal driving force is dangerous, ugly, monstrous, terrifying—everything that we've learned to call *evil*. So maybe (as Milton Friedman said of Henry Ford) he's a bad man who does a lot of good. But if he does a lot of good, can he really be so bad?

Good Motives and Good Actions

Dexter's unique. He's a sympathetic character whose fundamental motivation is totally creepy, while the consequences of his actions are predominantly benign and protective.

For thousands of years, the ruling assumption has been that if you want to encourage good actions, you'd better encourage good motives. At first blush, this makes sense. If people feel it's wrong to kill other people, for instance, they're less likely to kill other people. But there's always the possibility of motivation and behavior working in opposite directions. People may do the right thing for wrong reasons, or they may do something appalling for decent and good-hearted reasons.

Christianity gave a new importance to motives as opposed to actions. Jesus angrily denounces the Pharisees, the inventors of what we now call orthodox Judaism, those Jews who were especially concerned to follow every detail of the Jewish law, but no more than that. Jesus made such remarks as:

> You've heard that it was said, "Don't commit adultery." But I tell you that anyone who looks at a woman with lust has already committed adultery with her in his heart. (Matthew 5:27–28)

(What the actual? God's going to bill you for the goodies before you've even opened the wrapper? Might as well go the whole hog, then.)

So Christianity makes you responsible for your thoughts, even if unacted upon. The real test of a person's morality is not their actions nor the results of their actions but what goes on, unseen by their fellow humans, inside their skulls. By this standard, hypocrisy (outwardly being good while inwardly having bad thoughts) becomes one of the worst of sins.

A moral dilemma is no longer simply "What ought I to do?" but more importantly, "Am I thinking and feeling the right way? Are my intentions pure?" This opens up a vast new scope for self-examination, guilt, self-flagellation, and self-doubt, especially as thinking is, by its very nature, frolicsome and uncontrollable.

Enter the Man-Devil

In early eighteenth-century England, Dr. Bernard Mandeville was denounced as the most evil person alive. His enemies—almost everyone—branded him "the Man-Devil" (Get it?). Nearly all the most eminent thinkers of his day wrote ferocious denunciations of the Man-Devil. Just as anyone who wants to be recognized today as a stand-up guy has to denounce racism, Islamicism, or sexual abuse of children, so anyone who looked for minimum cred in the eighteenth century had to express their horror and detestation for the Man-Devil.

His bad reputation was only to be matched by Jack the Ripper, nearly two centuries later. Dr. Mandeville was Public Enemy Number One. No, he wasn't a ritual serial murderer. He was something far more dangerous than that!

The Man-Devil's great crime was to say something that had never been said before. He proclaimed that wicked behavior by individuals is good for society as a whole, or as he put it, private vices are public virtues. And he made it sound very convincing.

Far less is now known about the life of the mysterious Man-Devil than about anyone else of comparable importance at the time. But we do know that he made his living as a doctor specializing in nervous diseases. He was married and had children. He was at home in four languages and had read a lot in each of them. He died of the flu in 1733. As far as we know, aside from what he wrote, he led a blameless life.

This was an age of new media and information explosion. The thousands of London coffee houses were like today's Facebook. The thousands of London bookstores, with a printing press in the back and with a coffee house attached, were like today's blogosphere. Printers were the

IT nerds. The presses turned out a flood of new leaflets, pamphlets, and magazines, soaked up by the denizens of the coffee houses who debated them endlessly. Mass literacy had arrived, and with a sure instinct the masses turned to the vile and disgusting. The world had seen nothing like it before. Could the human mind possibly withstand the weighty burden of information overload?

Many of the new printed works were irreverent, mildly but persistently erotic, and satirical. Their goal was entertainment, but their authors understood, with the Dexter scriptwriters, that to truly entertain people you have to make them think.

The coffee houses charged one penny admission. "Runners" went round the coffee houses, from table to table, reciting the latest news reports. There was a turmoil of new ideas. No one could predict where it was all going. One coffee house, Jonathan's, started posting stock prices on the walls, and this coffee house eventually became the London Stock Exchange. People of different walks of life and social standing mingled and debated in the coffee houses (which, however, did maintain minimal standards: women were excluded, except for professional ladies who looked after customers in some of those little rooms in the back). A powdered wig and a penny a day—and you were online!

The new media were effectively unregulated and we all know what that means: something terrible is bound to happen. As the anarchist Dave Barry says, without government people will start having sex with dogs. Well, that didn't happen in eighteenth-century London, but something almost as appalling did occur: the coming of the Man-Devil.

A Poem that Will Live in Infamy

Dr. Mandeville came over from Holland at the age of twenty-nine, and fell in love with London. Within a few years, no one who met him would believe he wasn't a native Englishman. He wrote a number of satirical publications before he penned *The Grumbling Hive* in 1705. This is not a poem of polished elegance like those of Alexander Pope (who like nearly everyone else stole some of Dr. Mandeville's ideas while personally attacking the Man-Devil) but conversational and street-wise, in line with coffee-house chatter.

The Grumbling Hive tells of a fabulous beehive in which all the bees do, in miniature, exactly what eighteenth-century English people do. The bees are immoral though hypocritical: they practice all kinds of vice, while paying lip service to virtue. The hive flourishes, and becomes a beacon of prosperity, much like England.

> Every part was filled with Vice
> But the whole Mass a Paradise.

Then, overnight, the bees all become virtuous; they begin to practice what they preach. The economy of the hive collapses, and the hive is depopulated. A tiny remnant of the original population of bees leaves the hive and flies off into a dead tree-trunk. Since the bees remain completely virtuous, there is no indication that they regret the catastrophic consequences of their reformed behavior.

The Grumbling Hive did not immediately make Dr. Mandeville notorious. In 1714, he republished the poem with an extensive commentary, under the title *The Fable of the Bees, or Private Vices, Public Benefits*. Still no scandal. In 1723 he brought out a new edition with even more added material, including "A Search into the Nature of Society." A few months later, the Grand Jury of Middlesex referred this book, as a public nuisance, to the Court of King's Bench, recommending prosecution of the publisher.

No prosecution went ahead, but the hour of the Man-Devil had struck. *The Fable of the Bees* was reprinted five times in the next few years. Suddenly, everyone in Europe (and its outposts like the North American colonies) had heard of the Man-Devil, and every respectable person felt obliged to make outraged comments about him. All across Europe, people became aware of the horror perpetrated by the Man-Devil, as printed translations of his work appeared in every civilized language. When a French translation of *The Fable of the Bees* came out in 1740, a copy was ritually burned by the public executioner.

The leading philosopher of the moment, George Berkeley, living in Rhode Island at the time, wrote a vigorous denunciation of the Man-Devil (this was before Berkeley had been made a bishop and long before the town of Berkeley, California, had been named after him, immortalizing his name in a mispronounced form). Berkeley's attack unfairly misrepresents Mandeville's argument, but then, exactly what Mandeville's argument was is still being debated.

A few things are clear. Dr. Mandeville did not think that morality was a crock, and did not want to encourage people to practice vice. He thought that morality was useful, and that it made its impact by appealing to people's desire to gain the approval of others. He thought that people would always naturally practice vice (love themselves more than their neighbors and try to satisfy their own appetites before caring about anyone else). People need no special encouragement to practice vice: they are naturally vicious. Mandeville could have said that what was generally thought to be vice was not really vice, but was partly morally neutral, in itself neither good nor bad, and partly good. But that would have ruined the joke.

Only a few of the Man-Devil's literary contemporaries did not denounce him. One was Sam Johnson, compiler of the first dictionary. Reading Mandeville opened his eyes and changed his life. He reported that every young man believed *The Fable of the Bees* was a terribly wicked book, and therefore had to have a copy on his shelves. Another was Ben Franklin, on a visit to London, who had a few drinks with Mandeville and called him "a most facetious, entertaining companion." So in the flesh he seemed just as he does on the printed page.

The Man-Devil wrote many satirical pieces. It's not always clear just where he's coming from, for two opposite reasons. First, he's careful to avoid saying anything that would get him executed or imprisoned, so we can't always be sure when he's pulling his punches. Second, he's trying to be entertaining by being shocking, so we can't be sure when he's exaggerating his own audacity to keep up the reader's interest.

There's also the fact that what he wrote was mostly either in verse or in the form of dialogues, and in dialogues we can't be sure whether he completely agrees with what any one of his characters is saying.

Mandeville wrote a fun piece called *The Virgin Unmask'd*, a long conversation, with a touch of mild pornography, between an elderly woman and an adolescent female, in which the older woman tries to convince the younger to have nothing whatsoever to do with men, ever. Mandeville published this piece without finishing it, and we don't really know where he was going with it, except that it would be amusing to get there.

Among his other productions was a hilarious piece arguing for the provision of public stews. (A stew, at this time, was the popular name for a house of prostitution. Brothel—stew, get it? Those witty Londoners.) In this pamphlet "by a Lay-Man," pun intended, Mandeville pointed out that the suppression of prostitution would naturally lead to an increased incidence of rape. So harlots, by doing it for money, are incidentally helping to protect and defend virtuous women. As *The Grumbling Hive* put it,

> The worst of all the multitude
> Did something for the common good.

Or as Mandeville explained with mock earnestness:

> I am far from encouraging Vice, and think it would be an unspeakable Felicity to the State, if the Sin of Uncleanness could be utterly Banish'd from it; but I am afraid it is impossible. The Passions of some People are too violent to be curb'd by any Law or Precept; . . . If Courtezans and Strumpets were to be prosecuted with as much Rigour as some silly People would have it, what Locks or Bars would be sufficient to preserve the Honour of our Wives and Daughters? . . . some Men would grow outrageous, and Ravishing would become a common Crime.

At this time the penalty for rape was death, and neither Mandeville nor anyone else expected that was going to change.

Did Dr. Mandeville really want government-run bordellos? We can't be sure. His more serious arguments for this policy are phrased as comical parodies of the then-fashionable arguments for economic policies that promote national greatness. But the Man-Devil was nimble enough to make fun of arguments he actually believed in.

Later in the eighteenth century, most of those who could read (eighty percent of males and twenty percent of females) had read Dr. Mandeville, and even as they fumed with righteous anger, many of them pirated his ideas. The Man-Devil invented economics, sociology, social anthropology, sociobiology, utilitarianism, liberalism, evolution, post-modernism, psychiatry, sex education, the social philosophy of Rousseau, the ethical theory of Nietzsche, and the class theory of Marx. In the spirit of the Man-Devil, I'm exaggerating only very, very slightly. He also, sad to say, invented Keynesian economics and the theory of the stimulus package, the dumb notion, refuted many times since in a recurring nightmare, that government spending can get you out of a slump. But here, I like to think, the Man-Devil was just kidding around.

Many of Mandeville's ideas are developed fifty years later by Adam Smith in *The Wealth of Nations*, especially the idea that acting out of self-love and self-interest can lead to the public benefit. Smith wrote that:

> It is not from the benevolence of the butcher, the brewer, or the baker, that we expect our dinner, but from their regard to their own self-interest. We address ourselves, not to their humanity but to their self-love, and never talk to them of our own necessities but of their advantages.

Smith finally comes out with what Mandeville had only slyly hinted at: that so-called private vices are not really vices at all. It's ethically okay to love yourself, to be predominantly self-interested. Smith replayed a riff that had done the rounds of the coffee-house chatter: "A man is never more innocently employed than when making money." And Smith described how an individual could be

> led by an invisible hand to promote an end which was no part of his intention. Nor is it always the worse for the society that it was not part of it. By pursuing his own interest he frequently promotes that of the society more effectually than when he really intends to promote it.

In his first book, *The Theory of Moral Sentiments*, Smith had included an entire chapter devoted to a rebuttal of Mandeville. Smith, unlike Dr. Mandeville, had to make sure he could keep his university teaching post. While sharply criticizing Mandeville, taking the Man-Devil's provocative over-statements with deadpan seriousness, Smith commented that *The Fable of the Bees* couldn't have impressed so many people "had it not in some respects bordered upon the truth."

Mandeville's and Smith's theory that everyone will benefit if each person acts in his own self-interest can easily be misunderstood. A more complete statement of what Mandeville and Smith believed is that since most people are going to act predominantly in their self-interest anyway, laws ought to be designed so that, as far as possible, everyone will benefit if each person acts in his own self-interest. This is, they believed, the test of good law.

So the point Mandeville and Smith are really making is one about which laws are best. It's easy to overlook this because both Mandeville and Smith believed that the laws of England and Scotland in the eighteenth century had come quite close to being the best laws, and could easily be brought closer. Whereas Mandeville believes (or pretends to believe—you never quite know with the Man-Devil) that good laws are devised by clever politicians, Smith has a theory that law, especially judge-made common law, evolves and tends to improve as it evolves.

A country's laws fulfill a function like Harry's Code: they direct individual human appetites that are very far from benevolent into actions which benefit other people, without trying to change the appetites themselves. The Man-Devil's insight now dominates most of the world and is rapidly mopping up the few remaining hold-outs. If you want living standards to keep rising, then you have to give up the idea of making people morally better, in their inmost souls, by law. Instead, you design the law so that it takes people as they are, and gives them an incentive to be productive—to serve the good of other people.

We live in a world the Man-Devil has made. In some ways, the Man-Devil is like Jesus: he draws attention to the difference, and the possible antagonism, between inner thoughts and outward behavior. In other ways, the Man-Devil is just the opposite, a true Anti-Christ—he teaches us something we can never forget: that what really matters for humankind is not the purity of people's intentions but the actual results of their actions, results which may be, and most often are, no part of their intention.

A Second Look at Dexter's Motives

So far I've been assuming that Dexter is a psychopath hemmed in by a Code. His motives are foul, though his deeds are salubrious. This is the way Dexter thinks of himself. Dexter continually tells himself this, and as he does so, continually tells us. But could Dexter be deceiving himself and us?

The appeal of the show hinges on the fact that we both accept this story and simultaneously feel it to be false. We know that Dex is no soulless psychopath. How do we know it?

Here's one example. Dexter kills both Jorge Castillo and his wife Valerie. The chopped-up Jorge goes into the regulation six Hefty bags, but Dex doesn't chop up the wife because she's a bit of an afterthought and he can't afford the precious minutes. This dreadfully impolite and inconsiderate couple certainly deserve to be disassembled (though my inner economist can't help wondering whether it could possibly be profit-maximizing for them to murder *so many* of their clients), and there's the hilarious bit where Dexter asks them for the secret of their successful relationship, and then murmurs, "Thank you, that's very helpful," just before dispatching them.

Then what does Dexter do? He walks up to the door of the shed where the Cuban immigrants are imprisoned without food, water, or sanitation, and unlocks it. A brief pause. As we watch, we automatically think, "Thank God those poor people will now be able to get out, but maybe they won't notice the door's unlocked and will still spend hours of torment in there." Dexter obviously has just the same thought, and opens the door wider, before driving off to dump the Castillo corpses in the ocean. We see one immigrant open the door and peer out, fearfully and wonderingly.

Dexter has nothing to gain by this spontaneous action. He's very pressed for time, and the sooner the disappearance of the Castillos is reported, the more danger he'll be in. As it turns out, there was actually an eyewitness to Dexter's capturing the Castillos and loading their bodies into his car. Admittedly, Dexter couldn't be expected to know that someone would dive down to the ocean bed, recover Valerie's corpse, and replace it just where Dexter had killed her, but still, he has informed us that his motto is "Be Prepared." Someone with no empathy, a psychopath, or even someone who overrides his empathy in pursuit of pure self-interest, would have left the door locked and let the Cubans perish miserably, without giving it a thought.

Dexter keeps telling us he has no feelings, but we keep seeing that he does have feelings. It's true that his feelings are not entirely typical, and he's not fully in touch with them. Dexter, in fact, belongs to that procession of characters which includes Pechorin (Lermontov's *A Hero of Our Time*) and Meursault (Camus's *The Stranger*). These characters are all very different, but in their different ways they have problems with their feelings. Meursault has his head chopped off because he doesn't make a conventional display of the feelings he's expected to show in conventional settings, while Dexter, more intelligent and more controlling than Meursault, chops off other people's heads while working hard to simulate the appropriate feelings, to blend in and appear normal.

Dexter's interpersonal missteps are at worst only a slight exaggeration of stereotypical situations: the male who doesn't understand what women are feeling, the non-macho male who doesn't quite know how to make macho talk, the person at the funeral whose mind is on matters other than grief.

One of the first things Dexter tells us in the first episode of Season One is: "It has to happen." He has to kill, he has no self-control, his Dark Passenger must seize the reins. And in that first episode we see Dexter and Harry's conversation, in which Harry explains why Dexter must follow the Code. One of the remarkable things about this conversation is that Harry doesn't merely deliver the Code: he assures Dexter that his urge to kill cannot be cured, that he's fated to be a killer. Dexter is puzzled and wonders if possibly he might be able to change, but Harry nixes that one. And it's little Dexter, not Harry, who comes up with some semblance of an ethical rationale for Harry's Code: "They deserve it."

Why is Harry so certain that Dexter can't recover? Remember that at this point Dexter has not yet harmed any human person. Harry's an intelligent cop but he doesn't look like the type who would spend his spare time keeping up with the latest research into childhood development, and if he did, he would have come to a different conclusion anyway. As an infant, Dexter saw his mother cut to pieces in front of his eyes, and we're expected to suppose that this is what turned him into a serial killer governed by an involuntary compulsion. The plain truth, of course, is that most serial killers did not have extreme childhood traumas and most people who do suffer such traumas don't go on to become serial killers. At the age of three, seeing your mother horribly slain and then sitting for a couple of days in the pool of her blood is going to be upsetting, and your grades will probably suffer, but it simply will not make you a serial killer.

And when Dexter does begin killing humans, it's on the direct orders of Harry. Dexter has done nothing to commence a career killing humans, and is horrified when Harry instructs him to kill Nurse Mary, who makes a practice of killing her patients with drugs and is now trying to kill Harry. Dexter is horrified, but Harry firmly insists ("Popping Cherry," Season One). Harry makes it seem that killing Nurse Mary was necessary to save his life, but instead the police could have been informed of what she was up to, and she would have been suspended pending an investigation. However Harry had determined that Dexter must take the step of killing his first human. Harry quite deliberately sets Dexter on his path as a serial killer, while without Harry's pro-active intervention, there's no guarantee that Dexter would ever have slain a human.

So while we keep being fed the line that Dexter is a predetermined killer and that Harry gives him the Code which guides and constrains his killing, the facts of the narrative tell us that Harry both gives Dexter the Code and deliberately turns him into a killer. What's Harry's motive? We know that Harry the cop was breaking departmental rules by having sex with Dexter's mother, the CI (confidential informant) up to the time when she was brutally slain. Further dot-connecting is scarcely necessary.

Like many people, Dexter has bought the theory that he's subject to an irresistible compulsion. Since he firmly believes that, he doesn't seriously try to fight it. When he lays off killing for a few weeks, he feels irritable and concludes that he can't do without it. But of course he can. He just has to persist for a few more weeks—if he really wants to kick the habit. Then the urge will die down and become easier to control. Addiction is always a choice.

But maybe he doesn't want to kick the habit just yet. Maybe he's having too much fun. We certainly are.

4

SOME SECOND THOUGHTS ON ATHEISM

"God is dead," Nick said. "They found his carcass in 2019. Floating in space near Alpha."

"They found the remains of an organism advanced several thousand times over what we are," Charley said. "And evidently it could create habitable worlds and populate them with living organisms, derived from itself. But that doesn't prove it was God."

—Philip K. Dick, *Our Friends from Frolix 8* (1970)

"Atheism" comes from two Greek words, "a" and "theos." "A" means "without" and "theos" means "God." So "atheism" means "without God" and by extension "without any belief in God."

We don't have special words for a-mermaidism, a-leprechaunism, a-Loch-Ness-Monsterism, a-spoon-bending-ism, or even a-repressed-memory-ism, a-global-warming-ism, or a-class-struggle-ism, but we do have a special word for a-Godism, to wit: "atheism."

I'm not recommending we start using those other words, but I am proposing one new word: apneumatism. Apneumatism is not believing in *spirits*. Since, as far as I know, I coined this word, I'm going to decree that you can pronounce it "a-new-mat-ism," just as you already pronounce pneumonia as "new-monia." In many languages, including Greek, the word for "spirit" is the same as the word for "breath," hence "pneumonia."

Something that has struck me with greater force recently is that in my thinking, and I believe in that of most atheists, "atheism" in itself is rather a minor matter. It's something that flows from the more fundamental and decisive position of apneumatism. We are atheists only—or mainly—because we are apneumatists, not the other way around.

The Invisible World of Spirits

The vast majority of people who believe in God also believe in teeming hordes of spirits: angels, demons, ghosts, and other invisible critters. Muslims also have djinns or genies. Theists most often also believe that individual human beings *are* spirits, and that the spirits of dead humans survive in a spirit world, though Christians believe that when they rise from the dead, they'll be once again equipped with a physical body, which suggests that a spirit without a body would be seriously lacking something.

When you listen to a Christian or a Muslim arguing for the existence of God, bear in mind that he's really arguing for a vast realm of innumerable spirit beings, several different classes of angels, demons, and perhaps other entities like nephilim, plus the spirits (ghosts) of all the dead humans who ever once lived. The typical theist's imaginary world is not just a world with God in it, but a world containing billions upon billions of assorted spirits. And they're just the ones we've heard about.

I note in passing that this Christian's "God" is itself not one spirit, but three spirits, who often hang out together but occasionally do their own thing. The Christian doctrine of the Trinity, or as I affectionately call them, the Gang of Three, strictly implies that God is three spirits. Christians may be taken aback by this claim, but I see no alternative. That God is three spirits follows strictly from things that Christians have proclaimed since the fourth century C.E.

However, I have observed some Christians quite closely, and I have the impression that most of them, the rank and file, the folks in the pews, don't really believe in the Trinity. They pray to "Our Father" and would consider it in poor taste to pray to "Our Divine Triumvirate." It's true that the Orthodox have their "Jesus Prayer," but then the Orthodox, like the Catholics, also pray to hundreds of saints (which an objective cultural anthropologist would consider to be indistinguishable from minor gods). And nowhere does it seem to be popular to pray to the third member of the Trinity.

The Nature of Spirits

By most accounts, spirits are entities which are conscious and act with a purpose, but have no material form—or in some versions, they may take a material form, but they do not always need to or choose to. And perhaps there's the suggestion that the material form isn't really part of them, but an optional extension, analogous to a prosthetic limb.

There are numerous different notions floating around about the qualities and limitations of various kinds of spirits, and I don't want to pin anyone down to a precise conception. There are some believers in spirits, pneumatists, who think of spirits not as immaterial, but as composed of a very different kind of matter from the kind we encounter all the time in everyday life. This is one of those issues which at first blush seems substantive, but turns out to be a question of semantics. If you watch Miyazaki's wonderful movie, *Spirited Away*, and are asked whether the spirit world depicted is immaterial or consists of a special kind of matter—it does contain at least one big pile of poop—you tend to react by thinking about the definition of "matter" rather than about what goes on in the movie.

In many ghost stories, the ghosts can see us but we can't see the ghosts, except under rare and exceptional conditions. In one episode of *Supernatural*, Bobby, who is currently dead and therefore a ghost, tries hard to communicate with the regular live persons like Sam and Dean. Bobby looks just like he did when alive, including the clothing, beard trim, and haircut, except that he's kind of semi-transparent for the TV camera, a way of indicating he's invisible to those spirits who, like us, still have their physical bodies. When he tries to push a material object (in the everyday sense), he just goes right through it, but we're given the hint that if he tries very hard and puts in many days of practice, he might be able to develop the knack for actually affecting the physical world, perhaps by exercising the spirit muscles in his spirit arms, directed by the spirit commands from his spirit brain.

I deny that there are ghosts or any other kind of spirits. Why? I suppose the quickest answer is that there's no way to detect them *or any of their effects*. If spirits existed in a spirit world totally closed off from the familiar physical world, that would be one thing. But believers in spirits almost never believe that. They nearly always believe that spirits interact with the physical world, and not just on rare occasions, but every day, all over the populated Earth.

If a spirit somehow affects the physical world, there has to be some measurable impact in the physical world. There would have to be some physical occurrence, reliably detectable by precise instruments, which would enable us to say: something we didn't know about is doing something here, something not fully accountable by known physical conditions plus the laws of physics, and the explanation for that something could be a spirit. And we would be able to follow up with more and more precise recording and measurement of such occurrences.

A haunted house can serve as an allegory for the human experience with the spirit world. There are reports of strange goings-on in a quaint old house, and sure enough, when observers visit the house, they do report some strange goings-on. We attempt to measure these strange goings-on more exactly, by the use of precise instruments, registering sound, light, temperature, radioactivity, magnetic fluctuations, and other variables. As soon as we do this, the number of recorded strange goings-on sharply declines. Then we make our instrumentation more and more precise, and we study the ways of stage magicians, in order to be able to rule out any fraudulent tricks, and every time we do that, the number of strange goings-on declines a bit more. Finally, as we keep on tightening up our observational procedures, we reach a point where that number falls to zero, or as close to zero as can be classified as experimental error. There just are no strange goings-on, as far as we can tell. The house just isn't haunted, as far as we can tell. End of story (as far as we can tell).

That's a basic reason for denying that there are spirits, but there's something else. In observing the world, we notice that consciousness is always associated with a particular arrangement of physical matter, which we call a brain. As far as we've been able to find out so far, brains occur only in animals, and animals occur only on, or close to, the surfaces of planets with an extremely narrow range of specifications. This suggests the hypothesis: consciousness is produced by a certain kind of arrangement of matter, which occurs in animal brains, and as far as we know, nowhere else. Of course, it could be that consciousness is produced by brains and also independently by spirits, or it could be that consciousness is only produced by brains but they need a bit of assistance from spirits, but that doesn't help to explain anything we can observe, so we don't need it.

This is not to deny that there are limits to what we know, and even limits to what we can possibly know. Prior to the nineteenth century scientists had no notion of the electromagnetic spectrum. Nothing in the current state of science in 1800 pointed to the world being just chock-ablock with invisible rays. There was no manifest Great Riddle demanding an answer. Sir William Herschel demonstrated the existence of invisible infrared light in 1800. Johann Ritter identified invisible ultraviolet light the following year. After many other discoveries, in 1895, Wilhelm Röntgen made a photograph of the bones in his wife's hand, and the world suddenly became aware of the ability to look at the insides of bodies without cutting them open.

It's conceivable that we're overlooking some other vast area of reality. I would even say it's almost certain—though that doesn't mean that any conjectured vast unknown area, picked at random from our fond imaginings, is particularly likely to exist. We might stumble upon some indication of spirits affecting the physical world, and we might find there is a vast world of spirits, immaterial (or material in a strange and heretofore unsuspected way) and yet capable of interacting with everyday matter. And we might not.

The Genesis of Belief in Spirits

Historically, there's a big difference between the hypothesis that there are spirits and the hypothesis that there are invisible electromagnetic rays. We humans began by believing in spirits, in fact we hominins almost certainly believed in spirits long before we were humans. Belief in spirits was simple common sense to most cultures for hundreds of thousands of years.

Where did the idea of spirits, and the idea of a God, come from? I must admit that my view of this is completely unoriginal, entirely conventional, and not completely satisfying. I don't know who first formulated it. Despite its unprepossessing pedigree, I find it convincing as to fact, though oddly unsatisfactory—it can probably do with a bit of tweaking here and there, or maybe some kind of transformative makeover.

Belief in spirits arose because it's human nature to attribute conscious purpose or intention to entities, even when we now know that these entities are incapable of any conscious purpose or intention. Belief in one big boss spirit arose because people attribute to spirits the social organization of humans, and so belief in a single God can only arise after people have begun to witness great empires with the concentration of power in the hands of a single person, like Sargon or Hammurabi.

Why is it human nature to believe in spirits? I was once walking through Chicago's Loop when there was a prolonged spate of very powerful gusts of wind. I observed a woman shout at the sky, in a highly exasperated tone, "*Okay!* I get the *point!*" I've even observed myself getting angry at an inanimate object, when due to my own clumsiness or miscalculation, it did something unfortunate or painful to me (yes it did, the nasty brute). Do you remember the scene from *Fawlty Towers* where Basil's car keeps breaking down, and he responds by giving it a good thrashing?

From a strictly Darwinian point of view, it seems fairly obvious that there would be reproductive profit in being keenly aware of other persons' motivations. In the human social group, individual reproductivity would be enhanced by being able to manipulate other people (this would have a higher reproductive income than being able to shoot arrows or wield stone axes), and this social ability would be enhanced by having some insight into the way other individuals are motivated. So helpful would this ability be, that it would be better to wrongly attribute motivation in many cases than to fail to attribute motivation in cases where it might be a reproductive gain.

An additional possible motivation for belief in spirits is to explain what happens to someone's personality when they die, especially when they die with their body, to all appearances, still intact (except for the "breath"). Yet another possible motivation is to account for dreams, hallucinations, and other "weird" experiences.

The *Tanakh* (the *Old Testament*) bears the powerful imprint of the great empires. Before there could be any conception of Yahweh, there had to be a conception of Sargon (the writers of *Genesis* didn't know about Sargon; that was already too long ago, but they did know about Hammurabi).

If belief in God originated from experience of powerful real-life political dictatorship, this helps to explain something that would otherwise be baffling. Viewed objectively, the notion of an immensely powerful and knowledgeable being (we can drop absurdities like omnipotence and omniscience) insisting that everyone constantly sing his praises is bizarre in the extreme. Imagine a being who knows all about quantum gravity, because he has made it by spinning it out of his own mind, being consumed with the desire for little creatures he has created to keep voicing their adoration. Does an entomologist care what ants and bees think about him?

But God's narcissistic personality disorder makes perfect sense once we recognize that belief in a single spirit dictator arises historically by copying experience of a single material political dictator or emperor. Under real dictatorships, prudence dictates that everyone constantly praises the dictator; the subjects are all continually in competition with each other to praise the dictator.

Despite the birth of monotheism thousands of years earlier, Christianity originated in a world which was predominantly polytheistic, or perhaps some of them were more "animistic," believing in nature spirits which didn't amount to "gods." Despite the Trinity, Christianity always explicitly insisted that there is one God. Islam arose as an improvement on Christianity, getting rid of the idolatrous Trinity (as well as original sin and the sacrifice of an innocent human to erase the sins of guilty humans), and both derived in part from Judaism, a religious tradition which was heavily conditioned by experience of the ancient autocracies.

In the rise of monotheism to world dominance, there may also be a role for sheer historical contingency. The predominance of monotheism in the world today is largely the result of Christianity and Islam. Both Christianity and Islam were extremely intolerant belief systems, compared with the polytheism which had previously predominated. Christianity and Islam engaged in missionary work, in conquest, and in the killing of infidels. Earlier religions tended to be bound to a locality and to be wide open to syncretism. In the competition between belief systems, intolerant monotheism would tend to supplant tolerant polytheism.

I admit I am a little dissatisfied with this account. It has some of the shakiness we associate with the early Marxist idea of primitive communism or the feminist idea of an ancient matriarchy. But whereas ethnography can't find primitive communism and can't find matriarchy, it does find many cultures in which there are numerous spirits but no big boss spirit, and numerous cultures in which there are many spirits along with a big boss spirit, but very rarely or never any cultures with belief in a big boss spirit but no other spirits, unless we count eighteenth-century European intellectuals as a "culture." So, though the theory could probably do with some tweaking, the main point stands: belief in many minor spirits is more fundamental, and until recently was far more prevalent, than belief in God.

This Season's Arguments for God

Outside the academic disciplines of philosophy and theology, popular arguments for the existence of God come and go according to various cultural influences, sometimes including inputs from philosophy and theology. In an age in which science carries far more authority than theistic religion (and that is always true of industrialized capitalism), such arguments take the form: "Science is wonderful and can explain a lot, but here's one thing science will never be able to explain . . ." Currently there are three leading candidates for that one thing: morality, some types of biological complexity, and some intellectual aptitude, either consciousness or reason.

The claim that morality depends upon God has a few different forms. There is the idea that the existence of morality is something that can't be explained without God. This doesn't look even faintly promising. Infants spontaneously display an urge for social co-operation. Humans evolved as animals that lived in packs, so they genetically inherit various impulses to conform to the pack's culture and to act for the good of other pack members.

It may be asked how *objective* morality arises, and my answer is that there is no objective morality, in the sense that physics can be objective, a set of purely factual statements; there is objective morality in the same sense that there is objective medicine, a system of ideas depending upon the assumption of certain values, like preferring health to sickness and life to death. What those values are in the case of ethics is more subtle and elusive, which is why ethics is more interesting than medicine. The values are inherited from our evolutionary past, both genetic and cultural.

Another moral argument is that without belief in God, people won't be motivated to act morally. There's something paradoxical about this argument, as it says to the atheist, "Without belief in God, people won't be moral, so you ought to adopt belief in God." This assumes that the person addressed, who does not believe in God, cares about whether people act morally, and therefore it assumes that someone concerned with morality need not believe in God, the negation of the argument's explicit conclusion.

Also, it involves the false premise that people can choose what they are to believe. Belief is always involuntary. Furthermore, the argument contradicts ethnography: we know about hundreds of different cultures which do encompass moral rules, with a variety of different beliefs about God, including such religious traditions as Buddhism and Jainism, which reject belief in God and are highly ethical—and including some cultures where a theistic belief system coincides with general implementation of moral rules that "we"—meaning I and most of my readers—consider to be appallingly bad.

This kind of argument is also a fundamental non sequitur from the outset, inasmuch as we want to believe, and can only believe, what we consider to be true, not what we judge will have good consequences if people believe it. Such an argument could be adapted to conclude that we should pretend to believe, since this will encourage those of lower intelligence to falsely believe, thus rescuing morality. But aside from being itself immoral, this strategy is unnecessary, because people are innately moralizing animals; there is no danger—and no hope—that moralizing itself will disappear.

Another relevant consideration is that leading theistic thinkers have generally held that morality, or at least a huge component of it, can be derived purely by reason, without any appeal to divine Revelation. Aquinas basically took this view—he thought there were some bits of morality that relied upon Revelation, but most of morality did not, and that would be enough to maintain a tolerable community.

All attempts to reason from morality to God are pretty hopeless, and quite obviously so.

Design Arguments

Darwinism does not directly imply atheism, and there are in fact many well-informed Darwinists who believe in God. Yet Darwinism does tend to work against theism, in that it offers a refutation of the most popular argument for God's existence: William Paley's design argument. Darwinism shows how properties of organisms that look, at first glance, as if they must have been designed, could conceivably have arisen by an evolutionary process involving a large element of natural selection.

Richard Dawkins has voiced the opinion that he couldn't imagine being an atheist before 1859—without Darwin's theory, we would have no reasonable alternative to belief in God (*The Blind Watchmaker*, p. 5). It follows that the refutation of Darwinism would provide support for the existence of God. I think, to the contrary, that proof of a design input to the natural world would clearly suggest that there can't be a God, as defined by Abrahamic theologians, unless the big boss spirit permitted some more subordinate and less capable spirits to fool around with biology.

The school of thought known as Intelligent Design argues that some of the complexities of living things, and some key stages in evolution, are far too improbable to have occurred by physical laws plus natural selection. Intelligent Design proponents do not question that the vast majority of characteristics of living things could have arisen by physical laws plus natural selection. The proponents are always looking for those rare, exceptional cases.

So far, most people in the relevant fields have not found such arguments convincing, but it is imaginable that at some point an apparently conclusive mathematical argument might be produced.

Suppose someone were to give us a mathematical proof that natural selection (we'll speak of natural selection alone for the sake of brevity, ignoring other evolutionary processes) could not have produced the complexity of living things over a period of four billion years, starting from a single-celled organism (the origin of life is a separate problem).

Would this compel us to become theists or pneumatists? Well, first, there could be some purely natural ordering principle that Darwinism has overlooked. This is the position taken by Stuart Kauffman. I don't see anything in Kauffman's ideas suggesting that this ordering principle would not be fully decipherable in principle by physical laws; it's just that we don't know all these laws yet.

A soap bubble or a snowflake exhibit an orderly structure, in full conformity with the laws of physics and explicable by them and

Kauffman's idea seems to be that there are many more such inherent ordering processes in physical entities which we have not yet identified or explained in terms of laws. So even if we could prove that the complexity of life couldn't have emerged by natural selection, we could look for some so far unknown physical processes that might give a more complete picture.

Whereas Kauffman says that there are physical laws we don't yet know about which are favorable to the development of complex structures, Thomas Nagel says that the universe is so constructed as to favor the emergence of mind or consciousness. This has to imply that the laws of physics (including the ones we don't know yet) tend to favor the existence of consciousness.

But suppose that both the universe's bias toward order and the universe's bias toward mind were also found to be inadequate. Suppose that, by some dramatic accumulation of new knowledge, we were compelled to accept that there just had to be some input of conscious design into the evolutionary process. Would this amount to evidence for God? I think it would clearly amount to evidence *against* the existence of the Abrahamic God.

We can't just accept some set of observations while averting our eyes from equally clear observations that accompany them. What we certainly can easily see, even in just the biological realm, is plenty of evidence that any designing that has been going on has to be limited, fallible, and incoherent. As we look at the record of evolution in the fossils, we observe this at every turn.

For millions of years there were plants but no flowers. Then flowering, and pollination, and a new role for insects, abruptly came into existence. We're tempted to say that flowering was "discovered," implying that whatever process was doing all this didn't "know" about this possibility before the "discovery."

The dinosaurs ruled the Earth for 165 million years, and were then wiped out, except for some of their progeny which became birds. The disappearance of the dinosaurs led to the rise of mammals. From the standpoint of a Divine Plan, what was the point of the dinosaurs? Okay, let's say the Creator was having a bit of fun, or allowing some play time for more minor spirits.

When we look at the course of evolution, do we see evidence of a highly competent, highly knowledgeable designer with a definite aim? We certainly do not; in fact we see very solid evidence of the contrary. If we accept hypothetically that evolution requires some design input, what we see is evidence of a designer or designers who are either not very powerful or not very knowledgeable, or both.

And, of course, there are the well-known cases where it appears that the "design" of an organism does not go for a redesign that would be obvious to a human engineer, because the redesign can't be accomplished in the only way that natural selection can work, by small incremental steps. Standard examples include the recurrent laryngeal nerve of the giraffe and the panda's thumb. Another case is the "obstetric dilemma" in human births. Humans are far more prone to childbirth deaths than any other animal, apparently because there was selective pressure for bigger brains and therefore bigger skulls, but no way of arranging for a new exit passage for the baby, sidestepping the restrictions imposed by the pelvic bone. (I give several examples of "bad design" in *Atheism Explained*, pp. 51–52.)

If we had to accept "evidence of design," it would not be evidence for the existence of God, or at least, for the God of the theologians. The whole process of the evolution of life betrays no sign whatsoever of any clear direction or purpose.

At this point we can expect to hear the standard objection that we only draw this conclusion because we don't know God's purposes; we can't see the big picture, as God can. But, as David Hume pointed out, all the arguments for God's nature are based upon appeals to our common assumptions and reasonable expectations, so it's not fair to disclose, when the discussion takes an awkward turn for theism, that God's doings are utterly beyond our comprehension.

Again, we return to pneumatism rather than theism. If we suppose that these piecemeal, uncoordinated, conflicting designers were spirits, evidence of design in nature would not amount to evidence of one big boss spirit, but rather plenty of evidence to the contrary—of several, perhaps many, puny little spirits each easily confused and each pursuing their own limited goals, sometimes at cross-purposes with each other. It would be more compatible with Shinto than Christianity.

But if we did have irresistible evidence of design in nature, there's also the possibility the designers would not be spirits, but something else. They might be evolved beings subject to the laws of physics and chemistry. Wouldn't that just put back the whole design question; wouldn't they also have to be the products, to some extent, of design? Not necessarily; they could have evolved in environments unimaginably different from ours, in which intelligent beings could evolve without any design input, then they could have turned their attention to injecting bits of design into the very different world which became ours. The hypothetical mathematical proof that we can't explain biology without design would only apply to our limited experience on planet Earth in the last four billion years, and to similar environments, and not to other possible places where an altogether different form of life might have evolved.

There's another possibility, which appeals to the science-fiction fan in me, that the designers really are tremendously intelligent and coherently motivated, but they are laboring under a colossal handicap. For example, they might live in one universe, with its own spacetime, and have found a way to have some influence on another universe, ours, with its own spacetime. (Yes, I know, but I'm assuming these guys are *really* talented.) To make this simpler to talk about, take the case where they died out billions of years ago and had to contrive something billions of years in the future, perhaps by "seeding" something within a supermassive black hole—which, according to one fashionable conjecture, is what gives rise, when it collapses, to a new universe.

Another way, perhaps more of a classic science-fiction way, is to think of different universes co-existing in different "dimensions," a somewhat woolly notion which I freely admit may work better in fiction than it can in physics. And then, an intelligent animal in one universe figures out a way to send a message into a different dimension, and we have the idea for a promising story.

Could Consciousness and Reason Have Come into Existence by Physical Evolution?

One argument, or clutch of arguments, which seems to be on the rise in popular culture is the claim that some aspect of human existence, sometimes consciousness and sometimes the capacity for reason, could not have emerged from natural evolution.

Do we accept that if the brain is in a certain precisely defined physical state, it produces conscious experience? Of course we do, unless we're pneumatists who think that the brain requires a bit of assistance from spirits. Unfortunately, the intellectual climate is such that people who acknowledge this obvious fact often also talk as if we're about to discover exactly how the brain gets this remarkable result. We don't, they suppose, know everything about how the brain produces the mind, but we expect to find out sometime around the middle of next week.

But this is hopelessly mistaken, and a sign of staggering presumption. No one has the slightest idea how the brain does it, and we may never have the slightest idea. This isn't in itself grounds for thinking there are spirits, about which we know less even than we know about brains. It is what I think of as realistic humility. And after all, among the few things we do know about brains is that they do exist, which is more than we can say for spirits.

In these discussions, we should avoid the assumption that if there is some human ability that we find valuable, it must have been directly selected for because of reproductive profitability. We can do all sorts of things that were not selected for genetically. We, or some of us, can perform handstands or cartwheels, or walk on a high wire over Niagara Falls, or sing a high note that will shatter a wineglass. No one supposes for a moment that these performances became possible because genetic selection favored doing handstands or cartwheels or walking on a high wire over Niagara Falls, or vocally shattering a wineglass. What we Darwinists would say is that certain broad abilities were favored by natural selection, and these abilities made it possible for humans to do these things if they put their minds to it. And this goes for intellectual accomplishments as well.

Once hominins have arrived (and long before that), evolution owes a lot to culture. Cultural practices evolve by a process that is largely cut loose from genetic selection, and indeed, as Christopher Hallpike taught us long ago, human cultures usually include many practices which are clearly biologically maladaptive.

In considering cultural evolution we generally start from the famous case of the Japanese macaque monkeys, where an individual member of the troop made an invention which was copied by the whole troop and thus became a part of the troop's permanent culture (in this instance, part of its technology). If such an evolving human or hominin culture exists, there will be genetic selection for qualities conferring reproductive success on those who are able to manipulate the social world to their advantage. Thus cultural selection feeds back upon genetic selection.

In my legendary article, "How We Got Here," I argue for the importance of "cumulative rational selection" in human and pre-human cultural evolution. Cumulative rational selection, as we known from the macaques of Koshima Island, does not presuppose any humanlike conceptual skills.

It seems to me that "reason" is a fairly straightforward development from conscious communication. Suppose that people have become able to communicate by uttering factual statements. They can make utterances conveying messages like "A sabertooth is near," "The baby's wandering too far," or "No one's watching" (so we can get on with making a new baby now that the sabertooth has eaten that one). Having developed the ability to make such meaningful utterances, humans are a long way from having developed a theory of logic, or even a glimpse of the possibility that such a theory might be developed. Yet they have all they need to develop such a theory, given thousands of years of camp-fire storytelling and chit-chat, followed by the emergence of city-states. If you understand any simple factual statement, you must necessarily understand its negation, and you must necessarily understand that the statement and its negation can't both be true. That's all you need to invent logic—that and a few hundred thousand years of cultural evolution. So an awareness of logic does not have to be favored by genetic selection; all that needs to be favored is the ability to make factual assertions.

Going one step back, could the ability to make simple factual assertions be the result of natural selection? Before language incorporating descriptive sentences, there could have been a much more rudimentary language of gestures and occasional noises. This could communicate a lot and could be reproductively profitable, and the more grammatical language could develop by cultural processes given such a beginning. I have known a number of dogs and cats, and each of them could quite deliberately convey definite pieces of information to me without making use of declarative sentences. I don't find it at all incredible that the communicative ability of dogs might evolve, by the interplay of both genetic and cultural selection, into the ability to make simple assertions of fact.

Thomas Nagel says that the universe must have an inbuilt tendency to give rise to mind (*Mind and Cosmos*, p. 67). But consciousness is not something we see blossoming in every nook and cranny of the universe. It is rare and peculiar. Frank Herbert wrote a sci-fi novel, *Whipping Star*, in which (spoiler alert) stars are conscious. This doesn't look promising, because consciousness arises in well-developed animal brains, which come into existence in organisms facing an environment requiring quick responses to ever-changing conditions. Stars just have to sit there and convert hydrogen into helium, there are few threats to their survival, and they are totally defenseless against what threats there are, like being sucked into a black hole. The life of a star is pretty humdrum, not the kind of existence which would benefit from the capacity to make quick decisions.

It doesn't look any more likely that the universe has a bias towards producing mind than that it has a bias towards producing, say, the aurora borealis. And it won't do to say that the universe had a preference for mind because that is an outcome we like.

A strange argument sometimes offered (by Nagel, by Hallpike, and by Derakhshani) is that human reasoning involves awareness of objective reason or objective truth, and this couldn't have come about by means of "purely physical" natural selection. I can't see any sense in this. It's advantageous to an animal to be able to distinguish between mutually exclusive alternatives, such as a dangerous or a safe situation or edible or inedible objects. A choice has to be made among options, and this choice can lead to life or death. The ability to choose one option over another, coupled with the phenomenon of belief, immediately implies the awareness that a belief may be correct or mistaken. The capacity for this awareness exists long before the evolution of language, and when language does emerge, the ability to make simple factual assertions immediately implies the awareness of truth and falsity. The ability to choose the true over the false, a good proportion of the time, must confer a powerful selective advantage.

We don't defend our belief in facts and logic by appealing to the manner in which we acquired the ability to know about facts and logic.

That is incompetent, irrelevant, and immaterial, as Perry Mason used to say. For that matter, if such a derivation were contemplated, we would be no better off with an evolved brain in a universe with Nagel's inbuilt tendency to promote consciousness than in the actual Darwinian universe, for the supposition that the universe has an inbuilt tendency to promote consciousness does not make it the case that mind will be possessed of the awareness of objective truth—unless we assume (as we should) that any mind automatically must be possessed of that awareness, in which case the tendency of the cosmos to produce mind would be redundant.

In *Atheism Explained*, I cast doubt on the notion that there could exist something "supernatural." Anything which interacts in some sort of regular way with the natural must be part of the natural. I now think we can extend this to the "physical." If there are spirits, interacting with the physical, those spirits must themselves be physical (as a few pneumatists have maintained; I seem to recall that Helena Petrovna Blavatsky took this view, but I only met her on the astral plane and the memory is a bit foggy). The discoverers of the electromagnetic spectrum did not suppose that they were charting a "spiritual" realm even though the realm they had discovered perfectly corresponds with Paul's "things not seen" or Cotton Mather's "invisible world." If we ever find out anything about spirits, we shall have found out something about hitherto undiscovered physical phenomena. I am not saying here that consciousness and thought go on in the brain without the intervention of spirits—though I do believe that. I'm saying that if I'm wrong on that point, and spirits do act on the brain pretty much as pneumatists claim they do, those spirits can only be physical, and if there is a big boss spirit, he can only be physical too.

Return to Civility

On one point, I completely agree with Thomas Nagel. Atheists and apneumatists should be polite and respectful to theists and pneumatists, and we should treat their arguments seriously.

I don't deny that the existence of a God who created the world is quite ridiculous. But I also think that the idea that little children, without knowing it, want to kill their fathers and have sex with their mothers is quite ridiculous. The idea that there can be more than two human sexes is quite ridiculous. The idea that a minute increase in atmospheric carbon dioxide could face us with a serious problem of global warming is quite ridiculous. The idea that eating fresh red meat can be bad for you is quite ridiculous. And (a white-hot memeplex as this volume goes to press), the idea that humans will soon be able to build machines possessing real intelligence, consciousness, and will is deliriously ridiculous to the nth power. Yet these tall tales are treated with far more respect by intellectuals *à la mode* than the arguments for Intelligent Design or anything with a theistic flavor.

In industrialized capitalist cultures, traditional pneumatist and "supernaturalist" belief systems ineluctably wither away, to be replaced by more recently spawned, more vigorous belief systems which are sometimes just as dotty, just as pregnant with hazards to humankind, and yet which masquerade as science.

As things stand right now, the Christians are not threatening to come after my family to burn us at the stake for heresy. But just recently our rulers were forcing Covid "vaccines" on defenseless little kids, with no benefit to those children or anyone else, while inflicting long-term health defects upon them, causing them suffering, and shortening their lives. And the Wokists are threatening to preach to my grandchildren and great-grandchildren, even while they're in kindergarten, that they should get ready to have bits of their anatomy chopped off, in a pitifully deluded endeavor to convert them from one sex to the other. We are beset today by ideology-driven enemies of humankind, hell-bent on doing a whole lot of harm, and unlike a few centuries in the past, these enemies of Enlightenment are no longer primarily the believers in God.

Sixty years ago, I viewed my arguments against pneumatism as akin to some kind of glorious campaign. Now I see them as a wee bit of intellectual tidying up, which some people may find helpful.

References

Dawkins, Richard. 1986. *The Blind Watchmaker*. Norton.

Derakhshani, Maaneli. 2023. Another Thing in This Universe that

Cannot Be an Illusion. In Sandra Woien, ed., *Sam Harris: Critical Responses*. Open Universe.

Dick, Philip K. 2013 [1970]. *Our Friends from Frolix 8*. Mariner.

Eller, Cynthia. 2000. *The Myth of Matriarchal Prehistory: Why an Invented Past Won't Give Women a Future*. Beacon.

Hallpike, C.R. 1987. *The Principles of Social Evolution*. Oxford University Press.

———. 2017. *Do We Need God to be Good? An Anthropologist Considers the Evidence*. Castalia House.

Herbert, Frank. 2009 [1969]. *Whipping Star*. Tor.

Kauffman, Stuart A. 1995. *At Home in the Universe: The Search for the Laws of Self-Organization and Complexity*. Oxford University Press.

———. 2010. *Reinventing the Sacred: A New View of Science, Reason, and Religion*. Basic Books.

———. 2019. *A World Beyond Physics: The Emergence and Evolution of Life*. Oxford University Press.

Kawai. M. 1965. Newly Acquired Pre-Cultural Behavior of the Natural Troop of Japanese Monkeys on Koshima Islet. *Primates* 6:1.

Kawamura, S. 1963. The Process of Sub-Cultural Propagation among Japanese Macaques. In C. H. Southwick, ed., *Primate Social Behavior*. Princeton University Press.

Nagel, Thomas. 2012. *Mind and Cosmos: Why the Materialist Neo-Darwinian Conception of Nature Is Almost Certainly False*. Oxford University Press.

Perakh, Mark. 2004. *Unintelligent Design*. Prometheus.

Percival, Ray Scott. 2012. *The Myth of the Closed Mind: Why and How Humans Are Rational*. Open Court.

Steele, David Ramsay. 1988. How We Got Here. *Critical Review: A Journal of Politics and Society*. Reprinted in Steele 2019.

———. 2014. The Bigotry of the New Atheism. The London Libertarian blog. Reprinted in Steele 2019.

———. 2019. *The Mystery of Fascism: David Ramsay Steele's Greatest Hits*. St. Augustine's Press.

5

COLD COMFORT FOR PACIFISTS

Eric Laursen, *The Duty to Stand Aside:* Nineteen Eighty-Four *and the Wartime Quarrel of George Orwell and Alex Comfort*. Chico, California: AK Press.

In 1972 Dr. Alex Comfort had a colossal hit with *The Joy of Sex*, making him suddenly rich and famous. Thirty years earlier, in World War II Britain, the young Alex Comfort had a heated dispute in print with George Orwell.

Orwell was an enthusiastic supporter of the war against Hitler, while Comfort was opposed to the war. Comfort was an anarcho-pacifist, representing an ideological standpoint then briefly fashionable among young English writers. Orwell had published several books and dozens of articles, but he had yet to write *Animal Farm* or *Nineteen Eighty-Four*. So, outside narrow literary and political circles, neither man was very well known.

Comfort, seventeen years Orwell's junior, had produced a couple of novels, several poems, and some works of anarchist theory. His most enduring work came a few years later, *Authority and Delinquency in the Modern State*, which makes a good case that politics is an artificial game preserve for the kinds of anti-social predators whom it is a function of normal social life to curb and discourage.

Later, Comfort was to make his name as a medical researcher and a gerontologist—a scientific theorist of aging. He could little have dreamt, in 1942, that his novels, his poems, and political writings would never attract a wide readership, that his medical studies would be known only to specialists, and that he would yet become, at least for a few years, the most famous man in the world—"Dr. Sex." He could also scarcely have imagined that, despite outliving Orwell by fifty years (Orwell died in

1950, Comfort in 2000), and despite becoming briefly a household name, even his extraordinary fame would ultimately be far surpassed by Orwell's.

We don't know how Orwell would have changed his views had he lived longer. He was susceptible to alterations of political allegiance, some sudden and some gradual. His anarchist critics drew attention to his several switches of political orientation, to which Orwell's response was, as so often with him, not entirely candid. We do know what actually happened to Comfort: he was less intellectually volatile than Orwell, and maintained essentially the same anarcho-pacifist outlook for the rest of his life.

The Orwell-Comfort debate occurred in 1942, most importantly in the pages of the American *Partisan Review*, at that time run by former Trotskyists and open to various kinds of anti-Communist leftwing thinking. There was a brief continuation of the debate (in verse!) the following year, in the British socialist weekly, *Tribune*. The editors of *Partisan Review* were themselves split on whether to support America's war against the Axis powers. The leading figure, Dwight MacDonald, was firmly anti-war.

A striking fact about debates over "pacifism," especially when they occur during a war or during preparations for a war, is the way that discussion of the most fundamental, abstract principles tends to become disconnected from the practical choices facing decision-makers. In the early 1940s there was only one major policy choice for Britain: to pursue the war against Germany, or to accept Hitler's repeated offers of a peace deal. There were quite strong arguments on both sides. In retrospect, with the Soviet Union enslaving half of Europe after 1945 under horrific conditions comparable to the Third Reich, the arguments for peaceful accommodation with Hitler look somewhat better today than they looked back in 1942.

This disconnectedness is maintained by Laursen, who gives the impression that there was some third alternative to supporting Churchill's war or reaching an accommodation with Hitler. But just suppose the impossible, that "pacifism" were to have steadily increased in popular appeal in the 1940s. Then there would have come a point (twenty percent pacifist support? twenty five percent? thirty percent?) where the government would have felt obliged to fire Churchill and bring back Halifax to start talks with Ribbentrop. What third option could there be? Yet the anarchists did not campaign for a peace settlement. They would have nothing, on principle, to do with the evil British government, not even to stop the slaughter.

If we consider the claims made by both sides in this debate, we find that they mostly talked past each other. Orwell argued that if you were a pacifist, you were objectively "pro-fascist." He threw in the additional claim that pacifists had a psychological tendency to become sympathetic to fascism. Orwell therefore called pacifists "fascifists," a term he liked to pretend he was quoting as a phrase already in currency, though it appears to have been a piece of abusive terminology he had personally coined. In common with the Left in general, Orwell used the word "fascist" primarily to refer to National Socialist Germany.

There is certainly something in the suggestion that if you oppose your own government when it is in conflict with x, then you must be to some extent objectively helping x. But to put that fact into perspective, this was a war of choice for Britain. Britain declared war on Germany and insisted on continuing that war after France had capitulated. Britain rejected all of Hitler's eager offers to negotiate a peace. A negotiated peace would have saved millions of lives. Orwell, like other supporters of the war, spoke of the danger of being invaded by Germany, without mentioning the fact that Germany had no interest in invading Britain except to stop the war which Britain insisted on pursuing against Germany.

The anarcho-pacifists appeared less concerned than Orwell with the practical results of their arguments, more concerned with doing what was morally right. Under the cover of fighting fascism, Britain and the U.S. were equaling and even sometimes out-doing fascist atrocities, especially with their campaign of "area bombing," actually the extermination bombing of working-class communities (working-class for preference, because there being less floorspace per person, each bomb would kill a bigger number of non-combatants). Orwell responded (in his exchange with the pacifist Vera Brittain) by cheerfully declaring that it was a good thing war deaths were now more randomly distributed among the population.

Anarchists and other anti-war leftists would often say that in the event of a German invasion, they would support armed resistance against the Nazis, but they would not support the Churchill government's war against Germany. The ILP leader and Member of Parliament, James Maxton, continued to maintain this position throughout the war. It was inherently unpersuasive, because getting a German army across the Channel and into Britain was something like eighty percent of the task of occupying Britain. It made more sense to stop them coming than to wait till they arrived to fight them. We now know that for Germany to try to invade and occupy Britain would have had virtually zero chance of success. At the time, it was widely believed to be both feasible and likely.

Laursen gives a fair account of the Orwell-Comfort confrontation and the surrounding circumstances. There are one or two small inaccuracies—Laursen follows numerous other writers in stating that Orwell switched from anti-war to pro-war following Hitler's invasion of Poland. But we have no reason to reject Orwell's own account that he abruptly underwent this conversion upon awakening from a dream about the coming war, on the morning of August 22nd, 1939, ten days before the invasion of Poland, and a few minutes before he read the press reports of Ribbentrop's visit to Moscow.

Comfort at the time, and various anarchists since, tend to over-rate the extent to which Orwell and Comfort were thinking along the same lines and therefore might have come closer to agreement. Orwell got on well with individual anarchists, with whom he shared a lot of leftist assumptions along with a detestation for the Communist Party. But it was no surprise to anyone that the anarchist Freedom Press declined to publish *Animal Farm* when it was offered to them, because of its author's statist ideology. After 1935, Orwell had absolutely no truck, and virtually no patience, with any kind of anarchism or pacifism. His thinking is more closely aligned with Arthur Koestler's and even James Burnham's: social order always rests on coercion and the future inescapably lies with large-scale, centrally-directed organization.

Laursen attempts to restate and defend Comfort's conception of anarchist society. But the type of social order envisioned by Comfort (similar to other British anarchists like Herbert Read and Colin Ward) cannot possibly exist. British anarchists of the 1940s were socialists. They saw anarchist society as being controlled by small autonomous groups not mediated by commercial transactions. The possibility of (for example) an investor receiving an interest return on the production made possible by his savings is excluded from their system. Yet they assumed that their anarchism would permit modern industry and high living standards.

These two features of imagined anarcho-socialism cannot co-exist in reality. Modern industry depends upon the transmission of information through market prices. Any anarcho-socialist society could only be one of primitive technology and low living standards. Orwell, in fact, pointed this out in his 1945 review of a book by Herbert Read, though Orwell gave the wrong reason; he supposed that machine production was ineluctably leading to a centrally-directed economic system.

In Orwell's view neither capitalism nor anarchy had any conceivable future. His pressing intellectual problem was how to prevent what he saw as the inescapable collectivist system of the future from extinguishing democracy and all personal freedom, as in *Nineteen Eighty-Four*. This problem simply did not arise in the minds of anarcho-pacifists like Comfort, because unlike Orwell they saw no inevitability in a centrally planned economy. And on this point, they were right.

6
Is It a Fact that Facts Don't Matter? (2018)

Facts don't matter, or so Scott Adams keeps telling us.

This looks like an outrageous claim. He sometimes qualifies it by saying that "Facts matter for outcomes but not for persuasion" and sometimes seems to back away from it by saying that "Facts are over-rated" (implying they do matter at least a little bit).

And despite his flat assertion that facts don't matter, Scott spends much of his time on his blog and on Periscope disputing matters of fact. He tells us that he was one of the few to predict Trump's victory—he assures us that this is a *fact*, and that *it matters a lot*. More generally, he tells us that Persuasion is "a good filter because it predicts well"—he tells us that this is a *fact*, and that it *matters a lot*. And of course he repeatedly informs us that "facts don't matter," which if true must be a *fact that matters a lot* (and that would be a *performative contradiction*, but hey, Scott's impatient with technicalities so we'll steer clear of them).

In fact, Scott can't talk for five minutes or write for two pages without making his argument depend on matters of fact which really do matter for his argument. So how can it possibly be that facts don't matter?

Well, maybe he thinks that facts don't matter for most people, though they quite obviously do matter to him? Or maybe we can make some sense of his strange claim that "facts matter for outcomes but not for persuasion"? Or perhaps he means only that politicians sometimes win elections despite making a lot of factually inaccurate claims? Or perhaps he's practicing what he sees as Donald Trump's "anchor" strategy— making a seemingly outlandish claim to attract attention and situate the negotiation, a claim which he will later dial back to a more moderate statement?

The Two Meanings of "Facts"

What are facts? Dictionaries give several alternative (and sometimes in-compatible) definitions of the word "fact." However, these alternative definitions can be grouped into two basic ideas:

1. **"Facts" are the way things really are (or were), independent of what anyone thinks.**
2. **"Facts" are statements which have been certified as true, either by common consent or by some authority, such as a consensus of experts.**

It can be confusing that there are these two common uses of the word "fact," as they are often contrary in meaning. In sense #1, it's possible for everyone to be wrong about a fact, or just to be totally unaware of it, whereas in sense #2, nothing can be a fact until someone has become aware of it and considered it to be a fact.

A little thought shows, in fact, that the vast majority of facts in sense #1 can never be known by anyone—for example, think about such facts as the precise configuration of molecules inside a distant star, or how many beans were in that can I opened a year ago. The universe contains an infinity of facts in sense #1, and very nearly all of them are forever unknowable.

Furthermore a fact in sense #2 may not be a fact in sense #1, because common consent or the judgments of experts may be mistaken. Facts in sense #2 sometimes change. It used to be a "fact" in sense #2 that conti-nents do not move, that homosexuality is a mental illness, and that it's hazardous to your health to go swimming immediately after a meal. None of these are "facts" in sense #2 any longer.

Assuming that we've now got these facts right, then the sense #2 facts we now possess always were sense #1 facts, and the older sense #2 facts were never sense #1 facts, though people thought they were. Sense #1 facts never change, as long as we stipulate the date—a sense #1 fact may stop being a fact at a point in time, but then it's still a fact that this fact was a fact before that point in time.

Although the two senses are sometimes opposed to each other, there is an intimate connection between them. We're concerned about sense #2 facts because we think that they're generally likely to give us sense #1 facts, at least a lot of the time. If we thought that a sense #2 fact had only a fifty-fifty chance of being a sense #1 fact, we would lose interest in sense #2 facts.

Confusion may arise if we don't keep the distinction clear between sense #1 and sense #2. When Kellyanne Conway said that she would look for some "alternative facts," this went viral and was taken by many to imply that she thought we could pick and choose our reality, like O'Brien in *Nineteen Eighty-Four*. But close attention to that actual exchange between Kellyanne and Chuck Todd, and the other comments by President Trump and Sean Spicer, reveals that Kellyanne, Sean, and the president were very definitely talking about sense #2 facts. They weren't disputing for a moment that sense #1 facts are objective and independent of what anyone believes, though in this particular disputed case, whether Trump's Inaugural crowd was bigger than Obama's, it looks to me that the Trump people were probably sincerely mistaken.

The attribution to Trump and his supporters of the view that facts in sense #1 can be chosen at will is not only wrong (not a fact); it's extremely weird, because there are indeed a lot of people who deny the objectivity or absoluteness of truth (post-modernists, social constructivists, anti-realists, and truth-relativists) and these people are all on the left. This is a characteristic belief of leftist intellectuals, and is never found on today's right.

Cognitive Dissonance

Scott Adams talks a lot about "Cognitive Dissonance," a concept which plays a big role in his theory of how people form their ideas. In *Win Bigly* (p. 48), he introduces Cognitive Dissonance by citing the Wikipedia definition. The basic idea is that Cognitive Dissonance is the discomfort or mental stress people have when they find a conflict between one thing they believe and something else they have come to believe.

The first thing to notice here is that this phenomenon of Cognitive Dissonance does not arise in most everyday cases where we find we have been mistaken. I was sure I had left my keys on the coffee table, but when

I look, they're not there. I start to search in the other likely places, and soon find them in my coat pocket. I had made a mistake; my memory was slightly faulty; no big deal. I'm not distressed. People revise their beliefs and acknowledge their mistakes all the time. Scott is demonstrably wrong when he says that Cognitive Dissonance "often" happens in "daily experience." It almost never happens in daily experience.

But there certainly are cases (a small minority of cases) where a major assumption is challenged by events, leading to emotional distress and sometimes to the production of what Scott calls "hallucinations," highly fanciful stories which reconcile the person's prior assumption with what has unexpectedly happened. Scott, in fact, soon forgets the Wikipedia definition and then begins to use his own definition of Cognitive Dissonance, in which "your brain automatically generates an illusion to solve the discomfort" (pp. 48–49).

So, for Scott, the crux of Cognitive Dissonance is an illusion. This presupposes a distinction between illusion and reality, and therefore presupposes that *facts matter a whole darn freaking lot*. Exhibit A for Scott's argument is, of course, the election of Donald Trump on November 8th 2016. Many people had thought the election of Trump, though an appalling hypothetical, was practically impossible, but it happened, and so these people experienced mental discomfort, and some of them began to believe very fanciful stories.

As Scott reminds us, these "hallucinations" (a term he extends to include any belief in tall tales) are more common among the party out of power. In the time of Obama, some Republican voters believed that Obama was a Muslim, while in the time of Trump some Democratic voters believed that Trump had "colluded with the Russians."

When we look at these exceptional cases of what Scott calls "Cognitive Dissonance," what do we see?

The first thing we notice is that this Cognitive Dissonance is brought about by the realization that something is seriously wrong: we find ourselves inclined to believe in two things which can't both be true, and we know that this can't be right. Sometimes, as with the election of Donald Trump to the presidency, the contradiction arises because we have to accept that something has happened which our prior beliefs implied could not happen.

A standard example would be a religious sect which preaches that the world is going to end on a particular day. That day comes and goes without any obvious disruption, and the sect has to decide what to make of this—they may begin to preach that the world did end on that date, despite superficial appearances, or they may conclude they got their calculations wrong, and fix on a new, future date when the world will end.

The awareness that something is seriously wrong arises because of our acceptance of facts. What it shows is that *facts are tremendously important*. Facts matter more than *almost* anything else could possibly matter! There is (as a matter of fact) just one thing—only one!—that matters more than facts, and I'll tell you what it is in a moment.

Without our acceptance of facts, this Cognitive Dissonance could not arise. It's only because we accept that Trump did in fact become president-elect that we perceive a clash between this acceptance and our prior theory which told us it could not happen. This Cognitive Dissonance also requires that we recognize the law of logic which states that we can't simultaneously accept a statement and its negation. So, we can't accept that "Trump was elected president" and "Trump was not elected president." The understanding that elementary logic is supreme is innate in all competent humans, in all cultures and social classes, at all historical times.

When we come up with what Scott calls an "illusion" to reconcile the new facts with our prevailing assumptions, what we're doing is accepting the newly discovered facts while trying to preserve as much of our prevailing assumptions as we can, without self-contradiction, especially those assumptions we see as most fundamental. *This is a rational response.*

Coming to Terms with the Reality of Trump

After Trump had been elected but before the Inauguration, Scott predicted that Trump's opponents in the first year of the Trump presidency would go through the following stages:

1. **They would at first say that "Trump is Hitler."**
2. **About halfway through the year, they would concede that Trump**

is not Hitler, but would say he was incompetent, perhaps even crazy.

3. **By the end of the year, they would concede he was highly competent and therefore effective, but would assert that they didn't like his policies.**

Scott is justly very proud of this series of predictions, which have broadly come true (though he didn't foresee the eruption of the "Russian collusion" story, nor did he foresee the brief revival of the "Trump is crazy" theory following the release of Michael Wolff's book *Fire and Fury* in January 2018). Scott's latest prediction is that people will soon start talking about America's new "Golden Age."

However, as Scott's account makes clear (but Scott himself apparently doesn't notice), the fulfillment of these predictions depended on *the over-arching importance of brute facts.* According to Scott's account:

1. **The disappearance of the claim that Trump is Hitler results from unavoidable awareness of the *fact* that Trump has not done any Hitler-like things.**
2. **The disappearance of the claim that Trump is incompetent results from unavoidable awareness of the *fact* that he accomplished more than most presidents in his first year.**

By Scott's own account, then, in these two cases, the facts are absolutely decisive. He just takes for granted, without any hesitation, that people had no alternative but to acknowledge these facts.

When Trump was elected, we can imagine the anti-Trump believers "hallucinating" that Hillary had been declared winner, that Trump had conceded, that Hillary gave the Inaugural Address on 20th January 2017, and that Hillary was now in the Oval Office, carrying out the duties of president, no doubt superbly. But not one of the millions of Hillary supporters reacted in this way. Quite the opposite, they wept and wailed, bemoaning the undeniable fact that Hillary had lost the election. Clearly, *facts are sometimes decisive,* according to Scott's own account.

Another way the Hillary supporters could have failed to accept the demonstrated fact of Trump's election victory would have been to "hallucinate" that on November 8, 2016, the world was occupied by space aliens who abolished the United States of America along with its Constitution and election procedures. These space aliens now directly governed what had been the U.S. and we all became subject to their edicts. Not one of the millions of Hillary supporters opted for that theory!

Why did all the millions of Hillary supporters, without exception, fail to adopt one of these theories, or any of numerous other fanciful yarns we could dream up? *According to Scott's own account,* there was just one explanation for this: all these millions of people had to accept the facts. *The facts were irresistible.*

Having accepted the unwelcome *fact* that Trump was now president, the Hillary supporters responded to this unwelcome *fact* by claiming that Trump was Hitler. Although inaccurate, this was not entirely arbitrary. It was essentially a continuation of what many of them had been saying before the election. They had been saying that if you elected Trump you would be electing Hitler. No doubt to some of them this was hyperbole, but they didn't mind taking the risk that many others would interpret it literally, and now they found themselves hoist by their own hyperbole.

As the months went by, Trump failed to do anything remotely like Hitler. He did not set up concentration camps, outlaw all political parties except his own, murder his critics or rivals, or act in any way outside the previously existing law. He criticized Obama for having usurped the legislative role of Congress, complied with the decisions of courts, and did not propose that judicial review should be abolished. Nor did he grow a mustache.

The involuntary acceptance of facts caused changes in ideas. We can easily imagine that the Hillary supporters might have "hallucinated" that concentration camps were under construction, that all political parties except the Republicans had been outlawed, that Hillary, Bill, Barack, Michelle, Elizabeth Warren, John McCain, and Michael Moore had been assassinated in a "June Purge." *But not one of the Hillary supporters reacted like this.* Instead, they all accepted that Trump was not Hitler after all, and moved on to the theory that he was "incompetent" or even "crazy" and that the White House was "in chaos."

This was also factually inaccurate, but again, it was not entirely arbitrary. It returned to charges made against Trump during the election campaign. Trump's decisive management style, his plebeian bluntness of speech, and his readiness to let people go who hadn't worked out could easily be represented as someone just flailing around. His tweets could be described as impulsive, ill-considered responses to immediate provocations. It took a while before perceptive people, with the help of Scott Adams, came to understand that the Trump tweets were essentially strategic and adroitly crafted: Trump was counterbalancing the hostile propaganda pouring out from CNN and MSNBC; he was reaching a hundred million followers several times a day, and he was doing so (as he occasionally pointed out) for free.

The "incompetent or crazy" theory was killed by the demonstrable fact that Trump was effective; more than most presidents he was getting things done. Of course, we may not *like* some of the things he was getting done (and when it comes to the Wall, protective tariffs, and the wars in Syria and Afghanistan, I don't), but, as Scott rightly insists, that's a separate matter. More than half the country does like them.

Notice that, once again, acceptance of the fact that Trump was fully competent was involuntary. It was thrust upon the reluctant Hillary supporters by factual evidence that could hardly be contested, culminating in the successful passage of the Tax Cuts and Jobs Bill in December 2017, which all experienced observers attributed in large part to Trump's management skills and capacity for hard work. By the time Trump achieved a rare perfect score on a standard test of cognitive ability, most people had already abandoned the theory that he was incompetent.

What Kind of a Genius?

Scott tells us that Trump is a Master Persuader. He goes so far as to claim that Trump could have taken a different policy agenda and won with it, because of his persuasive skills (*Win Bigly*, pp. 92–93). He even says Trump could have won by persuasion if his and Hillary's policies were simply switched.

While Trump's persuasive skills are certainly extraordinary, and Scott has helped me and thousands of others to appreciate that, I believe we can explain Trump's political success differently, and I very much doubt that Trump could have won with a substantially different agenda. I believe his choice of agenda was part of a shrewdly calculated political strategy. A linchpin of this strategy is the traditional working class in the Rust Belt states. These people had seen their real wages reduced, they had seen mining and manufacturing decimated as companies moved off-shore, and they had seen that the Democratic Party would do nothing for them, not even to the extent of paying lip-service to their interests or having candidates visit their neighborhoods.

Trump, Hillary, and the Issues

In the 2016 election campaign, Trump constantly hammered away at the issues, while Hillary ran away from the issues. This was obvious to all those who followed the speeches and the TV ads on both sides, but if anyone had any doubts, there was a scholarly study of precisely this point, conducted in March 2017 by the Wesleyan Media Project. This study corroborated what was evident to anyone who followed both sides of the campaign.

All of Trump's many rally speeches were densely focused on the policies he advocated. Only briefly would he make a nasty remark about Hillary's personality or past misdeeds, then he would swiftly return to his advocacy of very specific policies. The same was even more true of the TV ads for Trump. On Hillary's side, both speeches and TV ads gave very little attention to policy issues—far less than any other presidential candidate in living memory—and put all the emphasis on Trump's horrible and frightening personality. As the Wesleyan study cautiously put it, "Clinton's message was devoid of policy discussions in a way not seen in the previous four presidential contests."

Trump's rally speeches never wandered far from the specific issues, so that anyone following the campaign even casually became acutely conscious of Trump's policy proposals, whereas most voters had little idea of Clinton's policies. Trump made many commitments, broad and nar-row, about tightening up immigration, whereas Clinton rarely spelled out her own policy on immigration, and most voters had no idea what it was. Voters might assume that Clinton favored doing nothing to change immigration controls or even that she favored moving to "open borders." Dedicated policy wonks might be able to ascertain that Clinton also favored tightening up immigration controls, though *perhaps* slightly less severely than Trump, but voters who merely watched the news would never have guessed this.

Clinton just could not talk too much about immigration policy, for this would be to concede, in effect, that she shared a lot of common ground with Obama and with Trump. She could hardly boast about the steep increase in deportations of aliens under Obama, while denouncing Trump for his proposed deportations, much less could she promise voters that deportations would be accelerated once she was in the Oval Office. That would tend to go against the claim that Trump was uniquely evil for wanting to deport aliens. For similar reasons, she could hardly brag about Obama's facilitation of oil and gas pipelines and condemn Trump for also wishing to expand production of oil and gas.

There has probably never been a previous election in American history where one candidate's numerous policy proposals have been so familiar to the general electorate, while the other candidate's proposals were almost unknown. Clinton based everything on the proposition that she was personally superior to Trump—more specifically that Trump was a monster and at least fifty percent of his supporters (she meant a quarter of the population, the working class) were "deplorable" monsters.

Everyone who followed the campaign, even superficially, would know that Trump was advocating:

1. **A tightening up of controls on immigration, especially more effective enforcement of existing laws restricting immigration.**
2. **Repeal or renegotiation of trade agreements such as NAFTA and TPP.**
3. **Revival of manufacturing in the Rust Belt, partly because of #2 but also because of targeted protectionist measures such as penalties for companies which opened up new plants abroad, tariffs on imports, and a general government policy of "Buy American, Hire American."**
4. **Defense of the Second Amendment—Americans' constitutional right to own and carry guns.**
5. **Appointment of conservative Judges who would follow the Original Intent of the Constitution.**

6. A "pro-life" stance which in effect meant giving abortion policy back to the democratic process in the states, rather than a court-imposed "pro-choice" policy.
7. Repeal and replacement of Obamacare.
8. Abstention from wars (like Iraq and Libya) which don't yield any net benefit to the U.S.
9. Major reforms in the treatment of veterans.
10. Increased military spending.
11. A major drive to repair and modernize infrastructure.

Everybody knows that these were Trump's policies. Now, quick, what was Hillary's policy on each of these issues? You see? You don't have the foggiest notion. You might guess that she would keep Obamacare, though she said she would overhaul it, and in politics the line between overhaul and replacement is fuzzy.

Trump vacillated between extreme and moderate versions of these policies, but he never reversed them during the campaign. What was, in effect, Clinton's reply to these proposals? First, Trump is an evil person and we are not Trump. Second, we are entitled to be president because we are a woman. However, according to Clinton's leftist supporters, anyone who decides to be a woman becomes a woman, and therefore Trump could at any time become the first woman president simply by announcing "I'm a woman!"

Most of the time, Clinton avoided responding to Trump's policy proposals with her own. She did her best to avoid any comparison of the opposing policies, and to keep the focus on Trump's personality, a risky strategy as many people found her own personality unendearing and her own past conduct questionable. But don't forget that if she had won, this strategy would have been hailed as awesomely clever.

The thing that most caused me to rapidly revise my very dismissive view of Trump shortly after the election was not just that he won, but that he won in precisely the way he said he would win. He knew what he was doing; he had better intelligence about the voters. TV interviews with personnel of his polling firm, Cambridge Analytica, corroborated this interpretation.

My guess is that Trump, years before the election, had already seen that a dramatic comeback for American manufacturing and mining was

inevitable—indeed, was already in its early stages—alongside the ignorant conventional view that manufacturing and mining were in permanent decline. He could therefore not only make political capital from
the plight of the Rust Belt but also, once elected, ride the wave of manufacturing and mining revival. In business circles, people were already
talking about "reshoring"—the phenomenon of companies bringing their
plants back into the United States. This talk originated at the beginning
of the century but had mostly still not trickled down into the popular
media, and now it is doing so it will be difficult to separate from the
achievements of Trump, especially as Trump has admittedly done a number of things to give it a boost.

The inevitable comeback for American manufacturing was a commonplace among business analysts years before the election (see for instance the 2012 study, *The US Manufacturing Renaissance: How Shifting
Global Economics Are Creating an American Comeback*). Reshoring has
several causes, including the spectacular and continuing rise of Chinese
wages and the development of fracking, which guarantees amazingly
cheap American energy for many generations to come. During the campaign, anti-Trump commentators often showed their ignorance by proclaiming that the decline of manufacturing and mining were irreversible,
even as both were already rebounding robustly.

Obama did occasionally try to explain what was going on, but the
one line that resonated was "Some of these jobs are just not going to
come back." Oops. There go several thousand Michigan votes. And
Hillary: "Because we're going to put a lot of coal miners and coal companies out of business, right?" Oh, dear. There go several thousand Penn-
sylvania and West Virginia votes. The fact that these lines were taken
out of context and hurt the Democratic campaign shows that there is
cunning in Trump's apparent crudeness in making bold assertions and
almost never qualifying them.

The Obama administration officially began measures to promote
reshoring in 2011, but Hillary didn't make much of this during the campaign. This was in keeping with her avoidance of policy talk and her
haughty disdain for the working class, those dumb rednecks who, just
like Blacks and Hispanics, could be relied upon to vote Democratic without being offered any serious incentive to do so. And while Hillary knew

enough to understand that fracking is a tremendous boon to humanity and a guarantee of economic growth, she was no doubt afraid to drive voters to Bernie Sanders and then to Jill Stein by enthusiastically embracing cheap energy, underwritten by fracking. Obama had celebrated fracking but Hillary didn't dare to do so.

A general theme of Clintonism is that it relied on harnessing the energies of leftists while favoring ruling-class privilege. Hillary was embarrassed by any shining of the light on specific policies, because she wanted both the votes and the activist work of "progressives" and the financial donations of "neo-liberals" and "globalists," and she feared that frank talk about specifics could only scare away one or the other.

Scott occasionally mentions Hillary's discussions of "policy details" (p. 164), implying that this was a boring and fact-oriented preoccupation by contrast with Trump's nebulous and exciting "Persuasion." Nothing could be further from the truth. The Hillary campaign was simply astounding and unprecedented in its avoidance of any talk about policies, as the Wesleyan study proves. As far as most voters could tell, Hillary had just one policy: hatred for Trump's personality. This avoidance of policy issues is connected with another feature of the Hillary campaign, familiar from the book *Shattered*. Hillary never came up with a story as to why she was running. Trump was running to "Make America Great Again," and he would sometimes unpack it: "Make America Rich Again, Make America Strong Again, Make America Safe Again"—tightly linked to all the eleven policy proposals mentioned above.

The Democrats made things worse for themselves by talking about Trump's appeal to the "white working class." Plenty of Blacks and Hispanics had lost manufacturing jobs in the Rust Belt. Trump picked up unexpected Black, Hispanic, and Muslim votes, and among white workers he did especially well with former Obama and Sanders voters, beginning his long-term plan of permanently detaching the working class of all races from the Democratic Party.

Trump plays a long game. A tightening of immigration controls is popular with voters, including those Hispanics and Muslims who are already here legally. Purely from the standpoint of political opportunism, what's even better than being elected to tighten up immigration controls and then doing so? What's better is being publicly opposed at every step in struggling to tighten up immigration controls. This continually reminds voters that there are forces at work plotting to frustrate the president and the popular will, and therefore constantly broadcasts the urgency of continuing to support the president. The Sanctuary City–Sanctuary State movement might have been engineered to guarantee Trump's re-election by a landslide in 2020.

Trump finds issues where the majority is on his side, and where he's therefore likely to win in the long term, yet where he has to visibly battle against opposition. Even before he won in 2016—and he knew he was going to win—he was thinking of how he would manage his first term to ensure his re-election in 2020. As I have learned from my own earlier blunders in this area, the biggest mistake you can make about Trump is to suppose that he *ever* acts on impulse. Trump is a supremely self-controlled person who always acts methodically according to a long-range plan. Ignore this fact, and you may already have lost against Trump.

"People Are Not Rational"

As Scott repeatedly tells us, his contention that facts don't matter arises from his fundamental conviction that people are not rational. According to Scott, "humans are not rational. We bounce from one illusion to another, all the while thinking we are seeing something we call reality" (*Win Bigly*, p. 37).

The theory that people are fundamentally irrational is the fashionable one. We are constantly bombarded by books and articles from a wide range of sources telling us that people don't make decisions rationally but emotionally, and then invent false reasons for why they decided the way they did.

However, as we've seen, when Scott is not intoning the fashionable dogma that people are irrational, he keeps forgetting it, and keeps reminding us, unintentionally, that people do change their beliefs in accordance with facts and logic.

So what about the rare exceptional cases which Scott calls "Cognitive Dissonance"? What about the theory held by Hillary supporters in January through June 2017 that Trump was Hitler? Or the theory held after June 2017 that Trump was incompetent or crazy?

Though both these beliefs were seriously mistaken, I wouldn't call them irrational. The view that humans are rational doesn't require that they never make mistakes—quite the contrary: only a rational being can make a mistake.

So, can I defend the "hallucinations" of Cognitive Dissonance as rational? I believe I can. The first thing to note is that such illusions are generally short-lived. Scott's ideas about Persuasion focus on the short-range and the short-term. Theories about Trump as Hitler or Trump as mentally defective, as well as theories about "Russian collusion," have now largely evaporated.

What happens when something occurs that people's previous ideas had been telling them could not possibly occur? They adjust their previous ideas, and their first stab at adjusting their ideas may not be the long-range adjustment.

Karl Popper has explained how people develop their ideas through conjecture and refutation, in other words by making unjustified guesses and then disproving those guesses, and moving on to new and better (but still unjustified) guesses. That's how human rationality works. That's the only way it could work. That's what happens in the examples offered by Scott.

Can We Handle the Truth?

A recurring theme in Scott's writing and speaking is that we're not equipped to get at the truth. Remarks like this are scattered throughout his written and oral output: "The human brain is not capable of comprehending truth at a deep level" (p. 28).

Scott often talks about the fact that people of different opinions can be watching "two movies on the same screen." Another metaphor he uses is that of "filters." He says that he prefers to use the "Persuasion" filter, while other people may use other filters.

But can't we say that one movie or filter is to be preferred to another because it is more accurate? Here Scott equivocates. At times he implies that any such preference is a matter of taste. But, naturally, he doesn't want to let go of the notion that his Persuasion movie or filter has something to recommend it! If he did that, there would be no reason to pay any attention to his arguments.

What Scott repeatedly says is that we can never really know the truth, but we can prefer one "movie" or "filter" to another because

1. **It makes us happy and**
2. **It is predictive.**

So, Scott argues, we adopt a point of view not because we think it's true, but because it makes us happy to think about it and it gives us good predictions (pp. 38–47).

But if a theory (what Scott calls a "filter") makes us happy and makes good predictions, is that so different from being true? These are not exactly the same, but they do seem to overlap quite a bit—especially because a theory most often makes us "happy" by making sense to us, by striking us as a reasonable explanation. So, if someone had said in 2015 that a powerful coven of witches in Kazakhstan had cast a spell to ensure that Trump would win the Republican Party nomination and go on to win the U.S. presidency, this would have been predictive, but would not have made us "happy," only because we don't believe that witches can influence the outcome of elections by casting spells.

What makes us happy is largely a matter of our existing theories about the world. A new theory tends to make us happy when it fits with the totality of our existing theories—and this, I claim, is perfectly rational (though, of course, not infallible).

As well as Cognitive Dissonance, Scott talks a lot about Confirmation Bias. He sees this as an example of irrationality. But confirmation bias is rational! As Karl Popper pointed out, our theories would be useless if we gave them up too easily. If the power goes out in my apartment, I don't immediately abandon my belief in Coulomb's Law or Ohm's Law. I automatically save my most fundamental beliefs and give up more minor beliefs: in this case, my belief that the fuses were not overloaded.

While facts do matter, *theories matter more*. Our preconceived assumptions—our theories—tend to dominate our thinking, *and that's rational*, but sometimes these theories can be tested against facts, and sometimes the facts are decisive in causing us to change our theories. That's rational too.

If facts matter and theories matter, what about Scott's exalted idea of persuasion? Everyone knows that persuasion can have some independent effect. Philosophers have always known that persuasion has a role, complementary to theories and facts. Two and a half thousand years ago, Aristotle wrote a textbook of logic, his *Prior Analytics*. He also wrote a textbook of persuasion, his *Rhetoric*.

As Ray Scott Percival has argued (in *The Myth of the Closed Mind*), persuasion, advertising, and propaganda can all be explained within the theory that humans are rational. Here I will just throw out one hint. When he claims that "facts don't matter" and that "people are irrational," Scott always focuses his attention on the very short run. He looks at people's *immediate* responses to "Cognitive Dissonance." When he considers events lasting more than a few months, he always, *in practice* though not explicitly, acknowledges that facts can be decisive and usually are.

Election campaigns are comparatively brief events which take place within a framework of prevailing ideas that can't be challenged without political loss, and these ideas are often the outcome of influences working slowly over decades or centuries. For example, who was the first newly elected U.S. president to be openly in favor of gay marriage? The answer (surprising to some) is: Donald J. Trump. When Barack Obama was elected in 2008, he presented himself as a most emphatic and deeply principled opponent of gay marriage. If he had come out in favor of gay marriage in that year, it would have been too risky.

Between 2008 and 2016, public opinion changed so that it became more of an electoral liability than an advantage to oppose gay marriage. And this change was itself the culmination of slow changes in opinion over many decades.

7

DR. PETERSON! CLEAN UP YOUR THEORY!

Dr. Jordan Peterson has many claims to fame, but perhaps the most significant is his claim to reveal the meanings of stories, especially Bible stories such as Adam and Eve and occasionally stories from popular movies like *The Lion King*.

When Dr. Peterson was surfing his first great wave of celebrity, he went on the road with Dave Rubin and addressed huge crowds in packed halls across the world. Peterson would make a presentation from the stage, talking for two and a half hours at a stretch, largely extempore, explaining the meaning of a single story.

Stories as Entertainment and as History

Stories are told and listened to for many reasons. One of them is the sheer thrill and fascination of the story itself. When we read an Hercule Poirot mystery, we usually don't think it has something profound to teach us; we read it for its own sweet sake. In such cases we're inclined to say that the message of the story is the story. Although stories always do convey many other things, there are some stories where the reader is not primarily interested in those other things, but only in the story itself.

Another motive for reading or listening to stories is that they're taken to be literal historical accounts of what actually happened. Millions of people still take the story of Adam and Eve in this way, and if we do view it like that, then any search for a further meaning may seem less important, though we might be curious about some details of the story not disclosed in *Genesis*.

Stories with Lessons

There are also stories which, while assumed to be fiction, quite unmistakably carry a more general message. The simplest case is where the "lesson" of the story is perfectly apparent and well recognized by every-one. We all instantly get the point of the story about Brer Rabbit and the briar patch; it captures the common human situation where a person pretends to be averse to something he devoutly wishes for. You will oc-casionally hear the briar patch alluded to in discussions of national pol-itics.

Allusions to some such stories have entered into the language. We all know what's meant by "sour grapes," the response of someone who finds themselves unable to get what they wanted, and therefore console themselves by saying that it was probably not worth wanting. This comes from one of Aesop's Fables, from around 600 B.C.E. Each of his Fables ends with an explicit "moral" or lesson. And so we have the expression, "the moral of this story."

The moral, or meaning, or message Peterson finds in various stories are not like this. Their truth is not self-evident, even after they are pointed out, and the assumption is that it takes unusual insight to dig them up. Peterson conveys the impression that he's doing something dif-ficult and important by refamiliarizing his audience with these stories and then explaining what they mean. But how could it be so important?

Three Puzzles

There are three main puzzles here. First, since the meaning Peterson gives a story usually isn't obvious but obscure and debatable, how do we know when we've got the right meaning? Second, a related point but not quite the same, what does it actually mean to say a meaning is the correct one? Is the correct meaning the meaning intended by the originator of the story, or imputed by people who heard the story when it first started circulating, or by someone who has studied a lot of stories, or by someone who has cracked a code which unlocks the secrets of all stories? If none of these, then what? Third, since we can, after a lot of trouble, decipher the meaning of the story, we must be able to state the meaning without the story, so why do we still need the story? Does the story itself add anything to the bare meaning, except a bit of entertainment?

Peterson has stated that he didn't understand the story of Adam and Eve until he read *Paradise Lost*. This remark reveals a couple of things about Peterson's presuppositions. First, it assumes that the story of Adam and Eve has one specific meaning, which is other than that it actually happened (Peterson agrees that it didn't). Second, this meaning must be difficult to identify; it must be non-evident to the ordinary reader, since Peterson, like most of us, has been familiar with this story since childhood, and didn't know its meaning until he read *Paradise Lost*. Thirdly, the meaning Peterson has now arrived at is not something in the mind of the original author, or of the compiler who decided to include this tall tale in *Genesis*, or of any of the thousands of people who learned and studied this story for many centuries after that. We know this because the cosmology and theology of John Milton, the English Puritan who wrote *Paradise Lost* in 1667, are violently at odds with the cosmology and theology of the writers and compiler of the *Torah* and of the *Torah*'s devotees, especially pre-Exile devotees.

Nearly all Christian and some Jewish interpreters of this story believe that the serpent was Satan—this is implied in the *New Testament* (for instance, *Revelation* 12:9; 20:2). But "Satan" means something utterly different to Christians than it does to Jews. In Christian teaching Satan is an archangel who rebelled against God and became the source and sovereign of Evil. Christians call him Lucifer, but there's no such person in the *Tanach* (the *Old Testament*). "Lucifer," in a Latin translation of *Isaiah* 14:12, signifies the Morning Star, a metaphor for the Neo-Babylonian Empire, about to be replaced by the Persian Empire. It doesn't by any stretch of the imagination refer to a rebel angel. In the *Tanach*, Satan is a servant of God who acts, in accordance with God's instructions, to lead humans into sin—see especially the book of *Job*.

This reflects the deeper division that in ancient Judaism, God purposely creates evil as well as good (*Isaiah* 45:7), whereas in Christianity, probably influenced by Zoroastrianism, God creates only good, and evil comes from the evil god, Lucifer or the Devil, who wages continual war on the good God. In *Paradise Lost*, Satan establishes the city of Pandemonium ("all the demons"), his base of operations to invade the human world. *Paradise Lost* comprises twelve books, and the Garden of Eden appears only in the ninth book! What precedes that ninth book draws upon *Genesis*, but places everything in the context of the evil god Lucifer, unknown to *Genesis*.

Then there's original sin, which Peterson reads into the story (37:50). In Christianity, especially Protestantism, the story of Adam and Eve is bound up with original sin (all humans have inherited a sinful nature from Adam), but there's no place for original sin in Judaism. Islam too, like Judaism, accepts the story of Adam and Eve while rejecting original sin. Original sin is a peculiarly Christian coinage, propounded by Augustine of Hippo and taken to the extreme by John Calvin. If you understand the story of Adam and Eve as involving original sin, you place yourself in opposition to the writers of *Genesis*, your only source for this story. Peterson seems to acknowledge that original sin is exclusively Christian (*Maps of Meaning*, p. 314), but he doesn't recognize any incongruity in finding this thoroughly un-Jewish notion in a Jewish story.

The Null Hypothesis

It's not that all talk of meanings in stories is pointless. It's that we ought to be clear about what we mean when we claim that a story has a meaning, especially a meaning unknown to most people familiar with the story. The thing we have to account for is the claim that the supposed meaning of the story has some special status because it's the "correct" interpretation of the story. If I say to you, "Indecision can be costly, so don't overthink your actions," this might possibly be sound advice, but is it any sounder, does it carry any more weight, if I tell you that in my opinion this is the "real meaning" of *Hamlet*?

There is a "null hypothesis" in all this talk about the meanings of stories by Peterson and other Jungians. It is that Peterson, or whoever is doing the interpreting, finds an amenable moral, dictated by his twenty-first-century secular liberal worldview (in Peterson's case with a dash of Protestantism) that has some broadly plausible derivation from the story in question. This is as arbitrary as it is facile. We can easily come up with dozens of possible meanings that can be read into any story, and then pick the one we find most congenial to our own ethical outlook.

A defender of Peterson might retort: "Who's to say that Dr. Peterson isn't entitled to find a moral message in some story or other and then deliver that message, with the story thrown in as entertainment value?" Yes, of course he's free to do this. Out of all the many meanings that could be conferred on a story, Peterson picks one that tickles his fancy. For Peterson, stories are Rorschach tests. His interpretation tells us something about Peterson and nothing about the story. No problem! Until Dr. Peterson informs us that this is objectively the real meaning of the story, and something of urgent importance for putting people's lives in order and saving civilization.

God Said to Abraham, Kill Me a Son

One Bible story where the real meaning is seen as puzzling and controversial is the story about Abraham being ordered by God to get ready to kill his son Isaac as a sacrificial offering (*Genesis* 22). At the last moment, God changes the plan, and tells Abraham to sacrifice a ram instead. Peterson says, "The story ends happily," though the ram might have had a different opinion.

Many theologians have puzzled over this story, as God's behavior looks difficult to defend morally. Immanuel Kant maintained that Abraham could not be certain that God was talking to him, but could be certain that what he was being commanded to do was immoral. Kant's view was clearly not that of the storyteller, the author of this part of *Genesis*.

In two different places, Peterson offers two different solutions of his own to this puzzle. In his first solution, he maintains that ancient humans did not sufficiently appreciate the need to make sacrifices to get a future return (*12 Rules*, p. 170; "The Great Sacrifice," 38:57). The story brings home the message that we have to sacrifice something now to get something more in the future. So the point of the story is to give people what economists call lower time preference. He has also appealed to this theory to explain the story of Cain and Abel ("Cain and Abel," 3:49).

This interpretation has a serious problem. There's plenty of evidence that, thousands of years before the supposed time of Abraham (very roughly, 2000 B.C.E.), humans were routinely delaying gratification, making sacrifices for the future—they were saving and investing. The making of stone hand axes goes back to a time long before our hominin ancestors had evolved into humans. Fire-hardening clay to produce ceramic goes back around thirty thousand years, and building kilns to greatly improve the fire-hardening goes back at least eight thousand years.

For another perspective on the historical timing, *Genesis* tells us that Abraham hailed from the city of Ur. Whether this be true or not, the city states of Mesopotamia had, by the supposed time of Abraham, already enjoyed many centuries with an elaborate system of cost accounting, credit, interest, banking, mortgages, and negotiable debt instruments. They no more needed to be cryptically informed about saving and investment than today's Wall Street floor traders.

One source of fatally flawed theories about early humans is the assumption that they were stupid or afflicted with a kind of childish simplicity. In fact, we can find no reason to doubt that humans even (say) fifty thousand years ago had IQs roughly as high as humans today, perhaps higher. The key difference between them and us is that we possess more capital, including human capital or accumulated knowledge. This is on top of the fact that people fifty thousand years ago were enduring a glaciation, with much of the world's land surface covered in kilometers-thick ice sheets. Anyone of average IQ can just *see* that it pays to sacrifice a lot now to get a return on this investment in the future. No one, or at least no community with a typical range of IQs, has to be tricked into learning this palpable fact by some coyly coded narrative.

Arguing that saving for the future is a difficult notion to grasp, Peterson asserts that wolves eat all they can once they have a kill, and don't know how to make provision for the future ("The Great Sacrifice," 37:37). You might suppose that someone from the wilds of northern Alberta would have heard that wolves routinely go to the trouble of burying the meat they can't eat immediately, preserving it for later occasions. Perhaps wolves don't understand the reason for their own behavior, but hominins observing wolves and many other animals making provision for the future would have understood it.

Dr. Peterson's alternative, and utterly different, solution to the puzzle is to liken Abraham's willingness to kill his son with the willingness of parents to "sacrifice" their children by allowing them to leave home ("The Great Sacrifice," 1:00:56). Loosely speaking, they are both cases of giving up our children. Peterson identifies Abraham's willingness to slaughter his son with parents' willingness to see their children move out and make their way in the world, in other words justifying a troubling piece of apparent evil by vaguely analogizing it to something utterly different which happens to be amenable to cozy bourgeois sentiment. There's also the point that research into human happiness (known in the trade as subjective well-being or SWB) finds that parents become happier when their children move out, so in the typical case it's not even loosely a sacrifice. The empty nest syndrome is one of those myths of the present day, like the prevalence of a midlife crisis, which is contradicted by empirical research.

So what's the "real meaning" of this story? I see no reason to look further than the obvious interpretation, that it is morally required to submit yourself totally to the commands of God, even to the point of killing your children. We tend to find this repugnant; the writers and compilers of the *Torah* didn't. The story, along with other biblical references, reflects an awareness of child sacrifice as a customary practice that prevailed, or had recently prevailed, among the Israelites and other Canaanite cultures.

Peterson's Theory of Myths

Peterson has given us a clear explanation of how and why he thinks stories are important in Chapter 1 of *Maps of Meaning*, his first book, published in 1999. Peterson occasionally makes remarks showing that he still agrees with this explanation.

Here is Dr. Peterson's theory. The world is both a "forum for action" and "a place of things." Each of these are necessary; we can't do without both "modes of construal" (p. 1). The place of things is knowledge of facts and the forum for action is knowledge of values. Science can give us information about facts but it can't give us information about values (ethnology can tell us about the values people have in fact embraced, but it cannot recommend to us the values we ought to embrace).

The way Peterson talks about this, it seems as though only science can give us information about objective facts. But long before there was what we would call "science," there was everyday knowledge of objective facts, what we might call common-sense knowledge (I am taller than my brother; eating this kind of berry will give you tummy ache; village *y* is further away from here than village *x*). Any human in any culture has a vast store of such knowledge. All human cultures include a folk physics and a folk biology, which consist of factual assertions about objective reality. For that matter, many non-human animals know a lot of objective facts and some couldn't survive without this knowledge. I had a cat who knew that a certain sound (a can opener) indicated she would soon get food—this is knowledge of objective reality. Science is a refinement and elaboration of human common-sense knowledge; human common-sense knowledge is a refinement and elaboration of animal knowledge. These all refer to the world of objective, physical reality, as well as to the world of subjective states of mind.

Peterson tells us that science can't help us in the forum for action, because that requires values; facts alone are insufficient. We're informed about meaning or value from myths, stories which communicate values and meaning. In the modern world, we have the factual knowledge given to us by science, but we lack the meaning and values given to us by myth. Mythic stories, then, are "maps of meaning." By becoming more acquainted with these stories and their correct interpretation, we will possess a guide to action: we will have a better idea of what to do, how to live our lives. (A lot of the time, Peterson in effect assumes that "meaning" and "value" are more or less the same thing, which I think is a mistake. To save space, I won't pursue this minor point here.)

Peterson correctly asserts that facts alone cannot logically imply any course of action. Facts by themselves cannot motivate. But he doesn't seem to notice that the counterpart is also true. Values by themselves can never motivate. They always have to be combined with beliefs about facts. Both beliefs about facts and judgments of value are required to motivate any purposive action. So, there can be no "forum for action" which excludes beliefs about facts.

Peterson seriously holds that there was a time in human history when there was no "notion of objective reality" (p. 1). Rather surprisingly, but quite unmistakably, he believes that this was the case up until the seventeenth century! (p. 5) Peterson maintains that "The 'natural', pre-scientific, or mythical mind is in fact primarily concerned with meaning—which is essentially implications for action—and not with 'objective' nature." And he asks, "How, precisely, did people think, not so very long ago, before they were experimentalists?" (p. 3).

As we will now see, humans, like all mammals, have always been experimentalists, and awareness of objective facts about the physical world must always precede the construction of myths.

The Baby as Scientist

If a baby shortly after birth is shown a succession of white balls, followed by a red ball, the baby will look longer at the red ball than it did at the preceding white ball. This, and thousands of other experiments made possible by plentiful videotape and extremely accurate timing, have helped to propel a revolution in what is known about the mental processes of infants. Peterson sometimes cites Jean Piaget, who closely observed children beginning in the 1920s, but Piaget didn't have videotape and we now know from more rigorous and more numerous observations by Alison Gopnik and her colleagues that most of his conclusions were mistaken (*Words, Thoughts, and Theories*, pp. 2, 220–21).

An implication of the new research is that babies are like scientists; they continually pay close attention to the physical world and develop their own theories about it. A baby is programmed by its genes to find out about the world of material objects, by a process of adopting theories and then revising or rejecting them in the light of new observations. The essential points of this revolution are summed up in the already-classic book, *The Scientist in the Crib*, first published in 1999. As *The Scientist in the Crib* puts it, "Human children in the first three years of life are consumed by a desire to explore and experiment with objects" (p. 86).

This shouldn't be too hard to accept, since we easily observe that kittens and puppies are obsessed with finding out about the physical world by experimental trial and error. It's harder to see with human babies because they have a longer period of near-immobility, but in this immobile period we now know that they are observing closely and drawing conclusions from their observations.

Parents often bewail the fact that their toddlers are "into everything": they're driven by an instinct more powerful than hunger to understand the workings of the physical world. At the same time as they're learning about the world of physical objects, babies are also learning about other people, their minds and motivations. And we now know, for example, that a baby understands that they are a separate person, an independent self, at least soon after birth, and possibly at birth or earlier.

Dogs, cats, chimps, and humans are all born with some innate theories about the physical world (or, more strictly, with innate pre-programming to create such theories when stimulated by experience), and all of them revise these theories from practical experience in the first weeks, months, and years. After a few months outside the womb, dogs, cats, chimps, and humans have acquired a considerable amount of knowledge about the objective facts of the physical world. But then something happens which opens up a wide gulf between humans and other mammals: humans acquire a language capable of describing the world and arguing about it. This acquisition of a language also arises from an innate predisposition, revised and elaborated by practical experience.

Once they have acquired the rudiments of a language, humans can listen to stories and make up stories. And now they are ready to imbibe myths. When they start to learn about myths, their knowledge of objective facts about material objects is already extensive. It could not be otherwise. The story of Icarus can mean nothing to you unless you already know something about the Sun, flying, heating, melting, and falling.

The Alchemist as Scientist

Peterson frequently mentions alchemy, and follows Jung in seeing alchemy as essentially a non-empirical, magical pursuit, which reveals aspects of the collective unconscious, a kind of genetically programmed folk wisdom.

Alchemy, in the West, began in the third century C.E. and flourished in Europe from the twelfth to the eighteenth century C.E. (*The Secrets of Alchemy*, p. 4). Alchemy was not mystical or spiritual. It was chemical science, though naturally it embodied many chemical theories we now consider to be mistaken. No one had a satisfactory method for distinguishing elements from compounds. Techniques of purification were primitive, and many recorded alchemical experiments only worked because of impurities, along the lines of "Stone Soup" (pp. 141–43).

Alchemists were often concerned with trying to change one substance into another, most notoriously to turn lead into gold. Alchemists believed that all metals are compounds, not elements, and therefore there had to be a way to reshuffle the elements to change one metal into another. "Alchemy" and "chemistry" meant the same thing until about 1700 when a division appeared, due to social and political pressures—

for example the fear that being able to make gold from lead might undermine the currency and wreck the economy.

Alchemists believed that their knowledge should be kept secret from everyone except a few wise adepts. They therefore wrote their books in elaborate codes, in which mythological or symbolic figures were employed to represent physical entities. In an example cited by Lawrence Principe, a book of alchemy might include a drawing of a dragon attacking an eagle, signifying "Let the red dragon devour the white eagle." The red dragon means nitric acid; the white eagle means ammonium chloride. The red dragon devouring the white eagle signifies the chemical reaction of these two substances. This kind of symbolism was an encryption device, to keep knowledge of chemistry from falling into the wrong hands ("Learning about Alchemy with Larry Principe").

In the mid-nineteenth century, by which time alchemy was considered a thing of the past, a movement of popular thought arose, a rebellion against established beliefs, both science and Christianity. This new "Occult Underground" or counter-culture (which over a century later would be called New Age) embraced Eastern religion, magic, spiritualism, and all forms of occultism. Since alchemy was being dismissed by conventional opinion and by official science and religion, and seemed to be mysterious and profound, the occult underground was attracted to alchemy, and interpreted it in terms of spirituality and self-transformation. The fact that alchemy was dismissed, by those who knew very little about it, as a mishmash of mysticism and magic, only recommended it to these new occultists. (The author of *The Occult Underground* gives us fascinating information about the popular new occultism which took hold in the mid-nineteenth century, but he, like Dr. Peterson, gets alchemy exactly wrong.)

Many books appeared, rooted in magical or spiritual thought, "explaining" alchemy in this fashion, and since neither scientists nor historians of science were at that time much interested in alchemy, this erroneous explanation went unchallenged. It was copied from book to book, and became almost the only readily available theory of what alchemy had been. Then the Freudians and the Jungians arrived, and recast the magical or spiritual forces as forces in the unconscious mind. All these interpretations of alchemy as something other than experimental chemistry are still being copied from book to book for popular readerships, and all these books are endlessly reprinted, as though this interpretation had not been comprehensively demolished. Finally, along came Dr. Jordan Peterson, without taking the precaution of looking into any works on the history of chemistry published in the last fifty years, and repeated the old, thoroughly refuted, but still widely popular conception of alchemy.

For more than a half-century, historians of science have been carefully analyzing the alchemical texts, reproducing the experiments described, and building up a precise picture of the alchemical theories. They have shown that alchemy was a discipline dedicated to explaining the physical world by experimental and theoretical means. Among outstanding scientists who were committed alchemists were Tycho Brahe, Isaac Newton, and Robert Boyle. Historians of science have now re-introduced the old term, chymistry, to apply to both chemistry and alchemy, emphasizing the fact that (up until 1700) these were two names for one discipline.

Historical investigation of alchemy shows that Dr. Peterson is dead wrong. Alchemy was experimental science, and it went back more than a thousand years. But there's worse to come for Peterson's theory of myths.

Ancient Science

The first civilization to invent writing was Sumer, in what is now southern Iraq. No doubt there was science before Sumer, but it could not be permanently recorded. Sumerian civilization began around 4000 B.C.E., and was conquered by neighboring Akkad around 2300 B.C.E. Sumer and Akkad were eventually replaced by Babylon and Assyria. All these civilizations enabled and nurtured science. Their scientists could, for example, calculate the volumes of solid objects of various shapes, apply geometry and algebra to physical processes, and accurately predict the positions of the planets many hundreds of years into the future.

Science flourished in Egypt and in Greece, and then tremendous advances were made in the Greek-speaking world following the conquests of Alexander. Archimedes (third century B.C.E.), was one of the greatest scientists, greatest mathematicians, and greatest engineers of all time, with a large number of original discoveries, still incorporated into today's science. All ancient scientists knew that the Earth is a sphere, but in the second century B.C.E. Eratosthenes calculated the circumference of the Earth, correct to within two hundred miles.

With the rise of Rome, according to Richard Carrier, science continued to progress for a while, and reached a level roughly equal to that which would be re-attained by Europe in the sixteenth century. Roman scientific progress ceased after about 250 C.E., followed by centuries of retrogression. The revival of science in Europe beginning in the fourteenth century C.E. involved the recovery of ancient science, which had been largely destroyed within Christendom, but partially preserved by Islamic scholars writing in Arabic.

In China, independent of the West, there was spectacular philosophical, scientific, and technological progress in the period of "warring states," 475–221 B.C.E. Then China was unified under a single government staffed by a formally educated bureaucracy with a single ideology, neo-Confucianism. Philosophical progress ground to a halt; scientific and technological progress were slowed to a snail's pace (and perhaps there was actual retrogression). Europe preserved its political disunity and later became the dynamo of progress. A condition of progress is that there be no powerful centralized state enforcing conformity of thought over a wide territory.

Aside from experimental science itself, the objective nature of physical reality has been discussed in more general terms for thousands of years. Pre-Socratic philosophers (sixth and fifth centuries B.C.E.) were able to discuss issues like the nature of time, space, and matter, often entirely naturalistically. Some of them were pure materialists, maintaining that everything in the universe, humans included, consists of nothing but physical matter. Later there were works like Aristotle's *Metaphysics* (fourth century B.C.E.) and Lucretius's *On the Nature of Things* (first century B.C.E.). Lucretius held that nothing at all exists except "atoms and the void."

Dr. Peterson's contention that thinking about nature as objective and non-supernatural goes back only four hundred years is a breathtaking howler.

The Myth of Archetypes

Peterson often appeals to Carl Jung's theory of archetypes. Jung noticed that very often the same story patterns appear in different cultures and in the utterances of mentally disturbed persons. Jung concluded that there are "archetypes," unconscious predispositions in all humans, to produce the same story patterns in conscious thought. It's essential to the Jungian theory that these archetypes are genetically programmed, not merely transmitted through the culture.

Peterson uncritically swallows this theory and thinks that the archetypes generated by our unconscious have important things to tell us about meaning and values. This would buttress his claim that, when interpreting a story, he's finding something actually there in the story that can provide us with authoritative guidance about how to live our lives.

The archetype theory is unfalsifiable—how might the entire range of known stories be any different if there were no archetypes? There's no way to rule out alternative explanations for similarities in many stories: first, the stories could have been spread by cultural contact; second, there's a limited range of possibilities in human experience for basic story patterns; third, the stories could have been selected for by appeal to our aesthetic faculty (there are plot elements, known to Aristotle, Alexandre Dumas, and Joss Whedon, which make for an appealing story).

Archetypes are just a myth.

Is and Ought

Jordan Peterson relates his view of the need for myths to the philosophical problem of "is and ought." He sees the problem he perceives in many people not finding a meaning or a purpose in life as being associated with what he calls "the age-old problem of deriving the *ought* from the *is*" (*Maps of Meaning*, p. 13).

This is a serious misunderstanding about the history of philosophy. The problem of is and ought (or fact and value) was raised by David Hume in 1739. It then went unnoticed even by most of Hume's readers for well over a hundred years. Only in the mid-twentieth century did philosophers seriously begin to tackle this question.

The problem may be put like this. You can write down any number of sentences describing purely factual states of affairs, but you cannot logically derive from these statements, by themselves, any judgment about the morally right course of action. For instance,

1. An injection of substance *x* administered to person *A* will kill that person (a purely factual statement).
2. I ought not to give an injection of substance *x* to person *A* (a moral or ethical judgment).

Statement #2 does not logically follow from statement #1. But it would follow if we added the statement "I ought not to do anything which will kill person *A*"—a moral judgment, not a factual statement. It would also follow from some such moral judgment as "No one ought to kill any human being except under certain conditions," plus a factual statement that killing person *A* would not fall under those conditions.

Hume's question is purely conceptual and does not readily arise in everyday life, because we all normally take many goals or purposes for granted. If I tell you "This building's on fire," I can assume you'll want to leave the building. I do not have to add "I guess that you, like me, would prefer not to undergo a painful death by smoke inhalation and multiple burns, at least not this afternoon, and therefore the fact that the building is on fire, when combined with your system of values, implies that you should get out of here." All that can be left unsaid.

Hume's problem of "is and ought" is a serious philosophical development, but it has almost no direct application to practical matters, because we virtually never encounter situations where people can't bring themselves to make moral judgments, along with other value judgments. Quite the contrary, the worst atrocities usually happen, in part, because people are far too ready to make confident value judgments.

The human baby is born with extremely strong preferences or "values": it prefers to avoid discomfort and it prefers to get approval from the other humans it encounters. As human infants absorb ideas from the culture, they develop further values. We simply never observe, in any time or place, a whole bunch of people who spontaneously abstain from making value judgments and therefore can't decide what to do.

So, when Peterson says that "an impassable gulf divides what is from what should be" (*Maps of Meaning*, p. 1) this is true (if Hume is right) of the logical relationships among sentences, but is not true of actual human thinking and doing (as Hume was well aware).

Hume's problem of is and ought has little bearing on Peterson's problem of whence we get our values. And Peterson's problem is misconceived from the get-go because knowledge of objective facts always necessarily comes before knowledge of myths.*

Bibliography

Carrier, Richard. 2017. *The Scientist in the Early Roman Empire*. Pitchstone.

Dewrell, Heath D. 2017. *Child Sacrifice in Ancient Israel*. Penn State University Press.

Gopnik, Alison, and Andrew N. Meltzoff. 1997. *Words, Thoughts, and Theories*. MIT Press.

Gopnik, Alison, Andrew N. Meltzoff, and Patricia K. Kuhl. 1999. *The Scientist in the Crib: Minds, Brains, and How Children Learn*. Morrow.

Hume, David. 1985 [1739]. *A Treatise of Human Nature: Being an Attempt to Introduce the Experimental Method of Reasoning into Moral Subjects*. Penguin.

Lindberg, David C. 2007 [1992]. *The Beginnings of Western Science: The European Scientific Tradition in Philosophical, Religious, and Institutional Context, Prehistory to 1450*. Second edition. University of Chicago Press.

Neher, Andrew. 1996. Jung's Theory of Archetypes: A Critique. *Journal of Humanistic Psychology* 36:2.

Peterson, Jordan B. 1999. *Maps of Meaning: The Architecture of Belief*. Routledge.

* I thank David Gordon, Ray Scott Percival, and Barry Smith for criticisms of drafts of this chapter.

———. 2017. The Great Sacrifice: Abraham and Isaac. <https://www.youtube.com/watch?v=-yUP40gwht0&t=2772s>.

———. 2017. Cain and Abel. <www.youtube.com/watch?v=vMJnpww-pytg>.

———. 2018. *12 Rules for Life: An Antidote to Chaos*. Random House Canada.

———. 2021. *Beyond Order: 12 More Rules for Life*. Portfolio.

Principe, Lawrence M. 2011. Learning about Alchemy with Larry Principe. <https://www.youtube.com/watch?v=MbCol-h_ql0>.

———. 2013. *The Secrets of Alchemy*. University of Chicago Press.

Russo, Lucio. 2004 [1996]. *The Forgotten Revolution: How Science Was Born in 300 BC and Why It Had to Be Reborn*. Springer.

Temple, Robert. 1986. *The Genius of China: 3,000 Years of Science, Discovery, and Invention*. Simon and Schuster.

Webb, James. 1988 [1974]. *The Occult Underground*. Open Court.

8

SAM HARRIS
AND HOW TO SPOT DANGEROUS IDEAS

The thing that most struck me when I first read *The End of Faith* was Sam Harris's unashamed advocacy of intolerance, arising out of his preoccupation with dangerous ideas.

Harris made a point of putting on record—no one was twisting his arm—his opinion that it's entirely permissible, indeed right and proper, to kill people who have done nothing wrong, simply because they believe things which he judges to be dangerous.

You think I must be distorting what Harris says?

> Some propositions are so dangerous that it may even be ethical to kill people for believing them. This may seem an extraordinary claim, but it merely enunciates an ordinary fact about the world in which we live. Certain beliefs place their adherents beyond the reach of every peaceful means of persuasion, while inspiring them to commit extraordinary acts of violence against others. There is, in fact, no talking to some people. If they cannot be captured, and they often cannot, otherwise tolerant people may be justified in killing them in self-defense. (*The End of Faith*, pp. 52–53)

Several misunderstandings here. A moral judgment or a policy recommendation cannot merely enunciate a fact. Some former terrorists have given up their commitment to terrorism after coming to terms with their experience and being confronted with arguments, so terrorists are not always beyond the reach of peaceful persuasion. Killing someone because you believe they hold to ideas that might lead them to commit acts of violence in the future is not self-defense.

Harris insists that there can be no "private" ideas (p. 44). It follows that your innermost thoughts are the business of the police. And he says:

> I hope to show that the very ideal of religious tolerance—
> born of the notion that every human being should be free to
> believe whatever he wants about God—is one of the principal
> forces driving us toward the abyss. (p. 15)

Harris never does show this. He never even produces an argument that we're being driven toward any abyss by anything. But he does make plain that he's against religious tolerance—I like the old-fashioned term, "liberty of conscience." If you find yourself inclined to believe something of a religious nature, you not only have to decide whether it might be true; you also have to run it by Harris in case it's one of those conclusions that would persuade him that you need to be deleted. Harris's view that it's okay, or perhaps even morally obligatory, to kill folks who embrace dangerous ideas should be clearly distinguished from his general willingness to criticize Islam as an erroneous system of thought, like Christianity or Judaism—or, I would add, like Marxism, Psychoanalysis, or Postmodernism.

The Wokish wee folk have condemned Harris and have spitefully disseminated untruths about him, because he has drawn attention to the fact that Islam is, like Christianity, largely composed of falsehoods. He has also irritated the Wokish by dwelling on the fact that the 9/11 attacks and many other recent terrorist outrages have been perpetrated by Muslims. And he's not reluctant to call attention to the oppressive treatment of women and other groups within some traditional Muslim cultures, something which our progressive feminists consider iniquitous to mention, because . . . ? Well, ask them.

In being willing to criticize Islam as well as Christianity, and in pointing out certain facts about terrorist acts by some Muslims, Sam Harris is entirely in the right. However, I beg to differ with Harris with respect to three of his contentions: 1) that the liberal principle of liberty of conscience should be abandoned, as it applies to Muslims, or some subset of Muslims; 2) that it's morally okay to kill people who have broken no law because we judge (or someone judges) that their ideas are dangerous; and 3) that suicide bombings can be simply explained by the theory that Muslims do what the *Quran* tells them to do.

Harris's Two Theses

There are two theses running through *The End of Faith*. Harris sees these two theses as being entirely at home with each other. But I think they require separate treatment.

First, there is the thesis that there exists something called "religion," distinguished by accepting beliefs "on faith," which Harris unpacks as accepting beliefs on insufficient evidence or as accepting unjustified beliefs. Second, there is a peculiar problem with Islam, because Muslims revere the *Quran*, the *Quran* tells them to kill unbelievers, and this explains why there is suicide bombing.

At first glance these two theses may seem to be compatible, because identifying the *Quran* (or the *New Testament*) as the infallible word of God doesn't appear to be well supported by evidence. But as we look more closely, we notice that the two theses are mutually independent and don't sit very well together.

While Muslims might be supposed to believe things on inadequate evidence, Harris makes no attempt to show that they're more susceptible to "faith" than many other people, religious or irreligious. Although Harris doesn't quite commit himself on this point, he seems open to the idea that non-Muslims can be just as prone to accepting unjustified beliefs as Muslims. By Harris's own standards, everyone, or very nearly everyone, believes a whole lot of things without adequate evidence.

There's a difference between saying that Muslim ideas are dangerous because they are accepted on faith, and saying that Muslim ideas are dangerous because of their specific content. The latter is Harris's position, so faith drops out as an explanatory variable.

We observe that the vast majority of Muslims, even the most devout and fundamentalist ones, are not suicide bombers. It's true that quite a large number of Muslims have some sympathy with today's Muslim suicide bombers. I explain this in much the way that I explain why many Irish Catholics (encompassing Irish Catholic Americans), including some who would never directly support Sinn Fein, have some sympathy with IRA–Sinn Fein: they see these people as fighting (perhaps not always in the best way) for the defense of their own national ethnic population.

Muslims, like Christians, do take propositions on faith, meaning, as Harris tells us, that the truth of these proposition has not been justified. I thought I was going to have to take up a bit of space to explain to Sam Harris that no proposition can ever be justified, except within a theoretical framework requiring assumptions which cannot themselves be justified. But I'm now relieved to see that there's no need for this, because Harris has more recently stated that "Science and rationality generally are based on intuitions and concepts that cannot be reduced or justified" (*The Moral Landscape*, p. 204n21).

Motives for Suicide Bombing

In Harris's view, Muslim suicide bombers do it because the *Quran* tells them to—it's just that simple. In some cases we may want to say, "the *Quran* and the *hadith*," but, as far as I understand it, the *hadith* gain their authority from helping us to clarify the meaning of the *Quran*.

Robert Pape and his associates have presented a mass of detailed evidence on the motives of suicide bombers, and this evidence excludes the conjectured explanation for suicide bombing, that Muslims read the *Quran* and then do what it says.

Pape analyzed all the recorded suicide bombings between 1980 and 2003; later the database was continued to 2009. About a quarter of suicide bombings between 1983 and 2003 had been committed by atheists, mostly members of the Tamil Tigers (the Liberation Tigers of Tamil Eelam), a Sri Lankan group aiming at independence for the Tamil minority in Sri Lanka. Though of Hindu background, the Tamil Tigers were Marxist-Leninists, fiercely opposed to theistic religion. Another atheist group which perpetrated suicide bombings was the PKK (Kurdistan Workers Party), a Kurdish separatist group in Turkey, adherents of Marxism-Leninism, whose victims were Muslims.

So, when *The End of Faith* was being written, a quarter of recent suicide bombings were by atheists, not Muslims, and some of these targeted Muslims. Harris seems to have been unaware of this when he wrote *The End of Faith*.

After 2003, the Tamil Tigers and the PKK ceased to be operative, so that nearly all subsequent suicide bombings are by people of Muslim background, though many of these (around fifty percent) are atheist or more broadly secular-minded adherents of leftist ideologies. (These generalizations are drawn from Pape's two books, which summarize his detailed files on every recorded case of a suicide bombing.)

Two conclusions emerge very clearly from the data. First, groups which organize terrorist attacks mostly represent militarily weak ethnic populations who perceive their homeland to be under foreign occupation. They see themselves as resistance fighters conducting defensive warfare against an aggressive and brutal enemy. It would not be very promising to look into Catholic theology for the "terrorist outrages" of the French Resistance against German occupation in 1940–1944.

Second, suicide bombing has come into favor among terrorist organizations because it works; it's an entirely rational technique which achieves results. The announced goal of 9/11 was to get the approximately 25,000 U.S. troops to leave Saudi Arabia. The U.S. troops were removed from Saudi Arabia. The operation achieved its goal.

There were no suicide attacks by people of Muslim background in the period prior to 1981—and that in itself should raise a doubt about Harris's theory. The pivotal event in modern suicide bombing occurred in Lebanon in October 1983. A single member of Hezbollah (an organization newly formed in response to the Israeli occupation of Lebanon) detonated a truckload of explosives, taking out 241 U.S. marines, as well as himself. President Reagan withdrew the U.S. troops from Lebanon, so this operation was a complete success. Around the same time the French, who had suffered a similar though less spectacular suicide bombing, also withdrew their troops.

It has been estimated that on average someone prepared to die in an attack can take out twelve times as many of the enemy as someone who plans to escape with his life. Would Reagan have reacted the same if the death toll had been only twenty? Suicide bombings as well as non-suicide terrorist attacks are organized by intelligent, educated people who follow the news. The atheist Tamil Tigers were quick to draw the logical conclusion from the successful suicide bombing in Lebanon. (Some people would say that Lebanon 1983, while it was a suicide attack, was not a case of "terrorism" since U.S. troops stationed in a country whose population seriously doesn't want them to be there are neither innocent nor civilians. But Pape extends the use of "terrorism" to such cases, and I won't quibble.)

It shouldn't be necessary to remind anyone that all pro-war narratives, for example American or British movies about World War II, represent it as the summit of patriotic virtue and glory when someone strikes a blow against the enemy knowing that it will result in his own death. Celebrating the voluntary self-destruction of soldiers in wartime, patriotic Christians would often apply the famous saying of Jesus: "Greater love hath no man than this, that a man lay down his life for his friends" (John 15:13).

Nor should it need to be recalled that a major part of Allied military operations in that war was devoted to the mass slaughter of non-combatants (the "area bombing" of working-class housing in German cities and similar bombings of civilian dwellings in Japan, culminating in Hiroshima and Nagasaki). The stated aim of this systematic extermination of civilian non-combatants was to "break the morale" of the enemy population.

History is studded with suicide attacks, though these were limited in effectiveness before the invention of dynamite in 1867. We're told that Samson, with God's help, killed himself and three thousand Philistine men and women by collapsing the building they were in (*Judges* 16:30), no doubt a prophecy of 9/11. A high percentage of Roman emperors were assassinated or violently injured in assassination attempts, usually by people who knew this would automatically mean their own deaths. The assassination of Tsar Alexander II in 1881 and of Russian minister Plehve in 1904 were suicide bombings. Suicide squads and individual suicide bombings were frequently employed in the Chinese wars from 1911 to 1949, both between different Chinese war lords and against the occupying Japanese. The Japanese military employed the famous *kamikaze* suicide bombings against the U.S., beginning in October 1944, and the Luftwaffe flew "self-sacrifice missions" (*Selbstopfereinsatz*) against the Soviets in the Battle for Berlin, April 1945.

Suicide attack is the continuation of a policy of non-suicide attack by suicidal means. If the suicide attackers could do as much damage to the enemy without suicide, they would always opt to do so. In nineteenth-century Europe there were anarchist suicide assassins who were generally atheists. These killings are not usually labeled suicide attacks but it's clear that the attackers often didn't expect to survive the attacks. This phenomenon became a theme in Victorian popular culture, reflected in "The Stolen Bacillus," by H.G. Wells and *The Secret Agent* by Joseph Conrad.

A Dangerous System of Ideas

Suicide bombing is horrible, but it's a vanishingly tiny part of "man's inhumanity to man." Suicide bombing (with the exceptions of the *Selbstopfereinsatz* and *kamikaze* pilots, and even those were cases of last-ditch desperation) is done by weak groups out of power, whereas more than 99 percent of major atrocities are carried out by strong groups in full command of a state.

So, by way of a change, let's turn our attention to the hundred-ton titanosaur in the room—Bolshevism, alias Marxism-Leninism, alias Communism, alias the Fraternal Socialist Camp. Communism killed 90 million innocent people. (I talk about killings for brevity, though we have to understand that for every killing there are dozens of less bothersome inconveniences, such as imprisonment and torture, visited on the Communists' hapless "human material.")

Communism, in the twentieth century, killed hundreds of times more innocent victims than Christianity and Islam combined in their entire historical existence. There are various ways of putting this in numerical perspective; I'll mention just one example. The Spanish Inquisition (Ha! You didn't expect *that*) lasted 356 years, from 1478 to 1834. Estimates of the total number executed by the Inquisition range from 1,250 to 5,000. Compare this with 15,000 killed *in two months*, under the Lenin-Trotsky government in the fall of 1918.

Everyone executed by order of the Holy Office of the Inquisition had their day in court, and most people accused were acquitted. The Bolshevik victims were just names on a list, picked up and disposed of, with a bracing proletarian disdain for bourgeois hang-ups like human rights or due process. Not that the Bolsheviks were proletarians, but they affected to be proletarians (we can call them trans proletarians). The

Bolsheviks had managed to divine the true interests of the proletariat, or so they devoutly believed, and had therefore—scientifically—anointed themselves the vanguard of the proletariat.

Harris's Unsatisfactory Response

Harris naturally attempts to answer the most obvious criticisms of his position. In support of his claim that there's something uniquely Muslim about suicide bombing, he points out that various non-Muslim populations have faced poverty and oppression without turning to suicide bombing (p. 109). This side-steps the key causal factor, occupation by foreign troops, and ignores the many non-Muslim suicide bombers.

In a direct comment on Pape's work, Harris calls it "obscurantist" to attribute nationalist political motives to Osama bin Laden (p. 261). Of course, a fundamentalist Muslim resistance fighter will justify his actions in fundamentalist Muslim terms, just as a Marxist-Leninist resistance fighter will justify his actions in Marxist-Leninist terms. Yet bin Laden scoffed at the suggestion that al-Qaeda was motivated by general hatred of the unbelieving West, emphasizing repeatedly that al-Qaeda was a response to Western military occupation.

> No, we fight because we are free men who don't sleep under oppression.... contrary to Bush's claim that we hate freedom. If so, let him explain why we don't strike, for example, Sweden. (bin Laden video, quoted in *Cutting the Fuse*, p. 51)

Harris asks, "Where are the Palestinian Christian suicide bombers? . . . Where, for that matter, are the Tibetan Buddhist suicide bombers? . . . The difference lies in the specific tenets of Islam" (p. 233). Does it really?

There have been some Palestinian Christian fighters against Israel and its Western backers. The best known is George Habash, founder and leader of the Popular Front for the Liberation of Palestine (PFLP). There were no Middle Eastern suicide bombers before 1981 but there were both Muslim and Christian Palestinian resistance fighters or "terrorists."

What about Christian suicide bombers specifically? I have not found a total count so I can't compare the number with other Palestinian suicide attacks. Christians comprise 1.5 percent of Palestinians living in the Middle East. It does seem from Pape's published materials that in all likelihood Palestinian Christians account for a decidedly bigger percentage than 1.5 percent of suicide attacks against Israel and Israel's Western backers. For example, in the resistance to the Israeli occupation of Lebanon, from 1982 to 1999, there were 32 successful suicide attacks where the ideology or background of the attackers can be identified.

Five were Christians (15.6 percent), while 22 were leftists with no commitment to religious extremism, leaving five whose outlooks were primarily Muslim fundamentalist (*Cutting the Fuse*, p. 196). So, in that admittedly non-probative case, Christians are more than ten times as well-represented among suicide bombers as their proportion of the Palestinian population. This is what we might expect, as Palestinian Christians are distinguished by a high average level of education, and education is a predictor of involvement in resistance/terrorism.

As for Harris's rhetorical query about the Tibetan Buddhists, it's well documented that the people who organize suicide bombings believe that these actions work more effectively against democracies than against totalitarian states. Totalitarian states can prevent their general population (and sometimes the outside world) from getting news about such events, and do not have to face domestic anti-war movements. There were very few suicide bombings against the Soviet occupation of Afghanistan, but very many against the later U.S. occupation. If China were to become a democracy, we should expect to see some elements in various ethnic groups within China become more violent, and some of them become suicide bombers.

Naturally, Harris tries to respond to the fact that atheists have been responsible for more and bigger atrocities than theists. He says that "communism was little more than a political religion." Communist beliefs "were both cultic and irrational" (p. 79; and see p. 231). But this amounts to equivocation. Harris made his name and his fortune by boldly proclaiming that Muslims are particularly prone to become mass murderers, because of what it says in the *Quran*; confronted with the fact that atheists are historically vastly more likely to commit mass murder than Muslims, his response is that Communism is a religion.

As far as Muslim suicide bombings go, the solution does not lie in killing devotees of the *Quran* before they get around to suicide bombing. That will reliably increase the incidence of anti-U.S. suicide bombing. The solution lies in ending military interventions against Muslim populations. (Surely it's a point in favor of such a policy that these interventions are, from the point of view of U.S. self-interest, costly and most often disastrous, even not counting the terrorist attacks they automatically provoke. What did the U.S. gain from the 2003–2011 Iraq war, which killed 100,000 innocent civilians?) No doubt there will still be occasional rare attacks in response to blasphemous cartoons or the like, but more than 99 percent of anti-U.S. suicide bombings will immediately and permanently cease, if the U.S. stops intervening militarily against Muslim populations. (In arguing for total non-intervention, I go further than Pape's group, who favor a more indirect and sensitive mode of intervention.)

Pape's theory propounded in 2005 elicited some serious criticisms, such as those of Assaf Moghadam and Scott Attran. Subsequent events have powerfully corroborated Pape's position (*Cutting the Fuse*, pp. 44–83); yet, in any case, Pape's competent critics did not endorse Harris's simple theory that suicide attacks are caused by doing what the *Quran* tells you to do.

Dangerous Ideas, Old and New

Within industrialized capitalist societies, theistic religion withers on the vine. We observe that this holds in all cases—the notion that the United States was ever an exception is a simple misunderstanding, arising from the fact that for two centuries the United States contained within its borders a third-world country: the South. Now that the South has industrialized, America is rapidly becoming exactly like Europe, as far as theistic religion goes.

Sam Harris ignores the big fact that the theistic or supernaturalistic belief systems of pre-industrial cultures are succeeded by the non-theistic, non-supernaturalistic belief systems of industrialized cultures. These latter "scientific" belief systems are just as much filled with absurdities and preposterous nonsense as the earlier belief systems. The Oedipus Complex, the class struggle, or intersectionality are just as much intellectual dross and drivel as the doctrines of the Trinity or blood sacrifice for sin. And they are just as likely to lead to atrocities, perhaps more so.

As a simple matter of fact, the historical atrocities deriving from purportedly scientific belief systems vastly outweigh the historical atrocities deriving from theistic or supernaturalistic belief systems. Does this mean that atheism is inherently more prone to commit mass murder than theism? Not necessarily. The greater death toll attributable to secular ideologies could be wholly or partly due to the fact that the rise of non-supernaturalistic ideologies coincides with the emergence of bigger populations and more efficient techniques to mobilize the state's mass-murder machine.

Voltaire's motto was *Écrasez l'infâme!*, crush the appalling monstrosity of ecclesiastical Christendom. It never crossed his mind that theistic belief systems would be replaced by new ideologies avowedly based on reason and science, and that these ideologies would turn out to be far more murderous, far more devastating for human well-being, than theism or supernatural belief had ever been.

The eclipse of theistic religion in the industrialized world has been much less of a gain for humankind than rationalists and freethinkers expected. There has been hardly any diminution of gross error in people's thinking, rather a limitation of one narrow type of error and the proliferation of many new errors, nearly always presenting themselves as scientific.

The driving narrative of Sam Harris and all the New Atheists is that we face a peculiar menace from theistic religion, which threatens to push us into the abyss, because it accepts propositions without sufficient evidence. Through my old atheist eyes, I see theistic religion as an enfeebled and increasingly irrelevant force in the world (as long as net global economic growth continues), being replaced by atheistic and purportedly scientific belief systems, which swallow just as many impossible things before breakfast, and threaten us with atrocities more horrendous than anything the theists could have dreamed up.

The Paradox of Tolerance

Harris's principle that we're entitled to kill people for holding dangerous ideas naturally brings to mind the Paradox of Tolerance, briefly formulated by Karl Popper in *The Open Society and Its Enemies* (Volume 1, p. 265n4). Popper holds that we ought to be selectively intolerant of intolerant ideas (though not routinely, but only under very rare and specific conditions), in other words, we ought sometimes to deny the usual liberal freedom of expression to those who advocate policies which would deny the usual liberal freedoms to everyone.

Popper's argument is superficially persuasive, but it falls apart upon closer examination. Its incoherence becomes visible when we pose the question "Who is the 'we'?" Is the "we" an extra-dimensional wraith, who can observe the growth of the intolerant group and intervene from outside the political process to restrict people's freedom of speech? Presumably not. But then we have the situation where the "we" is itself part of the political system, socially interacting with the intolerance-advocating group as well as other groups. And we have to assume that the "we" is able to deny freedom to the intolerance-advocating group while not being able to counteract the intolerance-advocating group by peaceful persuasion. Right off the bat, that looks unlikely.

Surely if the "we" is able to deny freedom to the group advocating intolerance, the "we" must be in a strong position, while the apparent inability of the "we" to combat the influence of the intolerance-advocating group by peaceful persuasion must imply that the "we" is weak. Furthermore, suppression of the group's activities might very well stimulate sympathy for the group, and play into the hands of those who say that tolerance is a sham, that the so-called tolerant are only tolerant as long as their key interests are not threatened, and so on. The government of the Weimar Republic prohibited Adolf Hitler from speaking publicly; whether this ultimately hurt or helped his chances of getting into power is debatable.

All in all, then, selectively practicing intolerance against those who would install an intolerant regime if they could, is not a superior strategy to defending the principle of liberty of conscience all the time. Ultimately, ideas expressed in words are the only weapon available to combat intolerance, just as ideas expressed in words are the only weapon available to spread intolerant ideas in the first place.

From Out of Left Field

Where are future atrocities going to come from? It's not obvious which ideas and which ideological groups are going to turn out to be the most dangerous.

Prior to 1917, the basic principles of Marxism were widely known. They included the following propositions: Minority coups or insurrections are wrong, and to be actively discouraged. (When I use words like "wrong" here, I'm translating from Marxese into English.) The socialist movement must be fully democratic and must take part in the democratic process to "win the battle of democracy." Even in non-democratic polities like Germany, Marx and Engels thought it wrong to use violence, as long as progress towards democracy could be made by non-violent means (Hunt 1984, pp. 325–336). Among other key tenets of classical Marxism, no socialist revolution is to be expected in a predominantly peasant society and the worst fate will befall anyone who tries to carry through a social revolution before the economic conditions are ripe for it.

These principles were fully accepted by all Marxists, including even the Bolsheviks. And when the Bolsheviks acted contrary to these Marxist principles by seizing power, shutting down the democratically elected assembly, and killing their intellectual critics, all leading Marxists in the world, without exception, denounced the Bolsheviks. Top of the targets on the Bolshevik hit list were those Marxists who remained true to elementary Marxist principles, notably the Mensheviks.

Before 1917 it would have seemed fantastic beyond all possibility of ridicule to hypothesize that by far the bloodiest empires in all of human history were about to be founded by a sect of Marxism, albeit a bizarrely heretical sect. If I were to predict now that five years in the future, the most murderous regime of all time will be set up by fanatical followers of Sam Harris, that would be about as plausible as a similar prediction about Marxism in 1912 (in fact a little more plausible, since Marx, unlike Harris, did not preach that people holding dangerous ideas should be wasted).

There's no litmus test to determine where the biggest danger is going to come from next—and no simple formula to decide in advance, when things get really bleak, who's going to be the ally who may possibly save your family's life.

Bibliography

Attran, Scott. 2006. The Moral Logic and Growth of Suicide Terrorism. *Washington Quarterly* 29:2.

Collard-Wexler, Simon, Constantino Pischedda, and Michael G. Smith. 2014. Do Foreign Occupations Cause Suicide Attacks? *Journal of Conflict Resolution* 58:4.

Conrad, Joseph. 2007 [1907]. *The Secret Agent: A Simple Tale*. Penguin.

Courtois, Stéphane, et al. 1999. *The Black Book of Communism: Crimes, Terror, Repression*. Harvard University Press.

Exposing Theism. 2012. Sam Harris vs Robert Pape on Religious Martyrdom. <www.youtube.com/watch?v=7sUbaHkCet0>.

Harris, Sam. 2005 [2004]. *The End of Faith: Religion, Terror, and the Future of Reason*. Norton.

———. 2010. *The Moral Landscape: How Science Can Determine Human Values*. Free Press.

Hunt, Richard N. 1974. *The Political Ideas of Marx and Engels I: Marxism and Totalitarian Democracy*. University of Pittsburgh Press.

———. 1984. *The Political Ideas of Marx and Engels II: Classical Marxism 1850–1895*. University of Pittsburgh Press.

Moghadam, Assaf. 2006. Suicide Terrorism, Occupation, and the Globalization of Martyrdom: A Critique of *Dying to Win*. *Studies in Conflict and Terrorism* 9:8. <www.tandfonline.com/doi/full/10.1080/10576100600561907>.

Pape, Robert A. 2005. *Dying to Win: The Strategic Logic of Suicide Terrorism*. Random House.

Pape, Robert A., and James K. Feldman. 2010. *Cutting the Fuse: The Explosion of Global Suicide Terrorism and How to Stop It*. University of Chicago Press.

Popper, Karl Raimund. 1966 [1945]. *The Open Society and Its Enemies. Volume I: The Spell of Plato.* Princeton University Press.

Smith, George H. 2013. *The System of Liberty: Themes in the History of Classical Liberalism.* Cambridge University Press.

Steele, David Ramsay. 2008. *Atheism Explained: From Folly to Philosophy.* Open Court.

———. 2010. Is God Coming or Going? *Philosophy Now* 78. Reprinted in Steele 2019.

———. 2014. The Bigotry of the New Atheism (by an Old Atheist). The London Libertarian blog. Reprinted in Steele 2019.

———. 2019. *The Mystery of Fascism: David Ramsay Steele's Greatest Hits.* St. Augustine's Press.

Wells, H.G. 2017 [1894]. The Stolen Bacillus. In H.G. Wells, *H.G. Wells Short Stories.* Flame Tree.

Williams, Jeffrey William. 2013. The Human Use of Human Beings: A Brief History of Suicide Bombing. *Origins: Current Events in Historical Perspective* <https://origins.osu.edu/article/human-use-human-beings-brief-history-suicide-bombing?language_content_entity=en>.

9

HERE'S WHY THERE CAN NEVER BE A MARXIST REVOLUTION

Karl Marx became a communist in the early 1840s. From this point on, he predicted that before long there would be a communist revolution which would begin in Europe and encompass the entire world. "Bourgeois society," founded on "the capitalist mode of production" would be done away with and replaced by "communism."

Communism would, from its inception, get rid of all private property and all forms of market exchange and would therefore have no money and no prices, no wages and no profits. It would also have no social classes and no state. The absence of classes follows from Marx's premise that under communism everyone will have the same relation to the "means of production." No one will be able to employ, or be employed by, anyone else. And, since Marx believed that the state only exists because of the division into classes, the disappearance of classes must mean the disappearance of the state.

These ideas underwent some modification, first by Marx himself, and then by subsequent sects, parties, and schools of Marxism, but the basic notion of a revolution which will do away with capitalism and replace it with a radically different form of society, without money and without a state, has persisted, and still motivates Marxists and neo-Marxists of many stripes.

I'm going to explain why this theory of communist revolution is false, mainly by explaining why communism cannot exist.

You may be thinking that this isn't a matter of great interest, because very few people now want to bring about Marx's idea of communism. I will address that claim near the end of this presentation. For now, let's just see why communism, broadly as Marx conceived it, is unattainable.

Not only is communism impossible, but the trends or "laws of development" which Marx thought he could discern in the capitalist system do not exist. Marx's economic theory of the way capitalism develops is fundamentally false. Capitalism has not developed in the way Marx expected and never could. It's a kind of intellectual optical illusion that causes Marxists to imagine that capitalism has developed, is developing, or ever could develop, along the lines predicted by Marx.

You might think that this second type of refutation is unnecessary. If communism cannot exist, then what's the point of also showing that capitalism cannot develop in the direction of communism? The impossible cannot be inevitable. That's right, but the two themes are closely related and, as it happens, if we look at the arguments Marx offers for communism, they are rarely if ever of the kind, "Here's why communism is feasible and would be an improvement over capitalism" and usually of the kind "Just look! Communism is automatically emerging out of capitalism, before our very eyes!"

To appreciate how desperately mistaken Marx was, you have to understand that communism shows not the slightest sign of emerging out of capitalism, and we can even say that the more capitalism develops, the more remote and unthinkable the very notion of communism must become.

In some cases, pursuing impossible goals can be harmless, or even helpful. In those cases, the closer we get to the impossible goal, the better. The great classical liberal thinker Immanuel Kant wrote an essay on "Perpetual Peace." Kant didn't think that the complete and permanent elimination of all wars was attainable, but he believed that the closer we could get to no wars, the better.

In other cases, an impossible goal means that the closer you get to that goal, the worse things become. The goal is impossible in a way that ensures that, the more strenuously you pursue it, the greater the human suffering. And such is the case with Marxian communism. Thus, we should not pursue communist revolution, not just because communism is impossible, but because any attempt to move in the direction of communism will make humans in general, everywhere on the planet, worse off.

Marx's Conception of Communism

When Marx first became convinced that capitalism would inevitably turn into communism, capitalism itself, or "bourgeois society" as he defined it, was in its infancy. The new class of "proletarians" or wage workers were a small minority of the population in every European country, though growing rapidly. Marx correctly surmised that the proletariat, the modern wage-laborers, would become the majority of the population, but he incorrectly surmised that these proletarians would be impelled by their circumstances to bring about a communist revolution.

Marx, and his friend Friedrich (later Frederick) Engels who collaborated with Marx and shared most of the same views, began by thinking that the communist revolution would occur quite soon, but as events unfolded, Marx and Engels concluded that they had been over-optimistic about the timing, and they repeatedly revised the timetable for the communist revolution.

Beginning in the early 1850s, Marx devoted himself to the full-time study of economics, or political economy as the subject was then known. Day after day in the Reading Room of the British Museum, he made himself the most knowledgeable person in the world on the history of economic thought. He planned to write a massive four-volume work revising and reconstituting all of economic theory. He completed and published only the first volume of this work, Volume I of *Capital*, in 1867. For the other three volumes he made many notes and wrote out many substantial passages, and in this incomplete but quite readable form they were edited and published after his death. (Volume IV, Marx's survey and critique of earlier economic theories, is now usually referred to simply by its own title, *Theories of Surplus Value*).

Capital, first published in German as *Das Kapital*, is an ambitious attempt to analyze the capitalist economy. At first glance, this book is all about "the capitalist mode of production." Communism is mentioned only rarely and briefly. Yet as we read more closely, we perceive that a major aim of the book is to prove that capitalism must, by its own spontaneous development, automatically lead to communism.

This can be clearly seen by reading Chapter 32 of Volume I. Why Chapter 32? Volume I has thirty-three chapters, but Chapter 33 was added in the hope of fooling government censors. At this time most European governments censored printed books, and Marx's expectation was that the censors might be lazy and just check the beginning and end of the book, thus concluding that it was a fussy theoretical work with no practical implications. Chapter 33 is therefore intentionally dry, unexciting, and of no great importance.

Chapter 32, a mere three pages, is the true finale of the book. If you want to read just three pages of Marx to tell you what Marx was up to, here they are. This is Marx's own "standing on one leg" statement of what he wants the world to know. After the academic timbre of the first few lines, this brief chapter morphs into a marvelous piece of stirring prose, all the more gripping for its professorial tone of voice. It distills the implications of the preceding thirty-one chapters, disclosing how capitalism, because of its own intrinsic and inherent laws of development, must necessarily and automatically lead to communist revolution.

The most vital element in Marx's claim that capitalism automatically leads to communism is his theory of the "centralization of capital." Marx is convinced that in market competition, bigger firms beat out smaller firms. The smaller firms go out of business or are acquired by the surviving bigger firms (*Capital* I, pp. 586–87; III, pp. 436–39). As Marx pithily expressed it, "One capitalist always kills many" (I, p. 714). The long-run trend, then, is for firms to get bigger, not just in absolute terms along with growth of output, but in comparative terms, in relation to the whole economy. Firms get bigger *and fewer*. The ultimate limit of this process is the ownership of the entire economy by one enormous firm (*Capital* I, pp. 587–88).

Thus, capitalism itself is doing the job of centralizing the control of all of industry, so that before communism arrives, industry will already be administered by immense organizations. Marx never once evinces the slightest suspicion that there might be problems associated with organizations far more gigantic than anything heretofore witnessed on this Earth. If he had any doubts, he could reassure himself that capitalism was evolving in this direction anyway. But here he was simply mistaken on the facts.

Marx did not suppose that within capitalism the ultimate limit of one big firm would be reached—the communist revolution was bound to happen long before that!—but he did think that this was a directional trend dictated with iron necessity by the inescapable laws of capitalist competition.

Commenting on the comparatively new joint-stock companies, Marx says that the joint-stock company is "the abolition of the capitalist mode of production within the capitalist mode of production itself..." (III, p. 438). Writing a little later, when everyone is talking about the "trusts"—associations of big firms which are trying to cartelize particular industries, Engels says:

> In the trusts, freedom of competition changes into its very opposite—into monopoly; and the production without any definite plan of capitalistic society capitulates to the production upon a definite plan of the invading socialistic society. ("Socialism, Utopian and Scientific," pp. 317–18)

This typifies early Marxist thinking. Every new economic development takes us closer to communism. Every newspaper headline screams that capitalism is about to disappear forever. Communism is so close you can taste it.

Engels goes on to say that as the trusts take over each industry, the state is obliged to take over more and more. This is the purely bourgeois state, before the workers' revolution. State ownership of industry, at least a large element of it, predates the revolution, so when the workers take power, all they will have to do is to seize control of an existing administrative apparatus. This is why Marx expresses the view that the transition from capitalism to communism will be far quicker, easier, and more peaceful than the historical transition from "scattered private property" to capitalism (*Capital* I, p. 715).

The trusts were a fleeting moment in capitalist development. Most of them failed very quickly. In actuality there is no tendency in a free market for competition to abolish itself by creating monopoly; that just cannot happen and never has happened. Trusts cannot be successful in taking over each industry because competition is not self-destroying but endlessly self-regenerating. As long as a trust's edicts are not given the force of law, an attempted cartel cannot prevent the emergence of new firms which rise up to challenge the cartel, nor can it prevent members of the trust from "cheating" and thus breaking up the cartel.

A Single Vast Plan

If communism is to be a society without private property, without market exchange, and therefore without money, how would the economy be organized? In some respects, Marx is quite voluble; in others, he is tight-lipped and taciturn.

Under communism, all of economic life, all of the production of goods and services, will be planned from a single center, for the whole of society. Industry will be governed and directed by what Engels calls "a single vast plan" ("einem einzigen grossen Plan"; Engels 2019, p. 367). First on a national level, then on a world level, the whole of national or global economic life will become, as Lenin later expressed it, "a single office and a single factory" ("State and Revolution," p. 479).

As Marx sees it, the most problematic feature of capitalism is that it is not subject to a single supreme plan. He refers to this overall planless-ness as capitalism's "anarchy of production." Under capitalism, anyone can start a business and can run that business more or less as they please, within very broad limits. Firms do occasionally collaborate, but much of the time they compete, each making its plans without consulting its competitors. Firms often keep secrets from one another. Sometimes the competition is rivalrous, in the sense that one firm's relative success entails another firm's relative failure.

Marx and Engels could not imagine that this was anything other than scandalously irrational and therefore horribly inefficient. Marx writes of "despotism in the workplace" and "anarchy" in society at large (*Capital* I, pp. 336–37), and he clearly supposes that this is a kind of paradox, an indefensible contradiction, which must be resolved by applying the principle of a single planning authority, now implemented in each workshop, to the whole of industry. Marx sees the factory as entirely rational internally, while the market gives free rein to "chance and caprice."

Anyone who has worked in a number of organizations, public and private, will tell you the opposite: chance and caprice are rampant within the organization, while the external pressures from the marketplace or the legal system seem by contrast like the only solid hope of order and sanity. Modern price theory and the empirical research it has inspired show that there is very little "chance and caprice" in actual markets.

If the anarchy of competition were to be replaced by comprehensive society-wide planning of production (which for brevity I'll call "central planning"), output of goods and services would, Marx supposed, immediately become much higher. There would be more wealth for everyone. In modern terminology, economic growth would be much more rapid and the average real income (the actual quantities of goods and services available to people) would be vastly greater.

Unlike capitalism in which numerous separate business entities pursued their own separate plans, communism must be planned as a whole. Since there will be no buying and selling, the people planning production will not be guided by pursuit of profit and will not be able to refer to the prices of things as given by the market. Instead, they will organize production by purely technical and physical criteria. Marxists routinely describe this by saying that under capitalism we have "production for profit" whereas under communism we will have "production for use."

References to the way this would be done are few, brief, and broad-brush. Here is one, by Marx:

> We will assume . . . that the share of each individual producer in the means of subsistence is determined by his labour-time. Labour-time would, in that case, play a double part. Its apportionment in accordance with a definite social plan maintains the proper proportion between the different kinds of work to be done and the various wants of the community. On the other hand, it also serves as a measure of the portion of the common labour borne by each individual, and of his share in the part of the total product destined for individual consumption. (*Capital* I, p. 83)

Here's a fuller account, thirteen years later, by Engels:

Society can simply calculate how many hours of labour are contained in a steam engine, a bushel of wheat of the last harvest, or a hundred square yards of cloth of a certain quality . . . It is true that even then it will still be necessary for society to know how much labour each article of consumption requires for its production. It will have to arrange its plan of production in accordance with its means of production . . . The useful effects of the various articles of consumption, compared with one another and with the quantities of labour required for their production, will in the end determine the plan. People will be able to manage everything very simply, without the intervention of much-vaunted "value." ("Anti-Dühring," pp. 294–95)

Under communism, how will consumer goods be allocated to individual consumers? Here Marx draws a distinction between the earliest phase of communism, immediately after the communist revolution, and a "higher phase" of communism. He assumes that several years of communism will yield an enormous superabundance of wealth.

In the initial phase of communism, individuals in return for their work will receive, not money wages, for there will be no money, but "vouchers" certifying that they had performed some stated number of hours of labor. They will then take these vouchers to the commonly owned store, and will be entitled to take a certain quantity of consumer goods in return. This is the system proposed by the early socialist theorist Robert Owen, who in Marxian terms can be classified as a communist.

Marx says that his "revolutionary watchword" is "Abolition of the wages system!" ("Value, Price, and Profit," p. 149) And yet his labor-vouchers look a lot like a wages system. Marx does not deny this. After all, this is "a communist society . . . just as it *emerges* from capitalist society, which is thus in every respect, economically, morally and intellectually, still stamped with the birth-marks of the old society from whose womb it emerges" ("Marginal Notes," p. 85).

In a later, "higher phase" of communism, there will be no labor-vouchers. The rule will be: "from each according to his abilities to each according to his needs." People will take from the common store whatever they want without having to show proof of how many hours they have worked. The higher phase of communism will abolish any conditional link between an individual's contribution to output and that individual's claim upon output. This becomes feasible because of the superabundance released by the abolition of capitalism. Marx believes that capitalism drastically restricts total output below its potential. His arguments for this belief are all unsound (*From Marx to Mises*, pp. 288–294).

Who would be the planners of production? According to Marx and Engels, the political structure of the communist society will be extremely democratic. They consider communism an extension of the movement for democracy (Hunt I, pp. 74–84; II, pp. 182–211). They do not conceive that communist society or communist economic planning will be administered by a party or by any kind of elite or leadership. But if we ask, for example, whether there will be one supreme world economic planning council, or several regional planning councils, whether there will be specialized managers or whether everyone will take turns at management, all such organizational questions are quite deliberately left unanswered.

Marx's Opposition to Communist Blueprints

Marx does not view it as a tentative suggestion that communism will have no private property and no market exchange, therefore no money, no banks, no stock exchange, no payments of rent, interest, wages, or dividends. He is firmly opposed to any form of "socialism" which does not totally abolish all market exchange. Anything less than this, he maintains, would still in practice be capitalism, perhaps capitalism in distorted and disguised form.

For example, in 1847 Marx wrote a book, *The Poverty of Philosophy*, attacking the 1846 book by Pierre-Joseph Proudhon subtitled *The Philosophy of Poverty*. Marx's terminology here is that he is a communist, and *not* a socialist, while Proudhon is a socialist and *not* a communist. The key difference is that Proudhon wants to retain the market economy, the system of prices and money, but to improve it in various ways to make it conform to standards of justice, while Marx, as a communist, wants the complete abolition of market exchange and therefore money.

Along with this absolute insistence on certain fundamental attributes of communism, Marx and many early Marxists often derided and ridiculed attempts to discuss just how the administration of communism would play out in practice. Any attempt to get into the nuts and bolts of how communism might work would be dismissed as "utopian." Marx famously disclaimed any intention of "writing recipes . . . for the cookshops of the future" (*Capital*, I, p. 26),[1] which may sound fine until the day approaches when you actually have to open these cookshops. And so, Marx and the early Marxists combine absolute commitment to certain defining features of communism with considerable haziness about the details, and a general refusal to talk about them.

This might seem defensible. To give a detailed description of how a kind of society totally different from anything we have ever observed might tackle certain problems decades hence would obviously be premature. And yet, if the practical feasibility of communism is a controversial issue, as it always has been, there seems to be no reasonable basis for a refusal to discuss hypothetical scenarios. Consequently, the policy of refusing to consider "details" of communism functioned as a protection against criticism. Marxists did not have to think of any problems that might arise, and might prove difficult, for a communist society.

Marx was early committed to the view that the "scientific" way to advocate communism was to produce arguments demonstrating that it was, as a matter of objective fact, the inevitable result of present developments. If you read what Marx says, it's quite evident that he's recommending communism, claiming it to be superior to capitalism and highly desirable, but he does not usually assert any of this outright. Instead he repeatedly intones 1) that bad things happen under capitalism, and 2) that communism is the only possible outcome of the way capitalism inevitably develops.

Marx does not describe communism as if it were a proposal that he has to defend against criticism but as an implacable fate, predestined by the inexorable laws of history, which in this case means the inexorable

---

1   The English edition quoted here mistakenly has "receipts" instead of "recipes." The German word *Rezepte* changed its meaning after the early 1870s when Marx wrote this passage.

laws of capitalist competition. This way of talking has proved to be immensely influential, though from a logical and economic point of view it is blatantly fallacious.

The Verbal Switch from "Communism" to "Socialism"

When Karl Marx died in 1883, his followers were a small group of intellectuals thinly scattered all over Europe. They may have looked unimpressive, as adherents of an obscure and wacky belief system, but they were about to become important historical players. In all European countries, there were growing socialist, usually called "social-democratic," parties, which were to become highly prominent as workers got the vote (often, as in Germany, the biggest political party in the country), and the leading thinkers of these parties would mostly consider themselves Marxists. All these parties had been founded in large part by non-Marxist socialists, but Marxism was proving itself far more persuasive than the various non-Marxist sects of socialism. In Germany, for instance, the followers of Marx proved to be more persuasive than the followers of Ferdinand Lassalle, who had done most of the legwork in developing the socialist movement's working-class following. The result was that on the continent (Britain was exceptional) these socialist parties came under the firm intellectual leadership of Marxists. One of the results was that the Marxists, finding themselves the respected intellectuals in parties long called "socialist" acceded to dropping the word "communism" and replacing it with the word "socialism."[2]

The Abandonment of Labor-Vouchers

After the death of Engels in 1895, the most respected Marxist theoretician was Karl Kautsky, dubbed by anti-Marxists "the Pope of Marxism." On most issues, organized Marxism continued to maintain the teachings

2   At no time did Marx or the early Marxists employ the terms "socialism" and "communism" to denote *successive stages*, with socialism preceding communism. This terminology was introduced by Lenin in 1917.

of Marx and Engels unmodified. However, the Marxist understanding of the earliest stage of socialism was revised. Organized Marxism, under Kautsky's influence, abandoned the belief that labor vouchers would be used in the initial stage of socialism. Instead, money wages would continue to exist, as they had under capitalism.

In a pair of lectures given in 1902, Kautsky spoke of "wages" in the new socialist society. He recognized that this would be a shock to his Marxist followers:

> What, it will be said, will there be wages in the new society? Shall we not have abolished wage-labor and money? (*The Social Revolution*, p. 129)

Kautsky goes on to explains that he doesn't think socialism could operate without money, which would remain indispensable "until something better is discovered." Kautsky's wording shows that he knows he is contradicting the traditional Marxian approach, but Kautsky's acceptance of money wages in the initial stage of socialism was rapidly accepted by nearly all Marxists.

Only a little thought is sufficient to raise serious questions about the practicability of labor-vouchers. Someone going to the store under socialism will typically not want to select just one item, but dozens of different items, so presumably each of these would have to be given its own "price" in labor-hours. But it is not feasible for these prices to be derived from the labor-time actually expended in making each product. It can easily be seen that there will be inefficiency, if either goods in the store are left unchosen by consumers so that they pile up over time, or if such goods are over-chosen (you see how artificial it is to avoid the word "bought") so that some consumers can get certain goods and those who come to the store later can't get them. But by "pricing" the goods in different amounts, corresponding to different amounts of different items that an hour's labor-time could be exchanged for, and allowing these values to be raised or lowered according to supply and demand, these problems don't arise (or only very rarely arise), just as in a regular market with everything priced in money.

"Pricing" different goods in different units of supposed labor-hours would solve a lot of problems, but it still leaves the key difference that according to Marx, the labor-vouchers are not money because they do not circulate and cannot be accumulated (*Capital* II, p. 362). They are franked or punched like a bus ticket and therefore can't play any further role. But once we consider the relations between the stores and the factories and farms, we see that it would be highly convenient to have the stores get vouchers from the consumers and make the stores use these vouchers to pay the producers of the goods. This is one of several ways in which the vouchers, contrary to Marx's intention, might begin to evolve into money. The socialist planning administration has to make decisions about precisely what is to be produced, in what quantities, and one obvious piece of evidence they would want to take into account would be the kinds and quantities of goods that consumers choose to take from the stores.

The social democrats' acceptance of the need for money to distribute consumer goods apparently leaves the whole organization of production unchanged. Marxists, while accepting Kautsky's concession to the necessity for money in the initial stage of socialism, still maintained that socialist production will be organized without reference to money or prices. It will still be "production for use and not for profit."

And yet this concession marks the first small step in a murky yet far-reaching process. Marxists begin by thinking of all financial categories as arbitrary, irrational, and dispensable. But anyone who studies economic theory is liable to conclude that there's nothing arbitrary about capitalist techniques; they are ways of solving problems which would have to be solved somehow in any alternative system, and this immediately prompts the questions: What are these alternative ways of solving these problems, and would they work as well as the capitalist solutions? If they wouldn't work as well, does this mean that socialism might be less efficient than capitalism, which would entail that average real incomes must be lower under socialism, thus contradicting the claim that socialism will have higher output than capitalism? If socialism has lower output, this implies that real incomes for the average person, or for the mass of people, can only be lower under socialism than under capitalism.

Kautsky's thinking was to evolve further over time, making more and more concessions to capitalist organizational forms in his conception of socialism, and allowing more and more scope for the market. The more you think seriously about how socialism would have to work in practice, the more you rediscover capitalism.

Mises's Outrageous Claim

In 1920 the Austrian economist Ludwig von Mises published his famous article, "Economic Calculation in the Socialist Commonwealth," in which he made the outrageous claim that a socialist economy is "impossible" and will forever remain impossible. He published this article at a time when the Bolshevik government in Russia was proclaiming that Russia was abolishing money for ever, and the rest of the world would soon follow. (The previous year, the Bolsheviks had renamed themselves "Communists." I spell communism with a small c to refer to the communism of Marx, or of non-Marxist communists like Morelly, Owen, or Kropotkin, and with a capital C to denote the Communist Parties, all controlled and funded from Moscow, which were set up in every country in 1919–1921.)

The conception of "socialism" considered by Mises is the prevalent one in 1920, reflecting the widespread acceptance of the picture drawn by Kautsky in 1902: socialism will allow money and prices in the distribution of consumer goods, but will not allow any market transactions in the sphere of industrial organization. Industry will be planned and managed without any profit mechanism and without any role for money prices.

What Mises meant by his outrageous claim was that there cannot exist a modern industrial economy yielding high levels of output without a functioning system of market prices, and these market prices cannot be confined to consumer goods but must extend to factors of production ("means of production").

Why are market prices so essential, according to Mises? Because they communicate precise and speedy information about the comparative scarcities of production goods such as raw materials, buildings, vehicles, and machines, different types of labor, and the shifting patterns of demand for consumer goods.

The aim of production in any society is to produce what the consumers want at least cost. Where there is a market, the people planning production can refer to market prices to help them determine which methods of production are more or less costly. A method of production may be technically feasible, but if it be too costly, then it is reasonable to prefer a different method with a lower cost.

The cost of producing some good is the reduction in production of other goods which follows from producing that good. The only practicable way to know the cost, in a society of any complexity, involves looking at money prices, but costs are not *defined* in terms of money prices. Cost faces anyone organizing a system of industrial production, even if we imagine a hypothetical system which has no money prices. It's just that, without money prices, no one can know what the true costs are.

If there's no way to decide whether a method of production is more or less costly, then the people planning production will not be able to avoid committing serious blunders in allocating resources, whereas with the help of market prices, the planners of production can see that these are blunders before resources have been committed to them. In a system without market prices, total output can only be appreciably lower than it would be in a social system which could make use of the information provided by market prices. Any sustained attempt to impose a single vast plan, replacing market prices, can only lead to the disintegration of modern industry, the collapse of the economy into primitive wretchedness, and the death of most of the population. The essential point of Mises's argument had been clearly expounded by Nikolaas Pierson in 1902, as an immediate response to Kautsky's lectures of that year, but Pierson's contribution attracted little attention at the time.

In *From Marx to Mises*, I explained why there can never be a substitute for the market. I outlined the various suggestions made by socialists to answer the economic calculation problem. Broadly, these are: to employ "calculation in kind," to use labor hours as units of account, to solve millions of simultaneous equations, and to create a kind of "simulated market" which would achieve the results of a market without any actual market. None of these proposals can work. Naturally, if any one of them had ever seriously looked as though it might conceivably work, it would have been tried.

The conclusion is that non-market socialism, as envisaged by classical Marxism, is not practically feasible in any industrial or post-industrial economy. The notion that modern industry could be operated without market prices and the pursuit of profit is ultimately just as absurd as the notion that physics or chemistry could operate without arithmetic. An industrial economy, with its potential for high output per head and thus high living standards for the mass of the population, is of necessity a market economy incorporating private property in the means of production. Nothing else is practically possible.

The finding that no planned system can hope to match the productive achievements of a market system is now known to be a special case of the general principle that the operation or the results of a complex or non-ergodic system cannot be simulated or predicted. For this reason, human-made machines applying computer technology can never become intelligent or conscious (as explained by Landgrebe and Smith, pp. 124–143, 160–191).

The Soviet Union, though notorious as a monument to spectacular inefficiency, might be cited as a counterexample to Mises's claims that socialism cannot exist and that an industrial system requires private ownership of capital. But do we really want to call the Soviet Union "socialist" in a Marxian sense? Here we can note that: 1) the Soviet economy was a money economy in which financial institutions played a large and steadily increasing role; 2) Soviet planners and managers had access to world market prices and Western technology; 3) there was an enormous internal black market, an illegal but nonetheless real free market, which provided some information to the planners and the managers; 4) state enterprises were required to aim at a profit denominated in money; 5) private businesses below a certain size were legally permitted; 6) there were private stores in every major city selling goods imported from the West to members of the ruling elite, with prices marked in dollars; 7) central planning did not in reality prevail, as plans were published after the start of the plan period and revised considerably month by month and year by year; 8) the Soviet Union was propped up by a substantial volume of aid from the West, especially during World War II.

The fundamental difference between the Soviet economy and even the most heavily regulated Western economies is that there was no transferable equity in the capital of most enterprises, so there were no internal capital or money markets. This big difference was key to the decline and fall of the Soviet system, due to its failure to innovate or to maintain economic growth.

In official Soviet theory, the Soviet Union was headed towards eventual "full communism," the system of moneyless, stateless socialism anticipated by early Marxism. In actuality, this hypothetical future was about as practically relevant as the Western belief that there would one day be a second coming of Christ. The only perceptible way to achieve economic growth and raise living standards was to import Western-style economic institutions, in other words to move in the direction of what was then seen as a Western-style economy, the only system feasible for any advanced industrial economy.

The Bolshevik coup of November 1917 and the eventual development of a "socialist" system supposedly operated by a succession of five-year plans is not an example of a Marxist revolution. This is both obvious and indisputable, because it did not lead to communism. Yet more than that, the Bolshevik seizure of power was in every particular unlike Marx's conception of a communist revolution.

The Bolshevik regime was resolutely anti-democratic; one of its earliest actions was to shut down the elected Constituent Assembly which was to have legislated into existence a democratic constitution.

The Bolsheviks tried to abolish money while keeping industry going; they failed miserably, leading to the New Economic Policy (NEP) beginning in 1921. Far from the state withering away, it became more obtrusive than ever. Far from the disappearance of social classes, there was a sharp division between the mass of the population and the rulers, even to the extent of special luxury stores for the ruling class, which the vast majority of the population were legally prohibited from entering.

In contrast with workers in Western countries, members of the Soviet working class had no rights or liberties. Genuine independent labor unions controlled by their members were not permitted to exist. The U.S.S.R., and its imitators like the People's Republic of China, murdered vastly more innocent people than any other regime or set of regimes in the history of the world.

Thus, at every point the Bolshevik seizure of power had nothing in common with the classical Marxist conception of a socialist revolution. It called itself Marxist? Well, if Karl Marx has taught us anything (and he has taught me a lot) it is that we ought never to judge any institution, much less an entire social order, by what it says about itself, but rather by what it actually does.

I have said that a market economy requires private ownership of all the major factors of production, including capital goods. A market economy can survive and grow given some amount of government ownership and regulation (though this is always a costly burden, tending to impoverish the population), but as this area of non-market determination is increased, the economy becomes progressively less efficient, and beyond a certain point, well short of "a single vast plan," there ensues total industrial collapse, civil breakdown, and mass starvation.

But can't we have everything owned by "the community" and at the same time allow different community-owned production organizations to trade with one another, thus combining community ownership with a market economy? Some people vaguely suppose that this might be possible, but it is in fact incoherent. The problem here is that for a market to emerge, the decision-makers in each production organization have to be able to make independent decisions, but that means that they must have effective property rights. It is precisely the fact that there is no "single vast plan" which allows a market economy to spring spontaneously into existence, and it is precisely the fact that there can never be a single vast plan which guarantees that the market economy will continue as long as humankind endures. The market is spontaneous and anarchic precisely because no person or group of persons is in control of the overall society-wide system. The market cannot confer its abundant benefits on humankind without being anarchic, unplanned, uncontrolled. If you try to control it, to the extent that you succeed, it ceases to be a market, and thus ceases, to that extent, to confer its benefits upon humankind.

The spontaneous, competitive process of the market yields information which could never have been discovered by a council of wise elders or a committee of workers' delegates sitting down and trying to formulate a "single vast plan." Ultimately this is because there prevails what Mises called the "intellectual division of labor," what F.A. Hayek called the "division of knowledge." The knowledge possessed by millions of independent agents can be drawn upon by means of the market, even though it is impossible to centralize all that knowledge in one place or one mind.[3]

It might be objected that the decision-makers in each production organization could be given some freedom to transact, but still denied "ownership" of the production organization. For instance, they would not be permitted to shut down the organization or to transfer control of it to a different group of decision-makers. But ownership means precisely the authority to make decisions about the disposition of resources. To gain the full benefits of the market, being able to shut down production organizations or start new ones, *without getting anyone's permission*, is precisely the sort of thing we want them to be able to do. We don't, for instance, want production organizations to be kept alive when their performance proclaims that it would be efficient to shut them down. If a production organization is operating at a loss, this means that the resources used by that organization would be more productive of consumer wellbeing if re-allocated to other organizations, which points to the contraction in size, and in some cases the shutting down, of that organization.

If we were to set up a system where "the community" allowed decision-makers in production organizations to make a range of decisions, while reserving major structural decisions to "the community as a whole," we would witness a continual tug-of-war between the "whole community" and the production organizations, and we can show that gains of efficiency and therefore more total products for everyone would, at every stage, flow from taking decision-making authority away from the "community as a whole" and giving it to the production organizations, or ultimately to individuals. (I looked at the early proposals for "market socialism" in *From Marx to Mises*, and the renewed discussions of market socialism following the demise of the Soviet Union in "The Market Socialists' Predicament.")

---

3   What the market accomplishes is made clearer by the Walrasian system, illuminating how millions of price-quantity relationships can be simultaneously brought into balance. Despite his keen insight into the market process, Mises weakened his theoretical and his rhetorical position by his total rejection of Léon Walras and ultimately of all use of mathematics in economics.

Here I have been avoiding use of the word "state," because we're talking hypothetically about how various arrangements would work, all the time provisionally accepting some of Marx's basic axioms of communism, one being that there is no state. In practice "the community as a whole," whatever its scope, has to be embodied in some formal organization, and that organization has to be able to rely on smaller units of the whole complying with its decisions. The "community as a whole" therefore has to be able to coerce smaller units to conform. And that means that the "community as a whole" can only be a state, and a terribly oppressive state at that.

Modern industry and production for sale are conjoined; they cannot be separated. Because an industrial society must always be a commercial society, any political attempt to abolish commerce and substitute "a single vast plan," or even to seriously curtail the domain of commerce, must always result in palpable income reduction and therefore serious suffering for the mass of the population. For this reason, an attempt to abolish the market and replace it with central planning will never be the goal of a genuinely popular movement, but always of a determined group of conspirators ready to crush popular dissent—though of course, a determined group of conspirators may, under certain circumstances, get a substantial percentage of people to support them by misrepresenting their true aims.

This gives us another reason why there can never be a Marxist revolution, for in the view of Marx and Engels and of all classical Marxists, the communist revolution can only be popular and democratic. "The proletarian movement is the self-conscious, independent movement of the immense majority, in the interest of the immense majority" ("Manifesto of the Communist Party," p. 495). Marx and Engels saw the communist revolution as the most advanced wing of the movement for democracy. When their *Manifesto of the Communist Party* appeared in 1848, there was no political democracy in any part of Europe; in every European country, the majority of the population had no political representation at all (Switzerland being the only debatable exception). Marx and Engels looked ahead to a point where political democracy would prevail; universal suffrage would be the immediate prelude to a presumptively peaceful communist capture of political power.

Capital Does Not and Cannot Centralize

In the history of capitalism, there is no observable trend toward central-ization of all capital in the hands of fewer and fewer firms. Quite the opposite: as total income increases, we observe that the number of firms increases. We see the emergence of some very big firms, but these, the biggest firms, survive in an environment of numerous smaller firms, and there is no observable tendency, in the actual history of capitalism, for these smaller firms to go away.

Today, nearly two centuries after Marx's prediction of the inexorable centralization of capital, over fifty percent cent of private-sector employ-ment and over forty percent of output, in the United States, comes from small businesses (defined as having less than five hundred employees). There are 33.2 million small businesses, and more than 80 percent of them have no employees—they are self-employed persons. The remain-ing less than 20 percent (the ones with from 2 to 499 employees) account for 46.4 percent of all US employees (Main 2022).

The situation is very similar in all industrialized economies, in Eu-rope, Asia, South America, and elsewhere. Nowhere do we observe any-thing remotely like Marx's prediction of fewer and fewer firms. We also observe that many big firms of the past have either gone out of business or been greatly reduced in size, especially in their size compared to the total economy, so we can't assume that sheer size is always a decisive competitive advantage.

If Marx could see this, he would probably be very puzzled by it. In his day the modern system of industrial capitalism was fairly new. It was observable that some very big firms had emerged, but the total economy was growing rapidly, and Marx did not think to look at the biggest firms comparatively over time, in relation to the size of the total economy. He took it as axiomatic that, in the competition among firms, there are ad-vantages, *and no disadvantages*, to being bigger than others. (And, al-though Marx pays attention to the new institution, the joint-stock company, he does not notice that the joint-stock organizational form means, by simple arithmetic, that if firms do get bigger and fewer, it doesn't follow that individual capitalists, "the magnates of capital," have to get bigger and fewer (*Capital* I, pp. 714–15.)

As Marx looked at capitalist industry in England and elsewhere, he saw numerous competing firms. He saw some firms growing bigger and many small firms going out of business. If a big firm always has advantages, and no disadvantages, in relation to smaller firms, it follows that differences in the sizes of firms are arbitrary, random, and—because the smaller firms can only be eliminated—temporary. "The smaller capitals crowd into spheres of production which modern industry has only sporadically or incompletely got hold of" (*Capital* I, p. 587).

The Optimal Amount of Planning

We now know much more than Marx or anyone else knew in the nineteenth century about the determinants of the size of firms. In a pioneering paper of 1937, Ronald Coase pointed out that a firm will co-ordinate production within a single organization when the cost of doing so is below the transaction costs of purchasing supplies in the market. We now think of this in relation to the familiar "make or buy?" decision. The sizes of firms are not arbitrary but are determined by real conditions. Firms can be too big, as well as too small. Free-market competition, as Coase cheekily observed, gives us "the optimal amount of planning."

Armen Alchian and Harold Demsetz criticized and extended Coase's work to encompass the advantages of team production, and Oliver Williamson showed the importance of "asset specificity," assets that have more value if taken together than employed in separate lines of production, in determining firm size.

Armed with the insights of Coase, Alchian and Demsetz, and Williamson, we can now perceive that there can be no overriding tendency for the comparative size of firms to increase indefinitely. To avoid misunderstanding, I should mention that government regulation of business nearly always has the effect of conferring monopoly privileges on some big firms by rigging the system against their smaller competitors. That's why big businesses are usually behind the movement for government regulation, or if they were not behind it initially, are very generous with their "expert advice" on the precise details to be implemented, once the movement reaches the point of legislation. This will create an economy with an inefficiently great predominance of artificially protected big firms, but still one that requires the continued existence of many smaller firms.

No successful, or even faintly promising, refutation of the Mises argument has been offered by anyone. A high-output industrialized economy is always necessarily a market economy, or in Marx's terms a system of "commodity production." But there are also other problems with the practical feasibility of Marxian socialism, notably Michels's Law of Oligarchy.

The Law of Oligarchy

The classical Marxian conception of socialism involves something that would later be called "participatory democracy." This democracy wouldn't be merely a matter of simply voting for representatives every few years; but rather, everyone would be actively involved in decision-making. The great achievement of Robert (later Roberto) Michels was to show, in 1911, before the term "participatory democracy" had even been coined, that attempts to institute participatory democracy can never attain the envisioned result.

Michels convincingly explained that all complex organizations give rise to a division between officials and ordinary members, or leaders and led. Michels did this partly by a general analysis of organizational possibilities and partly by studying what had actually happened to socialist movements and labor unions, which in those days still retained some notion that an organization could be run by the whole membership rather than by officials. The greater the size and complexity of any organization, Michels concluded, the wider the abyss between leaders and led. This is the "iron law of oligarchy."

Marx's socialism would involve the deliberate planning of all production on a world scale. Socialist central planning would necessarily entail extremely large and complex organizations. These organizations can only be bureaucratic oligarchies, pitted against the mass of producers, consumers, and voters. Only a tiny handful of the population would actually manage and direct these organizations.

This leads to a more general conclusion. The attempt to organize industry by means of central planning would not only precipitate a huge reduction in output and therefore mass immiseration. The attempt must lead to an all-powerful and extremely brutal state, just the opposite of what classical Marxists wanted or expected. Because of Michels's law of oligarchy, the officials of the central planning administration must become a new ruling class (or perhaps the front men for a new ruling class). In these circumstances, the state cannot wither away, but can only expand mightily.

Marxists before World War I believed in a future society which would be free, democratic, and centrally planned. They believed that such a society was bound to arrive because the inherent laws of capitalism's development and the circumstances of the working class would impel the workers to choose socialism (by definition centrally planned and non-market) as the way to pursue their interests. Thus, classical Marxists believed that resolute support for working-class interests would automatically tend to lead in the direction of a society which was free, democratic, and centrally planned.

However, reality says something contrary. Reality says that there can never under any circumstances exist a society which is free, democratic, and centrally planned. Reality (that tiresomely persistent fellow) also insists that it can never, under any circumstances, be in the interests of the working class to abolish production for sale and replace it with central planning. Any move in this direction must always viciously attack working-class interests.

Since any serious attempt at replacing the market with central planning requires an all-powerful state and the crushing of opposition, especially working-class opposition, Marxists who succeed in gaining political power are faced with a choice. Either give up the attempt to move toward a single vast plan, or give up any hope for democracy, personal freedom, or the furtherance of working-class interests. Western European social democrats took the first option, and continued to take it after 1917; the Bolsheviks took the second option.

The social democrats chose freedom, democracy, and the pursuit of workers' interests as defined by the workers, and this prohibited them from seriously embarking on "socialization" (a euphemism for gradual movement toward a single vast plan). The Bolsheviks felt they had to retrospectively justify their ill-conceived coup of November 1917 by pursuing central planning, and therefore quite inevitably had to round up and execute their political critics as a prelude to slaughtering many millions of workers. Their pursuit of centrally planned socialism put an end to Russia's formerly rapid economic growth. Bolshevism (including the Bolsheviks' imitators in other countries) retarded world economic development by more than a century. In Marxian terms, measured by developing the forces of production to improve the wellbeing of the masses, Leninism has been the most effectively reactionary force in modern history.

Marxian communism is supposed to witness the withering away of the state, but any serious attempt at central planning requires a huge administration, and since this administration has to be able to ensure compliance, it cannot avoid becoming a state. Marxists expected that the abolition of private property would do away with the need for a state, since there would no longer be a class of property owners employing a class of wage workers. But administering all of industry according to a single vast plan requires a vast organization, and from the Law of Oligarchy we know that this organization must inescapably be officered by a comparative handful of people, who must have interests opposed to the majority of the population.

The division into classes does not require private property in the classic sense. For example, a third of the land in medieval Europe was owned by the Church, which means that (in accordance with Michels's Law of Oligarchy) allocation of this wealth, and the employment of workers on this land, were under the control of the chief bureaucrats of the Church. The official name for Church property was "the property of the poor." There is plenty of precedent for a ruling class of officials rather than "private" individuals. Such would be the outcome of any attempt to administer the whole of world industry as "belonging to all the people in common." If you understand Michels's Law of Oligarchy, you can see that this is the only possible outcome. If you seriously try to imagine the communist administration in action, you can easily see that "everyone owning everything" is literally pure nonsense and in practice can only mean that the bureaucrats, whether they call themselves bishops or commissars, collectively own everything.

The law of oligarchy also gives us an insight into the socialist notion that capitalism exploits workers whereas socialism will not. As Marx points out, even his labor-vouchers proposal does not mean that workers actually receive goods that represent the same number of hours of labor as they have worked. This cannot happen, because provision has to be made for replacing and extending the means of production, and other purposes ("Marginal Notes," pp. 84–85). So, according to Marx's own conception of exploitation, workers under communism must continue to be exploited: part of the product of their labor is taken away from them. This will be countered by the claim that all the means of production are now owned by "society" or "collectively by all the workers." But by the law of oligarchy the control of administration can only be in the hands of a tiny minority of the population. It follows inescapably that, adhering to the peculiar Marxist definition of "exploitation" as "unpaid labor," exploitation has to continue under communism as Marx describes it.

The Class Struggle

In combination with the—purely imaginary—centralization of capital, Marx looked to the class struggle between capitalists and workers. The workers will become the vast majority of the population, and will become poorer, while the capitalists will become ever fewer and ever richer. In this unstable situation, the workers will be bound to win eventually. But what does winning mean, if any alternative to capitalism means lower real income for the average person?

I will make only a few brief comments on this scenario, since it has no direct bearing on the question of whether a communist or socialist economy, as defined by Marx, could work in practice. In Marx's narrative, the centralization of capital is more crucial than the class struggle, and as you now understand, the centralization of capital is a mirage.

Marx predicted that all other classes except capitalists and workers would be eliminated. Has this occurred? Here we face the semantic issue that Marx defined white-collar workers as members of the proletariat, just like the horny-handed sons of toil who lug things around. Certainly, if we consider to be proletarians all those who rely for their income mainly on selling their labor services to employers, then a majority today are proletarians. But Marx also thought that all proletarians would tend to become unified (the "class in itself" would become a "class for itself"), and this has not happened. The dentist and the janitor do not see each other as class brothers, but as almost different species of animal.

On the other hand, if we look at just the classic proletariat, the blue-collar workers, which does sometimes vaguely feel itself to have a common identity, then this group is a minority of the population and, over the last century or more, a slowly diminishing minority.

Marx expected that workers would become ever poorer. But in fact they have become ever richer, and there is (as a matter of correct economic theory) no upper limit to this, as long as there is an approximation to a free market. In particular, we observe that most workers are capitalists and most capitalists are workers, meaning that both white- and blue-collar workers are able to accumulate more and more savings for retirement. If you put money in any interest-bearing instrument such as a 401k, it's usually invested in employing people, and you get part of the profits, so you are a capitalist in Marx's sense. A worker with a 401k receives what Marx called "surplus value." Worker's retirement funds are now among the biggest capitalist organizations. Thus, instead of a widening gap between capitalists and workers, there is no gap at all, but a continuum.

Even ignoring the fact that most people are both capitalists and workers, there remains the fact that there can never be a class struggle between capitalists and workers. There never has been and never will be. This can be seen very easily.

We observe many conflicts between interest groups, but on each side of every conflict we see an alliance of capitalists and workers. For example, in a protectionist movement, the workers and capitalist combine together, in the industries which hope for protection against foreign imports, while the opponents of protection are both capitalists and workers in other industries, who will suffer income losses if they have to pay more for the products of protected industries. (What about a strike for higher wages? The strikers are arrayed against the workers prepared to take the job at the current wage.)

It's the same in any interest-group conflict: workers and capitalists on one side, workers and capitalists on the other side—never workers in general against capitalists in general. This is exactly what we should expect, given the fundamental reality that capitalists and workers, by the very definition of their economic roles, voluntarily co-operate for the mutual benefit of both.

Will Capitalism Last Forever?

A rhetorical argument often employed by Marxists against the Mises argument, or even against any suggestion that capitalism might last another thousand years, is to ask, "Can capitalism last forever?"

The argument is usually couched something like this. Throughout the course of history and prehistory, human society has passed through various successive stages. At one time, for example, there was something called feudalism, as in medieval Europe. But feudalism came to an end and was supplanted by capitalism. Since capitalism is only the latest in a historical sequence of "stages," it is myopically ahistorical to think that capitalism will go on forever.

The Marxist who frames this argument also says that capitalism will be succeeded by communism, which will then (uncontrollable coughing spasm) go on forever.

The Marxist manner of conceiving the stages of human social evolution is shaky in a number of ways.

Aside from these two "stages," which represent a radical tidying up of the messy details of history, it is usually claimed that the system preceding feudalism was "slavery," but on closer inspection, this "stage" begins to fall apart.

If we ignore the crude, schematic obsession with artificial "stages" and look at the sweep of human development, we see that Sumer, the first civilization to invent writing and therefore the first to leave detailed records, had an elaborate financial system of banking, interest, checking accounts, and negotiable debt instruments, five thousand years ago.

Furthermore, the great civilizations always emerged in a context where there was widespread trading and the use of money. Even before the emergence of our species, our hominin ancestors used money, and trade routes covered thousands of miles. Everyone today knows about prehistoric stone axes, but most people aren't aware that, since most folks don't live right by a flint quarry, stone axes were traded for thousands of miles using money. A prehistoric form of currency consisted of spondyluses, the shells of spiny oysters; these have been found thousands of miles away from the warm waters where they were harvested. Financial interactions long predate modern humans, predate human language, and helped to give birth to both the modern human species and human language.

What we observe in history and prehistory is that whenever people become better off by improved output, there is a tendency for the domain of "commodity production" to increase. Therefore it's no surprise when we see the universality of commodity production in a society where people are enormously better off than ever before.

As to whether capitalism will last forever, all that the Mises argument says is that the market economy and private property in factors of production will last as long as humankind. There are many institutional variations that might conceivably come into existence, compatible with private property and the market, including the possibility that corporations employing large numbers of workers might be replaced by a system in which everyone, or almost everyone, is either a self-employed professional or a member of a small partnership. Or there could conceivably arise a system in which most people lived in small communes, linked by trade with other communes.

Communism's Incredible Appeal

I will now answer the objection that the demonstration that communism is impossible is not very relevant because hardly anyone believes in communism any more.

First, once you have become familiar with this issue and thought through it, you can easily see, by simple extension of similar arguments, that a great many forms of socialism other than Marxian communism are very likely just not practically feasible. Communism is helpful as an extreme illustrative case.

Second, there are more believers in communism than you might think; for example, consider that the most influential Marxist writer today is the late Herbert Marcuse, who went along with various radical revisions of Marxism yet remained an unrepentant true believer in Marxian communism. And many active neo-Marxists today, like the leaders of Black Lives Matter, don't publicly proclaim their neo-Marxism, but rather work to create as much inter-community nastiness and hostility as they can, hoping that this will lead to civil strife and thereby to the destruction of capitalism.

Third, a kind of visceral communism persists in the phenomenon that people denounce commodification and call for decommodification. Given that "commodity production" (production for sale) is a permanent aspect of human life, made humans what they are, and is essential to avoid industrial collapse, then anyone concerned about human wellbeing in general must accept their fundamental responsibility to secure and defend private property and freedom of contract, and to resolutely beat back all assaults on these vital foundations of human well-being.

This phenomenon has a wider aspect. People who would never dream of literally propounding or defending communism will sometimes condemn existing social institutions by tacitly invoking an unstated standard of comparison, which when made explicit, looks a lot like communism. Unnecessary strife is caused by the prevalence of ways of thinking which ignore the fact that the domain of fruitful politics is hedged about by practical impossibilities.[4]

---

4   Today's most eloquent voice exposing this mental habit is Thomas Sowell, and this recurring cultural spasm seems to be an essential component of the intellectual phenomenon, to date not yet fully explained, vividly depicted by James Billington in his *Fire in the Minds of Men*.

A Postscript:
Could Marx Have Anticipated Mises?

Retrospectively, in the light of Mises's insight into the indispensability of a functioning market for advanced industry, we can discern the intriguing possibility that Marx himself, with the penetration he often displayed, came quite close to this conclusion. It appears that the conclusion never became entirely clear to him, because of his fierce commitment to totally marketless communism.

Marx maintains that we need a concept of value, defined as socially necessary labor-time in order to account for market prices, and he also seems to indicate that socially necessary labor-time will be the unit employed by the communist administration (in the absence of market prices) in order to plan national, and eventually worldwide, production.

If so, this would no longer be "value" since it is part of Marx's theory that the term "value" is confined to "commodity production," meaning production for sale. Marx conceives of "value" as a mystifying concept reflecting the fact that (in his judgment) people under capitalism are victims of forces they cannot understand or control (a phenomenon he calls "commodity fetishism").

So, communist society will no longer observe "value" but will employ socially necessary labor-time as a moneyless accounting unit. Marx tells us that book-keeping will be "more necessary in collective production than in capitalist production" (*Capital* II, p. 138). Book-keeping must be done in units and the suggestion is that the units will be units of socially necessary labor-time. In arriving at the measure of socially necessary labor-time, the planners will not be able to derive it from prices. There is even the suggestion that the planners will have an easy task, because they will not be distracted by prices; they will be able to directly observe quantities of socially necessary labor-time.

However, in a different context Marx understands that socially necessary labor-time can never be observed empirically, nor can it ever be calculated from any empirical measurements. In that case, we reach the Mises conclusion: the planners won't be able to plan because they won't have any units of account, so they won't know what to do.

Concerned to combat the common nineteenth-century idea that

prices should be made to conform to quantities of labor-time, Marx points out that we only become aware of the determination of prices by labor-values because of fluctuations of the market. Consequently, we cannot make prices conform to labor-values, because we do not have any way to arrive at labor-values except by observing the market. Marx doesn't seem to notice that it would follow from this that the planners of production in a marketless economy would not be able to identify anything corresponding to quantities of socially necessary labor-time.

This point was noted by the socialist writer and Marx analyst Stanley Moore. Moore saw that, according to Marx's own statements, the communist administration could not determine socially necessary labor-time, or "abstract labor," and therefore would not be able to do what Marx says they would do—plan production using labor-hours (Moore, p. 75; "The Poverty of Philosophy," p. 126; *Grundrisse*, pp. 157–173; *A Contribution*, pp. 83ff).

Why is socially necessary labor-time in principle always unobservable and unmeasurable? Here I have to explain a very important aspect of Marx's labor theory of value as elaborated in *Capital*. This theory of value is an explanation of how capitalism works, including how prices are determined. What Marx calls "values" are not equal to prices, but lie behind prices and are necessary, according to Marx, to explain why prices are what they are. In Marx's methodology, values lie behind prices in a way roughly analogous to the way mass (as defined in physics) lies behind the phenomenon of perceived heaviness or lightness: the former is required to explain the latter, but in practice a lot of adjustments have to be made to get from the former to the latter. Let's begin by doing what Marx sometimes does as a simplifying assumption: assume that prices are equal to values. Marx does understand that what he calls "values" can never be equal to prices, but he will sometimes treat them as equal, as part of a heavily simplified model. In fact, he basically does this throughout Volumes I and II.

The key point here is that, even in this heavily simplified model, "value" does not correspond with any measurable, concrete metric of time spent working. It's not possible to observe a worker, or a number of workers, or all workers, spending time working and arrive at the "value" (which in Marx's theory lies behind prices and, subject to certain adjustments, explains them).

The "value" of a product is, in Marx's system, *not affected in the least* by how many labor-hours it actually took, in the past, to create that product. Marx tells us that the "socially necessary labor-time" is the quantity of labor-time justified by market demand. In other words, at any time t, the socially necessary labor-time is not equivalent to the labor-time expended in the past, but is equivalent to the quantity of labor-time which will be expended in a hypothetical future equilibrium, given all the conditions at time t. If Marx had not insisted on this point, then his labor theory of value would have involved the assertion that observable labor-time, labor-time expended in the past, has some role in determining prices today, and this is so laughably wrong that Marx's economic theory would have been unable to convince most of those people it did convince.

Of course, Marx did not use the terminology of equilibrium and time t. Here's how he explains it:

> . . . suppose that every piece of linen in the market contains
> no more labour-time than is socially necessary. In spite of this,
> all these pieces taken as a whole, may have had superfluous
> labour-time spent upon them. If the market cannot stomach
> the whole quantity at the normal price . . . this proves that
> too great a portion of the total labour of the community has
> been expended in the form of weaving. (*Capital* I, p. 109)

How much labor-time is socially necessary is, according to Marx, always strictly determined by what the market can stomach.

Marx's conception of socially necessary labor involves a reference to what we now call market equilibrium. Since the system is always in disequilibrium, we can never, even in principle, observe the socially necessary labor-time. The socially necessary labor-time is the labor-time that would be allocated in equilibrium, if equilibrium ever could be reached. Since equilibrium can never be attained, because the data are always changing, we can only deduce the existence and the importance of socially necessary labor-time, and roughly guesstimate it, by observing the direction of what's going on in the market. However, the take-away is that socially necessary labor-time depends conceptually upon competitive market prices.

There are several additional complicating factors, among them the

"Reduction Problem": there are many thousands of different types of labor and in one hour, they each confer different amounts of "value." Marx handles this by saying that different kinds of labor add value as different multiples of unskilled labor, or "simple" labor as he calls it, and these multiples are derivable from product prices (*Capital* I, pp. 51–52). So, once again, Marx relies on the market to determine what counts as socially necessary labor-time.

Suppose that the labor of a dentist counts as 1.346 times the labor of an IT consultant; this is not something we can discover by analyzing the physical operations of dentistry or IT consultancy—nor by measuring how many hours of labor it takes to train a dentist as compared with an IT consultant. We can, at best, only get some kind of a handle on this ratio by observing their wages or the prices of their products. In other words, we don't know of a way to do this, even quite roughly, except by observing what happens in the market.

This is a question wholly separable from differences in income. Even if we were to decree that the dentist and the IT consultant get the same income per hour, we still—hypothetically, under this imaginary communist economy—have to cost an hour of the dentist's work as 1.346 times an hour of the IT consultant's work. But, it turns out, there is no way for us to figure out that this is what we ought to do. In the market, of course, there is no practical problem, because the different value-creating powers of different types of labor are fixed by the market, or as Marx says, "this reduction is constantly being made" (p. 51). (It's possible that the Reduction Problem was the only aspect noticed by Stanley Moore; as we've seen, this is merely one part of the difficulty.)

Another necessary adjustment is that unproduced resources have to be assigned a quantitative measure analogous to Marxian "value." Marx acknowledges that in capitalism, these resources have a price, but he has to call this an "imaginary price," since no labor has yet been added. These resources are in no way reducible to labor-time, yet they must be economized, which means their use must be treated as a cost and therefore accorded an "imaginary price," commensurable with socially necessary labor-time.

Marx's theory has the peculiar feature (this is its really distinctive postulate) that capital equipment, such as machines, vehicles, or factory buildings, cannot create any new "value." These are what he calls "dead labor" whereas new value is created entirely by "living labor." But this (as

Marx well knew and fully acknowledged) would have the consequence that labor-intensive industries would yield higher rates of return than capital-intensive industries, whereas we know from observations, and from reflecting on what's bound to happen, that the rate of return must be the same in all industries (because capital moves from industries with lower rates of return to industries with higher rates of return, until the rates of return are equalized).

And so we arrive at the inelegant and indefensible feature of Marxian economics that "surplus value," derived entirely from "exploiting living labor" has to be re-allocated, silently and invisibly, from labor-intensive to capital-intensive industries. To take the extreme example, a fully automated factory in Marx's theory would generate no profit, since no workers were exploited there, but would receive a share of the profits actually generated in other factories which did employ workers. This is all quite fallacious, but it is the defective theory Marx is working with.

In Marx's theory equilibrium price is not directly determined by "value" but (as we learn when we get to Volume III) by "market value," which is derived from the "price of production," which is in turn derived from "value." This has to be done because the rate of return on total capital invested must be the same for all industries (*Capital* III, pp. 153, 157–58). According to Marx, "price of production" can only be derived from "value," and that is his justification for embracing the concept of "value," even though "value" is never observed and never does equal price.[5] A corresponding adjustment would have to be made by the communist planners.

---

5   Marx knows from the outset that, in observable reality, product prices equal costs plus profit (p. 157), something which has of course been familiar for millennia. Because of his theory of value representing quantities of socially necessary labor-time, he has the task of explaining how values are "transformed" into product prices—the famous "transformation problem" which, it turns out, is mathematically insoluble, if the amount of "surplus-value" is to be the same as the amount of total profit. It is painfully obvious in Volume III that this transformation is only required because of Marx's arbitrary postulate that product prices must ultimately be governed by quantities of labor-time. (However, we should bear in mind that Volume III consists of unfinished work which Marx was not ready to publish.)

When Marx is doing all this, he is not thinking about how to plan a communist system, but about the determination of prices in a capitalist system. However in his account of the capitalist system, the key variable, socially necessary labor-time, is governed by market demand. Superficially, this variable looks like a technologically objective factor which explains everything, when in fact it is an artifact of market demand or what Marx calls "the forces of competition." (Rather similarly, "subsistence," which corresponds to the workers' wages, looks like a hard quantity, but is most certainly not so, as Marx concedes from time to time; he says it includes a "historical and moral element.")

If we strip Marx's theory of its evident errors, acknowledging that all resource inputs contribute to output and all help to generate the return on investment, and if we face the fact that each type of labor contributes different amounts, per hour, to the value of the product, then we arrive at the tautology that equilibrium price determines equilibrium price, or, more informatively, that equilibrium prices arise from the interaction of market demand with stocks of all available resources.

When analyzing the way the capitalist system works, Marx falls back on appeals to the "forces of competition." Once we move from analysis of capitalism to communist planning, there are no forces of competition. They can no longer do their work, because they don't exist. Consequently, it's a huge mistake to think that we could ever know anything about amounts of "socially necessary labor-time" in a communist system. We could try to observe and record actual expenditures of labor-time, but this doesn't get at the problem. We want to be able to decide what to do next, not merely record what we did yesterday.

The fact that socially necessary labor-time is not observable but is, in Marx's analysis, a theoretical construct needed to explain the observable processes of the market, means that if we eliminate the market, we do not know of any way to arrive at a determination of socially necessary labor-time. Consequently, statements by both Marx and Engels to the effect that, in the absence of the market and of any market data such as market prices, it will be much "simpler" to go directly to the quantities of labor, are false. There is no conceivable way to compute socially necessary labor-times when there is no market.[6] For that matter, there is no way to compute it precisely in the market either, but we don't need to. Equilibrium price is part of an explanation "in principle" of a complex system; no market actor has to think about it for it to be part of such an explanation. For predictive purposes we can simply assume we're in equilibrium, which is strictly false but might work well enough.

One consequence is that Marxists, not bourgeois economists, are susceptible to "fetishism," because Marxists are inclined to suppose that the abstraction "socially necessary labor-time" really exists and can somehow be observed.

We could set aside the irrelevant and immaterial reference to "labor" and simply say that the optimal measure of the cost of a factor is its equilibrium price. But there can be no notion of equilibrium price without the operation of market pricing in general. And it is only in the continual turbulence of market iterations that equilibrium price tends to emerge. So, even in a market, or an imaginary market, we cannot adopt the rule to wait until we can guess the equilibrium price before we make allocations. The allocations have to be made now, second by second, and it is the very process of making allocations that results, within the market, in equilibrium prices (not actual equilibrium prices, but equilibrium prices as a discernable tendency and as an explanatory device).

Just as Mises said, "The paradox of 'planning' is that it cannot plan" (*Human Action*, p. 700).

It may be possible to avoid this conclusion by maintaining that Marx did not really commit himself to the use of labor-time as a unit of account, or that if he did, this is a simple mistake which can be corrected by finding some other unit, leaving the rest of his argument intact. However, even then, our discussion would shed a cruel light on Engels's naive claim that formulating the single vast plan will be simplicity itself.

How did Marx manage to overlook this fairly obvious point? As I have argued (*From Marx to Mises*, pp. 149–150), it was because of his assumption that the missing data the planners would need was only missing because the capitalist producers were independent of each other.

6   I also elaborate this point in *From Marx to Mises*, pp. 144–50.

Owing to this preconception, he could not see that if all the producers pooled their knowledge, there would still be something missing—the data provided by market prices, in other words, nearly everything the planners need to know.

Marx was in the grip of the mental picture that under capitalism industrial decision-makers are in the dark because they are separate from each other, when in reality their mutual separation is the precondition for them to take part in a form of interaction which yields information they could not acquire in any other way.*

References

Alchian, Armen A. 1977. *Economic Forces at Work*. Liberty Press.

Alchian, Armen A., and Harold Demsetz. 1972. Production, Information Costs, and Economic Organization. *American Economic Review* 62:5. Reprinted in Alchian 1977.

Billington, James H. 2017 [1980]. *Fire in the Minds of Men: Origins of the Revolutionary Faith*. Routledge.

Coase, Ronald H. 1937. The Nature of the Firm. *Economica* NS (August). Reprinted in Coase 1988.

———. 1988. *The Firm, the Market, and the Law*. University of Chicago Press.

Engels, Frederick. 1989 [1880]. Socialism, Utopian and Scientific. In Karl *Marx, Frederick Engels, Collected Works*, Lawrence and Wishart/Progress, Volume 24.

———. 1987 [1876–1878]. Herr Eugen Dühring's Revolution in Science (Anti-Dühring). In *Karl Marx, Frederick Engels, Collected Works*, Volume 25.

———. 2019 [1876–1878]. *Herrn Eugen Dührings Umwälzung der Wissenschaft (Anti-Dühring)*. Henrikus Large Print Edition.

Gordon, David, and Ying Tang. 2022. What Jordan Peterson Should Have Said about Marxism. In Woien 2022.

---

* I thank David Gordon for valuable criticisms of drafts of this chapter.

Hayek, Friedrich A., ed. 1935. *Collectivist Economic Planning*. Routledge.

———. 1980 [1948]. *Individualism and Economic Order*. University of Chicago Press.

Hunt, Richard N. 1974. *The Political Ideas of Marx and Engels I: Marxism and Totalitarian Democracy*. University of Pittsburgh Press.

———. 1984. *The Political Ideas of Marx and Engels II: Classical Marxism 1850–1895*. University of Pittsburgh Press.

Kautsky, Karl Johann. 1910 [1892]. *The Class Struggle (Erfurt Program)*. Kerr.

———. 1902. *The Social Revolution*. Kerr.

———. 1925 [1922]. *The Labor Revolution*. Dial Press.

Kornai, János. 1992. *The Socialist System: The Political Economy of Communism*. Princeton University Press.

Landgrebe, Jobst, and Barry Smith. 2023. *Why Machines Will Never Rule the World: Artificial Intelligence without Fear*. Routledge.

Lenin, V.I. 1960 [1917]. The State and Revolution. In *Collected Works*, Volume 25. Progress.

Main, Kelly. 2022. Small Business Statistics of 2023. Forbes Advisor <www.forbes.com/advisor/business/small-business-statistics/#small_business_employment_statistics_section>.

Marx, Karl H. 1970 [1859]. *A Contribution to the Critique of Political Economy*. International.

———. 1973 [1857–1858]. *Grundrisse: Foundations of the Critique of Political Economy*. Vintage.

———. 1974 [1867–1894]. *Capital: A Critical Analysis of Capitalist Production*. Three volumes. Progress.

———. 1976 [1846]. The Poverty of Philosophy: Answer to the *Philosophy of Poverty* by M. Proudhon. In *Karl Marx, Frederick Engels, Collected Works*, Volume 6.

———. 1985 [1865]. Value, Price, and Profit. In *Karl Marx, Frederick Engels, Collected Works*, Volume 20.

———. 1989 [1875]. Marginal Notes on the Programme of the German Workers' Party [Critique of the Gotha Programme]. In *Karl Marx, Frederick Engels, Collected Works*, Volume 24.

Marx, Karl, and Frederick Engels. 1976 [1848]. Manifesto of the Communist Party. In *Karl Marx, Frederick Engels, Collected Works*, Volume 6.

McMeekin, Sean 2021. *Stalin's War: A New History of World War II*. Basic Books.

Michels, Robert. 1962 [1911]. *Political Parties: A Sociological Study of the Oligarchical Tendencies of Modern Democracy*. Free Press.

Mises, Ludwig von. 1920. Die Wirtschaftsrechnung im sozialistischen Gemeinwesen. *Archiv fur Sozialwissenschaften und Sozialpolitik* 47:1.

———. 1935 [1920]. Economic Calculation in the Socialist Commonwealth. Translation of Mises 1920. In Hayek 1935.

———. 1966 [1949]. *Human Action: A Treatise on Economics*. Contemporary Books.

———. 2011 [1922]. *Socialism: An Economic and Sociological Analysis*. Ludwig von Mises Institute.

Moore, Stanley. 1980. *Marx on the Choice between Socialism and Communism*. Harvard University Press.

Schumpeter, Joseph A. 1954. *History of Economic Analysis*. Routledge.

Sowell, Thomas. 1999. *The Quest for Cosmic Justice*. Free Press.

Steele, David Ramsay. 1992. *From Marx to Mises: Post-Capitalist Society and the Challenge of Economic Calculation*. Open Court.

———. 1996. Between Immorality and Unfeasibility: The Market Socialist Predicament. *Critical Review: A Journal of Politics and Society* 10:3 (Summer). Reprinted as "The Market Socialists' Predicament" in *The Mystery of Fascism*.

———. 2017. *Orwell Your Orwell: A Worldview on the Slab*. St. Augustine's Press.

———. 2019. *The Mystery of Fascism: David Ramsay Steele's Greatest Hits*. St. Augustine's Press.

Williamson, Oliver E. 1983. *Markets and Hierarchies: Analysis and Antitrust Implications*. Free Press.

———. 1998 [1985]. *The Economic Institutions of Capitalism: Firms, Markets, Relational Contracting*. Free Press.

Woien, Sandra, ed. 2022. *Jordan Peterson: Critical Responses*. Open Universe.

10

THE FIVE TIMES GEORGE ORWELL
CHANGED HIS MIND

What were George Orwell's political and social views? In many years of talking to people about Orwell, I have found that the best way to give an accurate and reasonably quick answer to that question, dispelling common misconceptions, is to focus on the occasions when Orwell changed his mind.

In his comparatively short life—he died at the age of forty-six—Orwell several times shifted or even reversed his position on important issues, sometimes very abruptly. Readers of Orwell will be misled if they try to put together statements he made at different times, not aware that these may represent violently opposed viewpoints. A simple example would be to take statements Orwell made about war during his militantly "pacifist" period, which lasted from June 1937 to August 1939, and try to combine these with statements he made after August 1939, when he had become enthusiastically pro-war.

There are five major turning points in Orwell's political thinking. They are:

1. Orwell's decision in September 1927 to quit the Burmese police force and devote his life full-time to writing.
2. Orwell's conversion, in mid-1936, from being explicitly anti-socialist to identifying himself as a socialist and a member of the Left.
3. Orwell's conversion, in May–June 1937, from being a Popular Frontist and Communist fellow-traveler to being an adherent of the revolutionary anti-Stalinist Left.
4. Orwell's conversion, in the early morning hours of August 22nd 1939, from being fiercely opposed to the coming war against Germany, to being equally fiercely supportive of this war.

5. Orwell's conversion, in the years 1942–1945, from revolutionary to parliamentary socialism.

These changes are all fully documented in my study of Orwell's thought, *Orwell Your Orwell: A Worldview on the Slab*. Here I will explain clearly and briefly what happened on each occasion.

The last four of these five changes were purely intellectual: serious alterations in Orwell's political worldview. The first may also have been predominantly intellectual, though it perhaps owed as much to Orwell's developing awareness of his own personal capabilities and values.

1. The Decision to Become a Writer

In September 1927, when he was twenty-four years old, Orwell came back to England on leave from Burma, where he had spent five years as an officer in the imperial police force. He now informed his astonished and appalled family that he was resigning from the Burmese police and had decided to remain in England and become, of all things, a full-time writer.

Until that upsetting moment in 1927, Orwell had apparently turned out well. His family was not at all wealthy but very respectable. They had sent him to a private "prep" school, where he won a scholarship to Eton, Britain's pre-eminent "public school." In Britain, "public school" was then and is now the term for an elite private school, at that time always a single-sex boarding school.

Orwell attended Eton from 1917 to 1921. A majority of top government positions were usually held by Old Etonians. By being an Old Etonian, Orwell automatically had a ticket into the British ruling class.

Orwell had been born in India, a true child of the empire. Orwell's father was a civil servant in British India, working for the department whose task was to inspect the opium crop to ensure its quality before it was exported to China.

This was a time when two-fifths of the Earth's surface was colored pink on the map, and most British people assumed that the British empire would continue for many decades to come, just as most Americans now fondly cherish the same confidence with respect to U.S. global hegemony.

Orwell came back from Burma a bitter critic of the British empire, and it looks almost certain that this must have played a major part in his decision to return to England. His first novel and one of his best, *Burmese Days* (1934), could hardly have been published while he remained a member of the imperial police force.

It's not clear whether Orwell immediately explained to his family in 1927 just what sort of a writer he was going to become—probably not. His plan was to periodically live among tramps, hoboes, down-and-outs, and then write up his experiences. Among those who followed English letters, this was a respectable tradition—Stevenson's *The Amateur Emigrant* (1895), London's *People of the Abyss* (1903), Davis's *Autobiography of a Super Tramp* (1908)—but it's doubtful the family would have even heard of these, for they were not especially literary.

In his new role as a writer, Orwell was disciplined and industrious. On the days when he wasn't actually on the road, living the life of a tramp, his typewriter could be heard clacking away for hours. He wrote numerous short articles and reviews for various magazines and newspapers, giving him a small but slowly growing stream of income.

In the Spring of 1928 he went to Paris with a modest amount of cash, and was swindled out of it by a girlfriend. In his written account, this became a male acquaintance, illustrating the point that Orwell's supposedly factual accounts are often fiction, only loosely based on real events. Having lost his money, he became a *plongeur*, a washer-up in restaurants, adding to his experiences of life at the bottom. Back in England, and again pursuing his plan of associating with tramps, he put these experiences together in his first published book, *Down and Out in Paris and London.*

The name on Orwell's birth certificate and on his gravestone is "Eric Arthur Blair." I have been calling him "George Orwell," a name he adopted in 1933 for *Down and Out in Paris and London.* It immediately became more than just a pen-name. From 1933 on, people who made his acquaintance knew him as George Orwell, not Eric Blair, and after his death, his second wife and widow called herself "Sonia Orwell."

Orwell heartily disliked the names "Eric" and "Blair"; we may surmise that, as someone concerned about tough masculinity, who looked with disfavor on homosexuality and birth control as pathologies of degenerate industrial society, he preferred the manly flavor of "George Orwell" to the limp-wristed sound of "Eric Blair." The theory sometimes propounded, that the two names represent two different aspects of his personality or worldview, is completely unfounded.

Although he continued to write numerous short pieces for magazines or journals, from 1933 to 1940 he published one book a year, four novels and four non-fiction works. This output was maintained despite five months fighting for the Republic in Spain and seven months visiting French Morocco primarily for his health, though here he was more able to work on his writing. Orwell had a chronic lung problem, not helped by lifelong heavy smoking, and was advised to spend time in a warm, dry climate.

2. Orwell's Conversion to Socialism

At the end of 1935 Orwell began a three-months-long visit to the north of England, with the intention of writing a book about the poverty he observed there. All his guides on this guided tour were socialists—ILP members, left Labourites, or Communists.

In the 1920s, when most of the world experienced prosperity, Britain was in slump, usually attributed to the return to the gold standard following the Great War. In the 1930s, different parts of Britain had contrasting economic experiences, some parts enjoying unprecedented prosperity while others appeared sunk in ugly and shameful poverty. Public attention was drawn to the "Distressed Areas" by the well-publicized "marches" of the unemployed and by the notable success of Walter Greenwood's novel, *Love on the Dole*. It was a natural publishing move for the author of *Down and Out in Paris and London* to visit the Distressed Areas and write about conditions there.

Orwell's report on the Distressed Areas was *The Road to Wigan Pier*, which took him nine months to write and was published in the Left Book Club. He handed in the manuscript at the end of 1936, just before leaving to fight in Spain. The first half of this book is a first-hand account of poverty in the poorest parts of Yorkshire and Lancashire. The second half is an exposition of Orwell's opinions on a wide range of politically charged topics. Before this, Orwell's views are often somewhat uncertain, but now we have a clear and quite full account of his opinions on socialism, capitalism, fascism, the empire, class divisions, and political culture generally.

Orwell, in common with the vast majority of self-identified socialists at the time, conceives socialism as a system in which "the State, representing the whole nation, owns everything, and everyone is a state employee," plus democracy and approximate income equality (Orwell, *Complete Works*, XII, p. 410). Up to 1936, Orwell explicitly rejects socialism, as can be seen from passages in his novel, *Keep the Aspidistra Flying* (1936). In *Wigan Pier*, Orwell announces himself as a new convert to socialism, and yet proceeds to make strong criticisms of socialists. In fact, he takes up far more space attacking socialists than defending socialism or attacking the right.

Orwell's conversion to socialism is also simultaneously a conversion to politics. Before *Wigan Pier*, he sees himself as a writer in the mold of George Gissing, a novelist and, to some extent, a social commentator and social critic with, of course, some political views. With *Wigan Pier*, politics become his central preoccupation, and henceforth he feels that all his writing must have a political point.

His main theme in *Wigan Pier* is that, while socialism is necessary, and indeed inevitable, socialists are going about their activity in the wrong way by laying too much emphasis on industrial progress and higher incomes. Orwell shares in the fashionable reaction against H.G. Wells, perceived by 1930s intellectuals as a simple-minded worshipper of technology and the proponent of a naive utopianism.

Orwell is a severe critic of what he calls "mechanical progress." He maintains that increased living standards are harmful because they make us soft. Men ought to be hard, and so, for example, Orwell derides the taking of aspirin. He suggests that there is little point in workers getting shorter working hours, because the pursuit of more leisure is an empty and absurd goal. "The implied objective of 'progress' is ... some frightful sub-human depth of softness and helplessness" (V, p. 187). He was later to develop this line of thought into a sustained attack on "hedonism."

In the 1880s and 1890s, socialism, as a creed for intellectuals, had received mortal blows, part of the cultural current we now call *fin de siècle*, involving a general loss of confidence in rationality and progress. The new anti-socialists did not reject socialism because they had an alternative vision of human improvement, but because they had lost faith in all such visions. By the 1930s, we arrive at the situation where political intellectuals are mostly left-wing while intellectuals primarily concerned with the arts are mostly right-wing—though they are right-wingers of a distinctive sort, reactionaries who agree with socialists in their contempt for liberalism and capitalism, but see the socialists as naive in thinking that there is any practicable alternative which would not turn out to be worse.

Orwell's argument in *Wigan Pier* is that of a reactionary artistic intellectual who has been very recently converted to currently fashionable political ideas. He retains from his former *fin-de-siècle* anti-socialism the conviction that industrialization is inherently ugly and corrupting, and he now thinks that socialists, though technically right about the need for a collectivized economy, are deluded in their optimism about the benefits of industrial development.

Orwell here gives us his famous rant against vegetarians, feminists, nudists, sandal-wearers, and fruit-juice drinkers (pp. 161–62). While this is no doubt Orwell's sincere response to these forms of deviancy, and would certainly have gained the amused approval of most leftists at the time, it also represents his view that middle-class degenerates are endangering the hoped-for political alliance between the less degenerate working class and leftist intellectuals.

There is one point which readers and commentators frequently get wrong: Orwell's attitude to the Communist Party. There are some harsh observations about the Communists in *Wigan Pier*, and readers tend to assume there is a straightforward continuity between this period and Orwell's later very dedicated anti-Communism. Some later retrospective remarks by Orwell himself tend deceptively to suggest such a view. Yet in *Wigan Pier* Orwell is quite definitely a Communist fellow-traveler, and then after May–June 1937, quite definitely not.

The Left Book Club was the high point of success of the Communist Party of Great Britain in its attempts to infiltrate and control the British Left. It was not merely a book club, but a continual stream of pamphlets, magazines, public meetings, discussion seminars, weekend schools, dances, socials, and other events. It was a vibrant church, dedicated to pursuance of the Popular Front.

All works selected for the Left Book Club had to be approved by a committee of three: Vitor Gollancz (the publisher), John Strachey, and Harold Laski. All three were committed fellow-travelers, and all three approved *The Road to Wigan Pier*, which became one of the most popular volumes of the Club. It was Gollancz, who had earlier contracted to publish the work which became *Wigan Pier*, who prevailed upon a somewhat reluctant Orwell to have it included in the Left Book Club.

Strachey had applied to join the Communist Party and been refused membership. He then produced a spate of capably written persuasive books expounding the Communist Party line, most notably *The Coming Struggle for Power* (1932), mentioned favorably by Orwell in *Wigan Pier*.

The Left Book Club was essentially a Popular Front book club and therefore a club for Communists and fellow-travelers. Nothing opposing the Popular Front, for example nothing by a Trotskyist, could have appeared in the Left Book Club (before August 1939, when there was suddenly no possibility of a Popular Front, the Communist Party no longer had any use for the Club, and the Club went into steep decline).

In the Popular Front period, the Communist Party of Great Britain was doing two somewhat discordant things. It was cozying up to the non-Communist Left in order to fight fascism by promoting the Popular Front, and it was attacking anything perceived as "Trotskyism" with obsessive zeal. What this meant in practice was that the Communists classified anyone who criticized them from the left as Trotskyists, to be demonized and destroyed, while warmly tolerating criticism from the right, as long as these critics would accept the principle of the Popular Front. Orwell's snippy comments about the Communists in *Wigan Pier* would have been familiar to any seasoned leftist as a standard kind of "reactionary" criticism which was no obstacle to mutual co-operation.

The rationale of the Popular Front was to unite the Left against the looming menace of "fascism." Orwell was completely on board with this objective. Despite his harsh remarks about the Communists, mostly related to their identification with industrial development and "the stupid cult of Russia" (p. 201), Orwell makes it clear that he supports the Popular Front movement. He refers to "the type of humbug who passes resolutions 'against Fascism and Communism' i.e. against rats and rat poison" (p. 206). So, there are people who oppose fascism and Communism equally, and Orwell says he is not one of them, because he sees that the Communist Party, for all its faults, is a vital ally in the struggle against fascism. The Orwell of *Wigan Pier* is most decidedly a Communist fellow-traveler. This was to change dramatically in less than a year, because of something that happened to Orwell on May 3rd 1937.

3. From Popular Frontist to Revolutionary Anti-Stalinist

The Spanish Civil War broke out on July 17th 1936, when military officers rebelled against the government elected in February. The left-wing government, Liberal Republicans with some socialists, were opposed by the insurgent generals, the Nationalists—called "fascists" by the left, though only a minority of them were actually fascists. The officers' rebellion had been prompted by numerous violent atrocities on the part of leftist gangs working together with the police and the government, culminating in the murder of the popular royalist politician José Calvo Sotelo on July 13th.

At the outset, the Republic controlled about sixty percent of Spanish territory, the rest controlled by the Nationalist officers and the diverse groups, *el movimiento*, which flocked to their support. Throughout the war, the Nationalists made territorial gains, culminating in complete victory by the end of March 1939, and the installation of General Franco as dictator.

Thousands of volunteers from Western countries volunteered to fight for the Left in Spain, and thousands of them were killed. Orwell wanted to join the struggle in Spain, at first with some unclarity about whether he would go primarily as a soldier or as an observer and writer. These were not sharply divided in his mind, because a major personal goal of Orwell's was to put himself in circumstances where he would have experiences he could write about.

To fight for the Left in Spain, you needed a letter of introduction from a recognized socialist organization. Orwell asked his fellow–Old Etonian John Strachey to set up an appointment with the Communist Party leader Harry Pollitt. Pollitt refused to give Orwell a letter of introduction. By this refusal, Pollitt unwittingly saved the life of the one man who was to do more than any other to bring about the downfall of world Communism.

There's room for doubt about the precise reasons for Pollitt's refusal, but one reason was that Orwell wasn't yet sure whether he was going to Spain primarily as a soldier or as a reporter, so he wouldn't commit to joining the International Brigade. He was not confident about his own usefulness as a soldier, thinking that he might be outclassed by Spanish volunteers, but as soon as he arrived in Spain he realized that he was far more qualified as a military man than almost all the Spanish troops on the Republican side. Orwell had received military training in the Burmese police force and before that the Eton OTC, and he had owned and used his own firearms, as many English middle-class youths did in the 1920s.

The result was that Orwell, turned down by the Communists, applied to the Independent Labour Party (ILP) and they gave him his letter of introduction. The ILP was a historically important but quite small organization, though still bigger than the Communist Party. At this point the ILP stood to the left of the Communist Party, being affiliated with the London Bureau, sometimes facetiously called "the three and a half international," small, but still bigger, for example, than Trotsky's Fourth International. As a result of getting the letter from the ILP, Orwell went to fight, not for the International Brigade, but for the militia of the POUM (Partido Obrero de Unificación Marxista), a tiny anti-Stalinist Marxist party with noticeable support only in Catalonia. The ILP and the POUM were inaccurately characterized as "Trotskyist" by the Communists.

Although Orwell found himself in the ranks of the POUM militia, his actual opinions were contrary to the POUM and completely in line with the Popular Front movement represented by the International Brigade. Orwell was posted to the Aragón front and took part in traditional trench warfare. He wanted to leave Aragón and go to Madrid, partly because the front in Aragón was comparatively quiet and he wanted to see more action, partly because Madrid was the most glamorous, because considered pivotal, center of the war.

The Communist Party was preaching the line that socialist revolution should be put on the back burner, and the Spanish left should unite with the democratic elements of the bourgeoisie to defend democracy against fascism. Orwell completely accepted this analysis, rejecting the POUM position that the way to win the war against fascism was to pursue the socialist revolution.

Posted on the Aragón front and occasionally exchanging some fire with the Nationalist enemy ("the fascists"), Orwell chafed under the comparative inactivity and longed to move to Madrid, where he could fight for the International Brigade. Moving to Madrid meant leaving the POUM militia and joining the International Brigade, controlled by the Communist Party and therefore by the Soviet secret police, the NKVD. If Orwell had succeeded in getting to Madrid, he might have been killed in the fighting. Failing that, he would certainly have been disposed of by a Soviet commissar for talking back. We would know him as an obscure young leftist writer, like a number of others who reportedly died in battle, fighting for the cause of democracy in the dialectical garb of Soviet state socialism.

At the end of April, Orwell took some leave in Barcelona. He planned to move to Madrid and take some other dissatisfied members of the POUM militia with him. He was delayed by a bout of illness and by waiting for new boots to be made (because of his outsize feet, Orwell needed his shoes to be custom-made).

Something unexpected now happened to upset his plan. When Orwell sat down to breakfast on May 3rd, he was a Popular Frontist and Communist fellow-traveler. On that day street fighting broke out, Barcelona-style, with rifles and grenades. The Republican government in Valenica, right-wing socialists (yes, right-wing, because of the Communists' currently anti-revolutionary line) allied with and therefore under the control of the Communists, sent Assault Guards, a kind of paramilitary police, to take possession of the public buildings which had been occupied by the workers in the heady "revolutionary" days of August 1936. "The workers" here means in effect the anarcho-syndicalists of the trade union movement, the CNT. The anarchist workers defended their buildings against the attack of the Assault Guards, and the tiny POUM fell in with the anarchists.

It was in this connection that Orwell made the famous remark: "When I see an actual flesh-and-blood worker in conflict with his natural enemy, the policeman, I do not have to ask myself which side I am on" (VI, p. 104), that side, of course, being the side of the workers against the police.

Orwell took part in some of the street fighting, which fizzled out as the workers had to go back to work, and then Orwell decided not to proceed to Madrid, but to go back briefly to the POUM front and from there apply to leave Spain and return to England. At the front, he was shot in the throat and hospitalized. When he recovered and came back to Barcelona, he found that a totalitarian state prevailed. Anyone associated with the POUM was liable to be arrested, tortured, and very likely killed by the Communists. Orwell and his wife (who had earlier got a job in Barcelona) then managed to hide out for a while, escape from Catalonia, and return to England.

Back in England, Orwell found that the inaccurate Communist account of what had happened in Catalonia was being widely disseminated, even by some respectable non-Communist publications. This account said that "Trotskyists" (the POUM) and anarchists, in the pay of Franco and Hitler, had started an uprising against the Republic. The major organ of leftist opinion, the *New Statesman*, refused to publish anything critical of the Communists' behavior in Spain, because of their assumption that this would weaken the Republic and help the Nationalists. Orwell wrote some short pieces about events in Spain and then the book *Homage to Catalonia*, which had minute sales at the time, but is now the second most read book on the Spanish Civil War (after Hemingway's novel, *For Whom the Bell Tolls*).

By June 1937, Orwell has become what the Communists would call an "ultra-leftist," bitterly opposed to the Popular Front and contemptuous of the Left Book Club. Some of this comes through in his novel, *Coming Up for Air* (1939). In retrospect, Orwell now decides that the POUM had been right and the Communists wrong: the way to pursue the class war and effectively fight fascism is to work for socialist revolution by violent insurrection.

Orwell now completely swallows the whole doctrinal package of the London Bureau. Part of this package was opposition to any "anti-fascist" war, such as a British war against Germany. Orwell was committed to virtually every detail of the London Bureau's position for two years and two months.

Orwell joined the ILP on 13th June 1938, and wrote a public explanation of why he had done so (XI, pp. 167–69), in part because the ILP could be relied upon to oppose "imperialist war," meaning Britain's coming war against Germany. In September 1938 he signed the leftist "Manifesto: If War Comes, We Shall Resist" (XI, pp. 212–13). According to this document, at the time of the Sudetenland crisis, the coming war would be the responsibility of British "economic imperialism."

Orwell's commitment to the anti-war position was such that he defended anyone who opposed the coming war, however much he might dislike the rest of their outlook. Accordingly he defended Aldous Huxley's literal pacifism, asserting that "Anyone who helps to put peace on the map is doing useful work" (XI, p. 154). Sir Oswald Mosley's British Union of Fascists had become the pre-eminent peace party, and Orwell wrote: "I don't know whether Mosley will have the sense and the guts to stick out against war with Germany" (XI, p. 341).

Orwell's position—the same as the ILP's—is that violent insurrection against the ruling class is required, but support for any war conducted by a national government is to be opposed. Though this position is often loosely described as "pacifist," it has no objection to violence per se, only to wars between nation-states, perceived as financially motivated conflicts between rival groups of capitalists.

So committed was Orwell to the revolutionary anti-war position that he wrote to his friend the anarchist Herbert Read, proposing the formation of an illegal underground organization to combat the war against Germany when it got started (XI, pp. 313–14; 340–41).

4. From Anti-War to Pro-War Overnight

Orwell wrote a six-thousand-word pamphlet opposing a war with Germany, though he could not find a publisher for it, and it was subsequently lost, possibly with Orwell's help. Bertrand Russell also wrote a book from a leftist anti-war point of view (*Which Way to Peace?*) and subsequently reversed himself, some months earlier than Orwell's reversal. This phenomenon of leftists moving from an anti-war position, continuing the narrow-Left stance of the First World War, to a pro-war position, because of the perceived unique menace of Hitler, was quite a common one.

In the early morning hours of August 22nd 1939, Orwell has a dream. In this dream, the expected war has begun. It will start in reality just twelve days later. Orwell doesn't tell us what precisely happened in the dream, but he reports that when he woke up, he knew he would act as a patriot, he would support Britain in the war against Germany (XII, p. 271). Although he describes this change of mind as though it were an emotional bolt from the blue, he states that he could offer persuasive arguments in support of the war, and he was indeed to do so in the days and months ahead, so it's a reasonable surmise that Orwell's pro-war standpoint has been silently germinating for some months past. Orwell has now abruptly adopted a new position which involves bitterly attacking everything he has been saying about fascism and war for the past twenty-six months.

After awakening from the dream, now suddenly a pro-war enthusiast, Orwell comes downstairs and looks at the newspaper headlines. They announce Ribbentrop's visit to Moscow to meet Molotov, which everyone at once broadly understands: Hitler and Stalin are about to form a friendly alliance partitioning Poland between them and giving Germany a free hand to conduct a war against Britain and France.

So Orwell and the Communist Party switch positions on almost the same day: Orwell from anti-war to pro-war, the CPGB from pro-war to anti-war. But not quite the same day, because many of the comrades take a few days or weeks to digest the full extent of the reversal they are now being required to navigate. The CP now argues that the war is caused by imperialism—with the emphasis on British imperialism—and they form a new front organization, the People's Convention, to campaign for "peace," meaning acceptance of Hitler's peace terms. There was no longer any need to fight fascism, now that fascism had made friends with socialism. And so, Orwell quipped, thing were now "all quiet on the Popular Front" (an allusion to the novel, *All Quiet on the Western Front*).

Despite their former Communist sympathies, most of the leading fellow travelers ceased to be fellow travelers and supported the war, even (after a few weeks of doubts and hesitations) John Strachey. We now enter a period when Orwell saw eye-to-eye with the most prominent intellectual leaders of the Left. At every point after 1936 Orwell was completely aligned with at least one major segment of the British Left, but now he was aligned with the dominant segment, an alignment to be somewhat ruffled following Germany's invasion of Russia on June 22nd 1941, following which a new wave of pro-Soviet sentiment swept over Britain.

From the start of the war until at least 1942, Orwell took the position that the only hope for winning the war was to have a socialist revolution in Britain. "Only revolution can save England ... I dare say the London gutters will have to run with blood. All right let them, if it is necessary" (XII, pp. 271–72).

This view can be seen as a transposition of the old POUM line from Spain to Britain. But it also arose from Orwell's firm belief that a collectivist nation must always be more efficient than a capitalist nation, therefore the former would beat the latter in war. Orwell saw German National Socialism as a form of collectivism, even sometimes calling it "Socialism" (XII, p. 159), though he usually reserved the term "Socialism," always capitalized, for a collectivized economy *plus democracy and income equality*. In Orwell's judgment, Britain could defeat Germany only by becoming equally collectivist. In line with the prevailing leftist mythology, Orwell also believed that if Britain did not undergo a socialist revolution, it would quickly go fascist.

The view that Britain would need a socialist transformation, or at least a measure of drastic equalitarian reform, before it could beat Germany, was quite commonplace, being proclaimed, among other voices, by the radio broadcasts of the popular writer J.B. Priestley. No such drastic reforms materialized, and yet the visible military advantage had shifted from the Axis to the Allies by 1942.

Even after Soviet Russia and the United States had come into the war, Orwell still maintained that Britain could not beat Germany without a British socialist revolution (XIII, pp. 307–08).

5. Bevanite and Pre-McCarthyite

By 1944 Orwell had to accept that he had been wrong. Britain was winning the war, despite the absence of socialist revolution. The earliest intimation of this in print occurs in early 1943 when he records "the

growing suspicion that we may all have underrated the strength of capitalism and that the right may, after all, be able to win the war off its own
bat without resorting to any radical change" (XIV, p. 292). It was as late
as October 1944 that Orwell frankly acknowledged that "up to at any
rate the end of 1942 I was grossly wrong in my analysis of the situation"
(XVI, p. 411).

Around the year 1947 Orwell also had to accept another change in
his views, on the matter of the empire, though in this case he made no
attempt to publicly admit or explain his errors. Orwell had always expressed outspoken opposition to the British empire, and yet it was an
odd kind of opposition, because Orwell nearly always added that the
abolition of the British empire just could not happen. Thus Orwell combined vocal hostility to the empire with vocal hostility to any suggestion
that the empire be abolished, which he emphatically asserted to be beyond the bounds of possibility. As a result, for example, Orwell never
campaigned for Indian independence, as did many leftists with outlooks
otherwise akin to Orwell's, such as Bertrand Russell and Fenner Brock-
way. Orwell's view of the empire implied that any such activity would
be a waste of time.

Orwell stridently maintained the claim that the empire raised the
living standards of people in Britain, including the working class, a view
which we now know to have been mistaken. In actuality the empire reduced the incomes of most British people of all classes, who were taxed
to support it, including the working class. It directly benefited a small
proportion of the population, such as those who got imperial jobs and
those who received subsidies for certain economic opportunities. The
empire was not, as Orwell liked to claim, "a money racket," at least not
for the great majority of the population, but rather a national glory
racket.

In 1947 India, Pakistan, Ceylon, and Burma were granted independence, fully implemented the following year. By any measure, India was
by far the most important part of the empire and was known to be such.
There's no record of just how Orwell came to terms with the realization
that he had been drastically wrong, for all of his political life, about the
possibility of colonial independence. Since he died before the healthy
growth of workers' wages in the 1950s and 1960s, following the "loss" of

most of the empire, he probably never did grasp that his views on the economic consequences of the empire were radically mistaken.

One new thought which might have become important had Orwell lived longer was his conclusion that dictatorships (and by implication all totalitarian systems) suffer from a handicap, because bad decisions become more likely with the absence of open debate. Hitler, for instance, did a poor job at fulfilling his own objectives, because as Führer he was insulated from criticism. Almost all the decisive things Hitler did from the invasion of Poland on, were blunders—and blunders which the German generals or other prominent Germans would not have committed.

Orwell somewhat muddled this insight by framing it as the ability of the non-expert common people to challenge the experts (XII, p. 306), missing the point that the experts are often divided, and the politically connected experts are privileged over the dissenting experts.

Orwell's great work *Nineteen Eighty-Four* was finished in 1948 and published in June 1949. For the last twelve months of his life, Orwell was a sick man in a sanitorium, unable to take on a new major work but able to converse with visitors and respond briefly to letters.

In the last years of his life, Orwell had clearly given up any expectation of violent socialist revolution, and was positioned on the left of the Labour Party. He had become a left-wing Labourite, a Bevanite, although the defining moment of Bevanism (the rebellion against National Health service prescription charges) was not to occur until fifteen months after Orwell's death.

Like many, perhaps most, left Labourites of that period, Orwell was a stalwart foe of Communism and fully ready to fight a new war against the Soviet Union. He disparaged what he called "appeasement" of the USSR (XVIII, p. 287). Orwell coined the phrase "Cold War" and never left any doubt that he supported the West in this confrontation. He did hypothetically favor another policy which, however, he did not think of as practically feasible, to try to help form a socialist united states of Europe, distinct from both America and the USSR (XVII, p. 248).

In 1947 Orwell reviewed James Burnham's *The Struggle for the World* (XIX, p. 96–105). Burnham argued that the world war between Communism and the West had already begun (here Orwell expressed agreement), and called for drastic measures, including use of nuclear weapons against

Russia, before Russia could develop nuclear weapons of its own. (The leftist Bertrand Russell proposed something similar around this time.)

Orwell was sympathetic to Burnham's program, but he argued against its more extreme elements by contending that Burnham's analysis exaggerated the imminence of the threat. Orwell maintained that the West had more time than Burnham would allow. In response to Burnham's depiction of the Western Communist Parties as a formidable force, apparently ruthlessly dedicated to Communist world conquest, Orwell pointed to the high turnover of membership in these parties. They were far weaker than they appeared on paper (p. 100).

Over fifty years after Orwell's death, it came to be publicized that he had compiled a list of public personages he knew or suspected to have Communist sympathies and had given a copy of this list to an old girl-friend of his, who now worked for a secret government department tasked with combating Communist influence. (In a twist suggestive of many fascinating plot developments, she was the twin sister of the wife of Arthur Koestler, the former Communist turned militant anti-Communist, though still, like Orwell, a committed leftist, author of the strongly influential anti-Communist works, *Darkness at Noon* and *The Yogi and the Commissar*.)

The public release of information about Orwell's list raised the question of whether he was a McCarthyite before McCarthy. Most of the people who engaged in this controversy had not yet caught up with the news that McCarthy has been proven factually correct: the people he had identified were not only, as he claimed, security risks who ought to be investigated, but provably were Soviet agents, including some individuals at the very peak of American political life (Alger Hiss, Harry Hopkins, Harry Dexter White).

Tail-gunner Joe made his first speech on Communist penetration of the U.S. government the month after Orwell's death, so Orwell was never aware of McCarthy. There can be no doubt that Orwell, had he lived, would have staunchly supported the Senator's quest to identify Soviet agents in government posts. McCarthy's opinion that the military and the executive branch should not be penetrated by hundreds of people who held allegiance to a foreign power rather than to their own country, and that such people should therefore be disqualified from employment in these areas of the government, is surely not terribly eccentric.

This account may still leave the broader puzzle: how could Orwell be a leftist whose complaint about the postwar Labour government was that it was not far more left and simultaneously be an ardent (or as the Communists and their sympathizers would picturesquely put it, a "rabid") anti-Communist?

This general combination of views was commonplace among Labour leftists at the time, including such people as Aneurin Bevan and Michael Foot, whose broad view of politics was highly congruent with Orwell's.

More specifically, we can explain Orwell's thinking in the following straightforward way. Orwell was firmly convinced that capitalism was in its final throes and could only be replaced by some form of collectivism. He was convinced of this on grounds of economics and industrial organization, though he knew absolutely nothing of economics or industrial organization, just as people today will earnestly assure you that we face a crisis of global warming, and couldn't tell you the first law of thermodynamics, let alone the Stefan-Boltzmann equation. Intellectuals may almost be defined as people who can easily be convinced of fanciful dogmas concerning matters of which they are comprehensively ignorant.

Orwell believed the coming collectivism could be either totalitarianism (which he also called "oligarchical collectivism") or democratic socialism. He therefore saw it as vital to make an attempt to combine collectivism with civil liberty, a combination he acknowledged might turn out to be unattainable (XII, p. 5)—in other words, he considered it a definite possibility that democratic socialism might just not be feasible and in that case there could be no escape from a totalitarian future.

Orwell fully accepted that totalitarianism, whether of the Soviet or Nazi variety, was far worse than capitalism, and at the same time he was firmly convinced that capitalism was at the end of its rope. As he succinctly put it, "The real question is whether capitalism, now obviously doomed, is to give way to oligarchy or to true democracy" (XVIII, p. 272).

Bibliography

Burnham, James. 1947. *The Struggle for the World*. John Day.

Caute, David. 1973 [1964]. *The Fellow Travellers: A Postscript to the Enlightenment*. Macmillan.

Evans, M. Stanton. 2007. *Blacklisted by History: The Untold Story of Senator Joe McCarthy and His Fight Against America's Enemies.* Random House.

Davis, Lance E., and Robert A. Huttenback. 1986. *Mammon and the Pursuit of Empire: The Political Economy of British Imperialism 1860–1912.* Cambridge University Press.

Haynes, John Earle, Harvey Klehr, and Alexander Vassiliev. 2009. *Spies: The Rise and Fall of the KGB in America.* Yale University Press.

Orwell, George. 1986–2001. *The Complete Works of George Orwell.* Twenty volumes. Secker and Warburg.

Romerstein, Herbert, and Eric Breindel, 2014 [2000]. *The Venona Secrets: The Definitive Expose of Soviet Espionage in America.* Regnery.

Steele, David Ramsay. 2017. *Orwell Your Orwell: A Worldview on the Slab.* St. Augustine's Press.

Strachey, John. 1935 [1932]. *The Coming Struggle for Power.* Modern Library.

Weinstein, Allen, and Alexander Vassiliev. 2000 [1999]. *The Haunted Wood: Soviet Espionage in America—The Stalin Era.* Modern Library.

11
ARE CRITICAL RATIONALISTS COMPLETELY OUT OF THEIR MINDS?

Michael Huemer has published a brief and blistering attack on the thinking of Karl Popper. He proclaims that Popper's ideas are "insane." He maintains that if you actually agree with Popper, "you are completely out of your mind," which implies that Popper himself was completely out of his mind.

Huemer titles his piece, posted on his blog, "You Don't Agree with Karl Popper." The point of this title is that, in Huemer's opinion, a lot of people (he mentions libertarians, many of whom admire Popper's ideas) think they agree with Popper, only because they don't fully understand what Popper is saying. If they did understand it, as Huemer does, they would find they wouldn't agree with it at all, unless they were completely out of their minds.

Huemer gives a summary of some of the ideas people attribute to Popper, and which he is willing to concede they can accept without being completely out of their minds. He then goes on to impute to Popper additional views which he considers to be seriously wrong, and which people can't accept without being completely out of their minds.

Here's his summary of the first set of views, the ones Huemer acknowledges that sane people, in his judgment, can readily accept:

> It's impossible to verify a theory, with any number of observations. Yet a single observation can *refute* a theory. Also, science is mainly about trying to refute theories. The way science proceeds is that you start with a hypothesis, deduce some observational predictions, and then see whether those predictions are correct. You start with the ones that you think are

most likely to be wrong, because you're trying to falsify the theory. Theories that can't in principle be falsified are bad. Theories that could have been falsified but have survived lots of attempts to falsify them are good.

Is this, as far as it goes, a correct statement of Popper's views? It's not wildly off, but there are some things which are not strictly accurate.

Most obviously, Popper did not hold that theories that can't in principle be falsified are necessarily "bad," merely that they don't belong to empirical science. He held, for example, that metaphysical theories, such as whether or not the universe is deterministic, can't be empirically falsified and are therefore not scientific, though they can be, and should be, seriously argued about. Popper wrote an entire book arguing against determinism and for indeterminism (*The Open Universe*), an issue which he insists does not belong to science. In his view there is no empirical test which could conceivably falsify determinism or indeterminism, and so this is an issue which belongs to metaphysics.

Another example is realism. Are trees, mountains, and stars things which exist independently of our awareness, or are they products of our minds and senses? Popper argues strongly for realism (*Realism and the Aim of Science*, pp. 80–158). At the same time, he maintains that there is no way of empirically testing realism. So, this is not a scientific question but a metaphysical one. It can't be tackled by empirical research but only by philosophical argument.

Popper holds that with some metaphysical theories, it may be possible to reframe them so that they become falsifiable. This may then lead to an advance in scientific knowledge. For example, the atomic theories of some of the ancient Greeks were not falsifiable. They were therefore, in Popper's terminology, metaphysical rather than scientific, though this does not imply that they were not meaningful, important, or interesting. Nor does it imply that they were not objectively true or false.

John Dalton's theory of the atom published in 1807 made numerous claims about atoms which could be tested by experiment: we could attempt to falsify them. Thus theories about atoms moved from metaphysics into science. Popper does not think this can happen to all metaphysical theories; he does not seek or expect the elimination of metaphysics. His view is that metaphysics will never be disposed of, and some metaphysics will always be required, even for and by science.

There are some non-falsifiable theories that may present themselves as scientific, so in that sense we might say that they're "bad," that's to say, not really what they claim to be. Examples include some of the propositions of psychoanalysis, such as the theory that all dreams represent fulfillment of wishes (*Realism and the Aim of Science*, pp. 163–174), or that all infants undergo an Oedipal phase of wanting to kill their fathers so that they can have sex with their mothers (Edelstein et al., *Therapy Breakthrough*, pp. 255–266).

Another possibility is that something might look superficially like a scientific theory, but on examination might turn out to be tautologous, and therefore not empirically refutable. And, Popper points out, truly scientific theories can always be turned into tautologies by interpreting them in such a way that they are immune to empirical refutation. Thus, "All swans are white" becomes a tautology if we add that anything not white cannot be a swan.

That "science is mainly about trying to refute theories" is a bit misleading as a statement of Popper's logic of science. Popper holds that science is about trying to find good and better explanations of the world, which involves comparing and evaluating theories according to several criteria, one of which is whether they agree with observations.

When Huemer says, "You start with the ones that you think are most likely to be wrong", I'm not sure what he means. You might perhaps be inclined to start with the theories that have the widest acceptance, since then you will make the most progress by showing them to be false. More generally, I suppose, you're most likely to start with theories which you find unsatisfactory. You may criticize a scientific theory in ways other than empirical testing, for example by arguing that the theory does not address a problem it was claimed to address, has hidden ambiguities or inconsistencies, or has components that can be eliminated without loss of empirical content (*Realism and the Aim of Science*, pp. 55–56).

Having looked at the elements of Popper which Huemer thinks we can accept without being completely out of our minds, let's now turn to those which he considers so terribly mistaken that agreeing with them is tantamount to insanity.

Huemer does not seriously attempt to give an outline of what he takes to be Popper's philosophy and then explain what he thinks is wrong with it. Instead, he identifies specific assertions he attributes to Popper, and he appears to think that these assertions are so outrageous, ridiculous, and self-evidently "insane," that it's enough to cite them and pull faces at them to convince his readers that Popper is completely out of his mind. Because of this procedure of Huemer's, I will list each of the distressing propositions Huemer imputes to Popper and try to say something helpful about each of them.

These assertions are a mixed bag; some of them are roughly the same as each other or overlap somewhat. Some of them accurately reproduce Popper's thinking; others don't. I list them here in the order Huemer gives them, without any attempt to sort them, rank them, or make sense of them. Double quotation marks indicate that Huemer is directly quoting Popper; single quotation marks indicates that Huemer is reporting in his own words what he takes to be Popper's position. No quotation marks indicates this is my paraphrase of something Huemer attributes to Popper.

I identify seventeen of these statements, which all express contentions Huemer attributes to Popper, and all of which allegedly constitute evidence that Popper is completely out of his mind.

1. '... the only legitimate kind of reasoning is deduction. Induction is completely worthless. ... His [Popper's] point is that *there is not the slightest reason to think* that *any* scientific theory is true, or close to true, or likely to be true, or anything else at all in this neighborhood that a normal person might want to say'.
2. 'There's no reason to think it's any more likely that we evolved by natural selection than that God created us in 4004 B.C. The Theory of Evolution is just a *completely arbitrary guess*'.
3. '... the goal of science must be to refute theories'.
4. "We must regard all laws and theories as guesses."
5. "There *are* no such things as good positive reasons."
6. "Belief, of course, is never rational: it is rational to *suspend* belief."
7. "I never assume that by force of 'verified' conclusions, theories can be established as 'true', or even as merely 'probable'."

}190{

8. "Of two hypotheses, the one that is logically stronger, or more informative, or better testable, and thus the one which can be *better corroborated*, is always *less probable*—on any given evidence—than the other."

9. "*In an infinite universe . . . the probability of any (non-tautological) universal law will be zero.*"

10. 'Popper is not just denying that we can be *certain* of these theories, and not just denying that they are *likely* to be true; he claims that they are *absolutely certain to be false*'.

11. 'When you get done testing your scientific theory, and it survives all tests, you can't say that it's likely to be correct; it's *less likely* to be correct, *even after you've gathered all the evidence*, than some unfalsifiable, unscientific theory'.

12. 'We have no reason to believe in science, and pseudoscience is more likely to be correct, and in fact the paradigmatic scientific theories are *definitely wrong. . . .*'

13. '. . . you can't logically deduce the falsity of the probability claim from observations. And again, that's the only thing you're allowed to appeal to. So, on Popper's view, quantum mechanics must be unscientific'.

14. The existence of vestigial legs in the bodies of some snakes is evidence for evolution, and this 'isn't a matter of deduction'.

15. '. . . Popper's philosophy entails that the Theory of Evolution and the asteroid-impact theory are unscientific, besides that we have no evidence at all for either of them'.

16. 'Of course, the obvious problem is that it's absurd to say that we don't have any reason to think any scientific theory is true'.

17. '. . . scientific theories are *less likely* to be correct than unscientific ones, *even after* they survive stringent tests'.

By my count, nine of these seventeen propositions are false—in these nine cases Huemer attributes a view to Popper which Popper most definitely does not hold. A couple of the propositions are a bit indeterminate, so only six of the seventeen are definitely correct. In those six cases where Huemer gives Popper's view correctly, I will generally defend what Popper says. The one case where I don't defend what Popper himself says, or at least the way he expresses it, is #6.

I will comment specifically on each of Huemer's seventeen allegedly Popperian positions, but before I do that, I will now give a very brief account of that part of Popper's philosophy which Huemer judges to be insane and which, in Huemer's view, you cannot accept unless you are completely out of your mind.

Critical Rationalism in a Nutshell

Before Popper, it was generally accepted by philosophers that science, as well as ordinary common-sense knowledge, relied upon a procedure known as induction. Induction is supposedly the way we get from the particular to the general, from the individual to the universal, from a limited number of observations to a universal law. For example, it is held that objects near the Earth will fall toward the Earth with an acceleration of 9.8 meters/second/second. Certain conditions have to be imposed. The object must be in a vacuum, otherwise the atmosphere will make a difference to the acceleration because of air resistance. But these conditions don't matter for our discussion here. We assume an acceleration of 9.8 m/s/s, then make an added calculation to allow for air resistance. Several additional and very minute adjustments have to be made for better accuracy. The point is that apart from changes in these stated conditions, the acceleration is always the same.

The question is: what entitles us to say that because we have observed a number of instances of falling bodies which conform to an acceleration of 9.8 m/s/s, the same will be true of all falling bodies near the Earth, for example, a thousand miles away from where we have made our observations, or a thousand years in the past or the future?

In 1739, David Hume pointed out that there is no logical operation which enables us to make this leap: to say that what we have observed of a certain finite range of instances will apply to other instances which we have not observed. We observe today in Edinburgh that sodium chloride dissolves in water whereas iron filings do not dissolve in water. There is no logically sound way to infer from today's findings that next week in Edinburgh, or today in London, we will not find that sodium chloride does not dissolve in water whereas iron filings do. Nor does the fact that things have behaved a certain way in the past, or in our neighborhood, even make it more probable that they will behave the same way in the future, or in a distant location—not an eentsy weentsy bit more probable. These are elementary logical points. They hold equally for the Aristotelian logic with which Hume was acquainted and for the modern logic developed by Peano, Frege, and Russell at the end of the nineteenth century. Consequently, there can be no valid method of induction.

Both science and everyday common sense require that we do form conclusions about what happens invariably, in all times and places. Therefore Hume's insight looks as if it must undermine both science and everyday common sense—as long as we cling to the notion of induction, the assumption that we can logically derive statements with a boundless range from a limited set of observations.

As a result of this discovery of Hume's, the philosophy known as empiricism was put in question. Empiricism holds that we get knowledge of the world only through the evidence of our senses, through observation, and through logical deductions from our observations, but since logic does not permit us to extend our conclusions beyond a list of our past observations, much of our knowledge (which is of a general or law-like character) can never be logically obtained by following empiricism.

Philosophers have attempted to tackle this problem in a number of ways, but nothing has shaken Hume's finding that, according to logic, valid induction is impossible and therefore gaining knowledge of the world by a purely empiricist approach is impossible.

Skipping over the history of the many failed attempts to find a reasonable basis for induction, which have always necessarily tended to move in the direction of saying that we know some things prior to any experience, we can now explain Popper's radically different approach.

Popper accepts Hume's conclusion that, in our search for general laws, we cannot support these laws by induction. The fact that some regularity has been observed on all occasions, around here and up to now, cannot logically offer any support for the proposition that the same regularity will continue to be observed in other places or other times. So, Popper entirely agrees with Hume's rejection of the possibility of valid induction.

Unlike Hume, who considered that we do use induction, even though it is logically indefensible, Popper goes on to say that we never do use induction; if we think we have arrived at a conclusion by induction, we are victims of a kind of optical illusion, whereby we falsely reconstruct the actual steps of our reasoning (*Realism and the Aim of Science*, p. 35). Consequently, Huemer's #1, that 'Induction is completely worthless', is a little misleading. Rather, in Popper's view, induction does not exist; there is no such thing as induction. It would be odd to say, 'Levitation is completely worthless'.

Against Hume, Popper says that we do not have to conclude that we cannot gain knowledge of the world and extend and improve our knowledge. We can do this by the method of conjecture and refutation. First, we come up with a conjecture (a surmise, guess, or hypothesis) about some apparent regularity in the world. Then we test that conjecture by comparing it with subsequent experience. Sometimes we find that our conjecture is contradicted by an experience or observation, and then we may decide to abandon that conjecture and replace it with a second conjecture. If we find that experience contradicts our first conjecture while not contradicting our second conjecture, we may conclude that our first conjecture has to be scrapped, while our second conjecture can survive being scrapped, at least for the moment.

So, returning to the question of what entitles us to say that objects *always* fall to Earth with an acceleration of 9.8 m/s/s, the answer is that we cannot soundly deduce this conclusion from our observations, but that since no observation has been found to contradict this guess, we have decided to stick with it. Obviously, this does not mean that it is true or likely to be true, though, as far as we can tell, given our present stock of knowledge, including all our past observations, it might be true. (However, in this case we have found a better theory, in which 9.8 m/s/s occurs as a special case: a general theory of gravitational attraction between two bodies, which enables us to say that the acceleration will be different on other planets and moons.)

Unlike induction, which must always be logically unsound, conjecture and refutation is logically impeccable. It would not be logically impeccable if we were to claim of our first guess that we have proved it from observation or experience, or even if we were to claim that it had a probability greater than zero. We have not proved it, in the sense of logically deriving it from observations, nor have we shown it to be more probable because it is consistent with all observations so far. As the controversy over "grue" should have reminded us, an infinite number of false theories are always entirely consistent with all observations so far.

We can remain logically correct if we simply say that we have made a guess at the truth, that our guess *might* be true, and that we're going to stick with it for the time being. That's what we can say about our first theory, then about a second theory which might replace our first theory, then about a third theory which replaces our second theory, and so on indefinitely. We stick to each guess up to a point, and abandon it when it apparently becomes incompatible with experience or observation. We then move on to a new guess, and the same process repeats itself, possibly without end.

Having come up with a guess, we at first stick to that guess, since we have nothing better. Our minds are pre-programmed by millions of years of evolution to search for patterns and generalities in the incoming flood of experiences. Now, in practice it may be that we become emotionally committed to our guess—we may *believe* in our guess—and we have in fact evolved to be prone to believe stuff (perhaps because it was advantageous to the survival of humans to stick to their guesses quite tenaciously, or perhaps because there is something in the very nature of consciousness that induces us to believe). But from a logical point of view, belief is extraneous, redundant, and immaterial. Logic is not psychology. Scientific method has nothing to do with belief, just as the proof or disproof of a mathematical theorem has nothing to do with belief.

As we move from one guess to another, our currently accepted guesses tend to get better—better in the sense of seeming to us, given the totality of our knowledge, to be more promising stabs at the truth. When we replace theory A with theory B because we have refuted theory A by finding a counter-example to it, we can conclude that theory A is false, whereas theory B might be true but is not necessarily true. We prefer theory B to theory A because theory B has not yet been refuted, while theory A has been refuted. If someone proposes theory C, we can look for some way in which the predictions of B and C are different, and then perform the "crucial experiment" which will tell us which of the two predictions comes true. We can never demonstrate the truth of our theory, but we can demonstrate that one theory is better than another because it tests out better, and we may be able to say that the theory we have provisionally accepted is the best we have been able to come up with so far. We therefore prefer it to any of its known rivals, even though we have no guarantee, and can never have any guarantee, that it is true.

Conjecture and Refutation in the Crib

Popper's process of conjecture and refutation, or trial and error, is the method used by human babies, as they learn about the world. The research of Alison Gopnik and her associates, which has been able to reconstruct by very strict attention to human baby behavior, what babies believe, even in the first few weeks of life outside the womb, shows that babies adopt a theory about the world, revise or replace it when it clashes with their subsequent experience, and do this sequentially and progressively, getting gradually closer to what we regard as the common-sense knowledge of grown-ups—which will then be further revised and in large part discarded by those grown-ups who pursue an education in science.

By the way, it seems that Gopnik did not know about Popper and did not realize how well her research fits the Popper conception. She refers to a baby's first guess as "induction." Since reading Gopnik, and being impressed by her congruence with Popper, I have found that other psychologists have argued along somewhat similar lines, notably Robert Siegler.

It was reading and pondering Gopnik's exciting results (*The Scientist in the Crib*) which prompted me to understand that, not only is the critical rationalist theory of conjecture and refutation the correct account, but all other accounts are absurd and preposterous. There is no other way in which conscious animals could conceivably have developed a culture involving progressive accumulation of knowledge, except the Popperian system of conjecture and refutation. But even if I were to be wrong about that, it would remain true that conjecture and refutation is in fact the only method by which knowledge does accumulate.

Over many years of thinking and talking about Popper, I have noticed some common misinterpretations which tend to lead people astray. Here I will just point out one of these: the assumption that Popper's philosophical account of the logic of science offers a recipe for doing science. According to Popper, there can be no recipe for doing science successfully, any more than there can be a recipe for creating a great work of art. The logic of science is not a cookbook for doing science, any more than a textbook of logic is a handbook for winning debates.

In particular, we ought to keep clear the distinction between the purely logical and the practical applications of falsification. Whereas no accumulation of observing white swans and only white swans can substantiate or even make slightly probable the universal statement that all swans are white, a single observation of a black swan automatically and necessarily refutes the statement that all swans are white. That is a simple truth of logic. But in the actual practice of science, it may be that a theory continues to gain acceptance despite the existence of a falsifying observation (Schilpp, pp. 1021, 1035).

A particular observation may be dismissed after failure to reproduce it. But even a reproducible falsifying observation may be acknowledged without abandoning the theory it contradicts. This will be recognized as a troubling anomaly, something that ought to be resolved somehow, but scientists will not always feel that they ought to immediately make the problem go away by abandoning the theory. Our preferred theory may have such merits that we're prepared to put on hold the problem that some observation conflicts with it—that, in simple terms, it appears to have been refuted.

Another qualification to the simplest model of conjecture and refutation is that certain methodological conventions must be adhered to if science is to work at all, the best-known of these being that, wherever possible, an experiment or observation should be reproducible by many different researchers on many different occasions. A different convention or set of conventions is required to cope with the fact that measurement is never perfectly precise, so we need practical rules to determine what degree of approximation of a result will agree or disagree with a prediction. And, as I will explain shortly, another convention is required to enable us to treat some predictions of probabilities as falsifiable.

Huemer's Seventeen Propositions

One thing which will immediately strike anyone who has read Popper and then looks at Huemer's seventeen propositions is that Huemer sometimes attributes to Popper views which Popper very definitely rejects or which contradict things Popper explicitly and frequently states. Nine of Huemer's seventeen propositions are false accounts of Popper's thinking: they are never stated by Popper and directly contradict what Popper repeatedly and emphatically asserts.

Huemer might reply that this just shows that Popper contradicts himself. But I'm not sure that would really harmonize with the tone of Huemer's polemic. The impression he gives is that Popper takes an unambiguous and consistent position which Huemer says is crazy. He doesn't convey the impression that he thinks Popper occasionally makes crazy remarks which are at odds with the main body of his less crazy philosophy.

In any event, it can be shown that these points where Popper's statements contradict Huemer's account of Popper's thinking cohere quite naturally with the rest of Popper's theory of science. They are not isolated departures from Popper's general account.

I will now comment on Huemer's seventeen points, moving from examples where Huemer incorrectly attributes some position to Popper to examples where Huemer reproduces Popper's view accurately and where I will defend what Popper says.

Huemer's #1 (that science has nothing to do with truth) is contradicted by Popper's numerous statements that science is trying to get at the truth. There are hundreds of these statements; you can hardly read a few pages of Popper without tripping over them. For example Popper writes (combatting instrumentalism, the view that scientific theories are merely tools for prediction rather than claims about objective reality): "in the search for knowledge, we are out to find true theories, or at least theories which are nearer than others to the truth—which correspond better to the facts" (*Conjectures and Refutations*, p. 226).

Huemer's #3 (the assertion that the goal of science is to refute theories) contradicts Popper's assertion that the aim of science is "to find satisfactory explanations," which means explanations "in terms of testable and falsifiable universal laws and initial conditions" (*Realism and the Aim of Science*, pp. 132–35). Popper sees the growth of knowledge, the progress of science, as the overthrow of currently accepted theories by better theories, which occurs by criticizing existing theories and offering competing alternative theories, which may turn out to be preferable.

Popper adds that it is reasonable, sensible, and sound policy to prefer the best theories we have, and we keep trying to improve our theories by a process of critical discussion and debate. In the realm of empirical science, refuting a theory empirically by showing that it contradicts observations is one, but not the only, important means to that end. We never arrive at a point where we can demonstrate that we have the truth, though we can hope to make progress towards the truth. Thus, in Popper's account, we can say that Einstein's relativity theory is better than Newton's theory of gravitation. Newton's theory was, in Popper's words, "a splendid approximation" (*The Open Universe*, p. 47), yet it was supplanted by Einstein's theory, also a splendid approximation, which has advantages over Newton's theory. Newton is a good approximation to Einstein in a range of circumstances, but not in all circumstances. Observation corroborates Einstein better than it does Newton, because many singular observations contradict Newton without contradicting Einstein.

In his #4, Huemer gives Popper's claim that all theories and laws are guesses, as one of Popper's self-evidently insane statements. Huemer does not explain why he supposes this is insane or what else theories and laws might be. The craziness is not self-evident to everyone. Consider the following quotation from a talk by the outstanding physicist Richard Feynman:

> Now I'm going to discuss how we would look for a new law. In general, we look for a new law by the following process. First, we guess it [*audience laughter*]. No, don't laugh, that's the truth. Then we compute the consequences of the guess, to see what, if this is right, if this law we guess is right, to see what it would imply and then we compare the computation results to nature or we say compare to experiment or experience, compare it directly with observations to see if it works. If it disagrees with experiment, it's wrong. In that simple statement is the key to science. (Feynman 2020. Ungrammatical expressions in the original.)

Another of the Popperian contentions which Huemer apparently takes to be self-evidently insane is his #5, that there are no such things as good positive reasons. (The context makes clear that Popper is talking about good positive reasons for accepting a theory.) Again, Huemer does not explain why he disagrees, or what he thinks might be a good positive reason. Maybe he's thinking of examples where a piece of evidence clearly supports a particular theory. What Popper would say is that, in such a case, the piece of evidence is incompatible with rival theories. It is therefore, despite what we may at first suppose, a negative reason; it supports a theory insofar as it contradicts that theory's competitors.

Huemer's #10 and #12 both have Popper claiming that scientific theories "are absolutely certain to be false." This is a serious misreading of Popper. Popper contradicts this proposition over and over again. Popper consistently maintains the view, advanced by the ancient philosopher Xenophanes, that we might very well arrive at a true theory, but we could never be in a position to demonstrate conclusively (or to 'know') that it was true (*Realism and the Aim of Science*, p. 33; *Conjectures and Refutations*, pp. 114–16, 151–53).

It seems to be a difficulty for some readers of Popper that he combines the objectivity of truth with fallibilism. Popper thinks (and I agree) that the truth or falsity of a theory is absolute and objective, while our being able to determine its truth or falsity can be very difficult, and in many cases impossible—especially when we're looking at general, law-like theories, which are the most fertile and useful. We should not confuse truth with guaranteed truth.

Huemer does not quote Popper as asserting anything like #10 or #12, and he doesn't try to show that #10 or #12 can be inferred from anything Popper says. Why then does Huemer make the totally ludicrous claim that Popper asserts that our best scientific theories are "absolutely certain to be false"? It appears that *Huemer simply assumes that a true theory cannot have zero probability*. Since Popper says that theories have zero probability (Huemer's #9), Huemer thinks he must be saying that those theories are false. If Huemer supposed that a theory with zero probability must be false, then he would think that his #10 and #12 followed from his #9. Huemer's supposition here is no doubt the supposition of many people. But it is incorrect, where infinity is involved (Cthaeh 2017; 3blue1brown 2020).

An impossible event necessarily has the probability of zero, but the converse is false. Any event has zero probability where the sample space is infinite. What applies to events applies to propositions specifying events, and so Popper has not made a leap in extending this conclusion of probability theory from events to theories.

If you possess a lottery ticket, one of a thousand tickets, your probability of winning (stipulating that precisely one ticket has the winning number) is one in a thousand; if your ticket is one of a million tickets, your probability of winning is one in a million, and so on. If your ticket is one of an infinity of tickets, your probability of winning is zero. This does not mean you cannot win, because, after all, you do have a ticket, one ticket must win, and your ticket is equally as likely as any of the other tickets to be the winner.

Since critical rationalism does not require that its adherents don't have beliefs—it just says that belief is a subjective psychological quality immaterial to the logic of science—a critical rationalist may very well believe that a theory is true, while acknowledging that it has zero probability. (But what if the universe isn't infinite? Well, it's still quite big.) As I inspect the contents of my own mind, I find that I do believe in conservation of momentum. So I believe, simultaneously, that conservation of momentum is true and that the probability of its being true is zero. But, remember, these are just my beliefs, which, like your beliefs, or anyone else's beliefs, always count for nothing.

By the way, if we adopt the metaphysical principle that nature is strictly governed by universal laws which can be grasped by humans, we may (with a few more steps) hope to be able to avoid the "zero probability" conclusion, but we don't know a way to demonstrate the truth of any such metaphysical principle. We can't validly deduce from observations that we don't live in a universe bereft of universal laws, or bereft of any that we could possibly discover. I'm guessing, though, that a lot of people do tacitly hold to some such metaphysical principle, which may help to explain why they seem to find it intuitively obvious that a well-corroborated theory like relativity or quantum electrodynamics must have a greater than zero probability of being true.

But can't we reasonably say that the current theories of scientific cosmology are more probably true (or closer to the truth) than, say, a literal reading of the first chapter of Genesis? Of course we can! But we should clarify what is meant by such a claim.

Popper points out that we often use words like "probable" and "likely" in ways that are not defined in terms of the calculus of probabilities—the branch of mathematics which we learn when we study probability theory. Confusion can arise when we start supposing that a use of the term "probable" which owes nothing to the calculus of probabilities is an application of the calculus of probabilities (*Realism*, pp. 282–83). We sometimes use "probable" or "likely" as a synonym for "rationally preferable" or "promising as a candidate for truth." We cannot meaningfully say that the probability that Genesis is correct is one number, and the probability that the Big Bang happened is a different and presumably somewhat higher number. That would be a strange thing to try to do, since we judge that the Genesis theory has been refuted.

But what about when one theory replaces another, as Einstein replaced Newton? Can't we compare the probability of Newton's being right with the probability of Einstein's being right? Well, although Popper himself took a dim view of arguments from the history of science, I can point out that this is just not what happens. There was a crucial experiment (precession of the perihelion of Mercury) which corroborated Einstein and falsified Newton. Other crucial observations have been consistent with Einstein and not with Newton. So, most scientists, some more quickly than others, came around to the view that Newton was false and Einstein possibly true. No one, in 1916, thought about the *probability* of Newton or Einstein being correct; they thought about making observations to determine which one was correct (or closer to being correct).

Huemer apparently presents #8 (that more informative theories are always less probable than less informative theories) as one of the things you can only accept if you are insane or completely out of your mind. And yet this statement by Popper is not really controversial. The point Popper is making is that theories with more content are to be preferred to theories with less content, and the theories with more content must be less probable than the theories with less content.

For example, the theory that all persons named Huemer are color-blind is more probable than the theory that all persons named Huemer are color-blind and left-handed, which is in turn more probable than the theory that all persons named Huemer are color-blind, left-handed, and bald. The theory that all cyclists in Chicago have antibodies for SARSCov2 is more probable than the theory that all cyclists in the Midwest have antibodies for SARSCov2, which is in turn more probable than the theory that all cyclists in the U.S. have antibodies for SARSCov2. These are elementary applications of a fundamental truth of probability theory.

The more informational or empirical content a theory has, the more it claims, the more improbable it is. We want theories that claim as much as possible, and the more they claim, the less probable they must be. A theory with more content prohibits more; it is bolder; it takes more risks. If we find we can adopt it, it is more useful because it yields more information. It follows that we look for theories that are as improbable as possible, since these, caeteris paribus, must be the best theories.

There is therefore a special sense in which scientific theories may often be less probable than pseudoscientific theories. If the pseudoscientific theories are vacuous, impossible to pin down, compatible with an unlimited range of observations, then the pseudoscientific theories will be more probable; in fact their probability of being true will be 1. They don't commit themselves to anything in the world because they are vague and waffly. They say so little that it is impossible to find counter-examples, and therefore impossible to disprove them.

Astrology is an example. Not counting the serious statistical work of Michel Gauquelin ('neo-astrology'), the problem with traditional astrology is that it's compatible with an indefinite range of imaginable observations; we can't think of any conceivable observation which could refute it. The same is true of Freudian or Jungian analysis. "Pseudoscientific" systems, like traditional astrology, Freudianism, and Jungianism, are generally characterized by including centrally important theories which are compatible with any conceivable observable events; they therefore have a maximally high probability of being unrefuted by observations. It's characteristic of genuinely scientific theories that they imply that many conceivable observable events will never, in fact, be observed, and therefore these theories could easily be refuted by observing one of these events.

Aside from that kind of example, due to a difference in content, I don't see that Popper's theory implies that a scientific theory must always be less probable than a pseudoscientific theory, as Huemer seems to be suggesting in his #11, and #17. Is it *always* true that a pseudoscientific theory is more probable than a scientific theory? That's an interesting question which might be worth pursuing, but, as far as I can recall, Popper has made no claim anent it. On quick reflection, it's not obvious to me that, say, Velikovsky's theory, normally considered pseudoscience, is more probable, because more vacuous, than standard cosmology.

Non-Lawlike Theories

According to Huemer, Popper holds that "The Theory of Evolution is just a *completely arbitrary guess*." This is an astounding misreading. In Popper's view, all theories are guesses but these guesses are rarely arbitrary. In science, they are usually attempts to solve problems. Perhaps the main problem Darwin attempted to solve was 'How can we account for the diversity of life forms, along with the varying degrees of similarity of some of them?' And there are various related problems, such as 'How can we account for the fact that different geological strata bear the fossils of different life forms?'

Guesses arise as solutions to problems, and different guesses compete with each other. Guesses which are better at solving problems tend to win out in competition with less successful guesses. So guesses which survive are far from arbitrary, though they always remain guesses.

According to Huemer's #15, Popper holds that evolution and the asteroid-impact theory of the extinction of dinosaurs are "unscientific." Popper didn't write about the asteroid-impact theory, but he wrote quite a bit about Darwin's theory and accepted it as a momentous achievement. (And he often pointed out that the growth of human knowledge—conjecture and refutation—is a form of natural selection, in which theories compete and die.)

These two theories, evolution and asteroid-impact, do have the peculiarity, however, that they are each accounts of a unique chain of events that happened just once—the evolution of life on Earth and (a subset of that) the extinction of the dinosaurs. These are theories which do not take the form of universal laws. They do require the application of a number of universal laws, from physics, chemistry, and biology. Much of what

Popper says about some scientific theories would not apply in these cases, since they do not possess a law-like logical structure, and Popper tends to be focused on theories which do possess a law-like logical structure.

Huemer asserts that "Real scientific theories . . . are not normally of the form 'All A's are B' (as in philosophers' examples)." This perhaps carries the innuendo that philosophers are making some sort of mistake by giving so much attention to theories of the form 'All A's are B' (or 'All swans are white'). But all scientific theories having the form of laws (or putative laws) do indeed take the form 'All A's are B'. All other theories, such as a theory, or story, of what happened at a particular time and place, involve applications of these law-like or universal theories. Philosophers are not slipping up when they give so much attention to theories of the form 'All A's are B'.

Nonetheless, theories of what happened historically, such as the theory of evolution, are still subject to conjecture and refutation. We can compare the theory of what happened with observations. The creationist theory in its most popular form can be refuted by many observations, including the existence of datable fossils gradually changing over billions of years.

In both the general account of evolution and the asteroid extinction theory, the theory in question has competed with alternative theories. The best-known alternative to evolution is special creation. Given evolution, the best-known alternative to natural selection is the Lamarckian theory involving the inheritance of acquired characteristics. In both these examples, we decide by refutation. Special creation, especially special creation less than ten thousand years ago, has been falsified. Though we now know that there is some role for inheritance of acquired characteristics ("epigenetics"), as a complete explanation for complex adaptations, inheritance of acquired characteristics has been falsified.

Alternatives to the asteroid extinction theory still have some following among the relevant scientific specialists: continental movement, volcanic activity, climate change, and competition from mammals are among the contenders. Here we don't look at probabilities, but at the possibility of refuting one or more of the competing theories. (We accept there was an asteroid impact at approximately the right time, because of the evidence of worldwide iridium deposits, but that doesn't prove that the impact was the cause of the extinction.)

Theories about a unique historical succession of events have the quality that in these theories the "problem of induction" does not arise. Since these theories take numerous universal laws for granted, and try to establish what happened in some specific instance, they don't make any attempt to proceed from the particular to the general, from the singular to the universal. They may make use of probability, but the use of probability is purely deductive. Probability is involved, but it is not involved in the process of arriving at a universal law. These theories are—like the theories of Sherlock Holmes in solving crimes—all a matter of observation and deduction, with no place for induction.

Huemer gives the observation that some snakes have vestigial legs as evidence in favor of Darwinian evolution and against creationism. As a somewhat facetious aside, let me point out that the most popular form of creationism derives from the first few chapters of Genesis, where we are indeed informed that snakes originally had limbs (as well as being highly intelligent and fluent in Hebrew), which they lost after a snake persuaded Eve to eat the forbidden fruit (*Genesis*, Chapter 3). So a fundamentalist Jew or fundamentalist Christian might not be fazed by the vestigial legs on some snakes.

A better example would be the feet on some fossilized whales. Creationists scoffed at the evolution story that whales descended from land-dwelling animals and ridiculed the claim that whales had ever possessed feet. After many decades of arguments about evolution, fossil whales with feet were dug up in Egypt, one of many examples where new observations have strikingly corroborated—in a highly "improbable" way—Darwin's theory.

Huemer seems to reason like this. Snakes' vestigial legs are not required by the theory of evolution; the absence of vestigial legs would not contradict evolution nor would it contradict the specific example of an evolutionary pathway, that snakes are descended from animals with limbs. Therefore, no refutation is involved in the finding that snakes have vestigial legs, nor would it be involved in the opposite finding.

There are numerous potential falsifiers to the prevailing account of evolution—to take the most popular example, if a fossil of a rabbit were to be found in pre-Cambrian strata. But Huemer's point is that the vestigial legs on snakes do help to support the theory that evolution occurred, and that snakes are descended from animals with limbs, simply because this is the kind of thing you might expect to find if evolution were true, even though such a finding is not required. Hence, we have here a case of the strengthening of a theory because of something that increases the probability of the theory's being correct.

All this seems quite persuasive, but I don't accept that it contradicts Popper's account because we're not dealing here with the attempt to arrive at a universal law. "Probability" here has no inductive implication. I might add that we're not compelled to approach even this matter in anything like the Bayesian manner. We can simply say that the vestigial legs in fossil whales constitutes an observation that has to be explained; a theory which offers a good explanation has an advantage; a theory which predicted precisely this would be even better (the theory did not predict that fossils of whales with vestigial feet would be found but it did assert that there were once whales with feet; finding precisely that kind of fossil is a good corroboration for that very prediction).

To avoid a possible misunderstanding, I should mention something that Huemer does not raise: that Popper at one time explicitly stated that the Darwinian theory was not a scientific theory, but a "metaphysical research programme" (Schilpp, pp. 133–143) because, he argued, it was not falsifiable. In taking this position he did not dispute the fact that it might very well be a true account of evolution, nor did he dispute that it had a productive role to play in guiding scientific research, nor did he dispute that many narrower components of the evolutionary story would be falsifiable (no rabbits in the pre-Cambrian). Later Popper reversed himself on this issue, and accepted Darwinism as falsifiable and therefore scientific (Radnitzky and Bartley, pp. 143–47).

Deduction and Probability

Huemer reports Popper as holding that "Induction is completely worthless; probabilistic reasoning is worthless" (Huemer's #1). Most of what we might want to call 'probabilistic reasoning' is not inductive. From the fact that a coin has a one-half chance of landing heads, plus the fact that a die has a one-sixth chance of landing 4, it follows that the chance of the coin landing heads *and* the die landing 4 is one-twelfth. This is presumably a case of probabilistic reasoning, yet there is nothing inductive about it. It is purely deductive—with the multiplication law for the joint probability of independent events as a premise. And then, we can take the whole of inferential statistics: there's no attempt at induction here. I assume that Huemer might call statistics probabilistic reasoning, yet it's all purely deductive.

Huemer gives quantum theory as an area where the predictions are probabilities, and he says that probabilities cannot be falsified, which is true. Therefore, the implication seems to be, quantum theory is not scientific by Popper's definition. He then says that quantum theory is "weird" so he will not rely on it as a counter-example to Popperian falsifiability, and goes on to his examples of evolution and the asteroid extinction theory.

Yet, as well as its predictions of probabilities, quantum theory makes some predictions which are not probabilities and are extremely precise. In fact, famously, the most extraordinarily precise prediction in the entire history of science, the anomalous magnetic moment of the electron, is made by quantum electrodynamics. So, in addition to its predictions of probabilities, quantum theory also makes amazingly precise non-probabilistic predictions, and quantum theory would therefore still qualify as scientific.

However, long before quantum theory, physics relied heavily on predictions of probabilities, notably in statistical mechanics—and there is surely nothing less weird than statistical mechanics. And even in quantum theory, we don't want to say that the predictions of probabilities, taken by themselves, are always unscientific.

From the beginning, Popper confronted the obvious problem for the falsifiability criterion that predictions of probability cannot be refuted. He pointed out that physicists themselves have never seen this as a practical problem, and have routinely viewed their statistically-based theories as refutable. Popper's theoretical solution to this problem is essentially along the lines developed by practical scientists: we adopt a methodological convention which requires us to disregard extremely low probabilities. (The solution is more precise and elegant than I can unpack here; see *Logic of Scientific Discovery*, pp. 190–97).

Duhem's Argument Against Falsifiability

Huemer advances the "Duhem-Quine Thesis" as a reason for dismissing Popper out of hand. In this case Huemer doesn't claim that Popper is insane or completely out of his mind. But since he does maintain that this argument very simply disposes of Popper's account of science, I will touch upon it here.

Pierre Duhem pointed out in 1906 that when we try to test a theory by deriving a prediction from it, a failure of the prediction can't conclusively refute the theory, because when we use a theory to predict, we always rely on other assumptions or hypotheses, assumptions not contained in the theory but necessary to derive a prediction. So, we never test the theory alone, but only the theory in conjunction with other propositions. Therefore, we can't be sure that an observation refutes our theory. It could be that if we changed one of those other propositions, the prediction would be confirmed rather than contradicted. These auxiliary assumptions may include such things as the reliability of our instruments as well as our assumed initial conditions or other background knowledge that we might take for granted.

Popper holds that, typically, a theory is not abandoned after one contradictory observation or even many. It is usually abandoned when there is an alternative theory which is able to prove its mettle by making correct predictions where its rival made false predictions. In Popper's account, the process of conjecture and refutation typically takes place in the context of two or more competing, rival theories.

Popper's view is that every effort should be made to make the theory falsifiable. It's always open to anyone to challenge the crucial experiment with a new interpretation which places the onus for the refutation on one of the accompanying assumptions and thus rescues the theory itself from refutation. Here, Popper says that it would be preferable if the person 'saving' the theory in this way would offer a new formulation to make the theory, along with the changed assumption, independently falsifiable.

Huemer also claims that Newtonian dynamics is not falsifiable because it does not say anything about the "total forces" acting on bodies. I'm puzzled by what Huemer is getting at here. Newton's theory doesn't rule out the possibility of non-gravitational forces which would have to be explained. If there is, for instance, a supernova (an exploding star) the shock wave pushes nearby bodies away. So this might be another force, a non-gravitational part of "total forces." The supernova itself is not part of Newtonian dynamics but does not contradict Newtonian dynamics. The effects of the explosion on nearby bodies would follow Newton. The same applies to any major non-gravitational forces not yet known.

When applying Newton's theory, it's normally part of the stated or assumed initial conditions and background assumptions that other forces which might move bodies, such as magnetic attraction/repulsion, or the propulsive effect of volcanic eruptions, are negligible. Within a planetary atmosphere, Newton has no trouble coping with the modification of gravitation by atmospheric density. It's always open to anyone to assert that some heretofore overlooked force has been partly responsible for some motion not accounted for by Newton. The mere existence of some forces other than gravity and momentum does not contradict Newton. In the absence of some motions not explicable by gravity and requiring the introduction of other non-gravitational forces, Newton's theory explains all routine bodily motions.

On the other hand, there's an infinity of conceivable observations which would clearly refute Newtonian dynamics. If, for instance, it were to be found that orbiting bodies were indeed elliptical but their speeds were constant (or if this were found to be true, say, for orbiting bodies outside the Milky Way, or above a certain mass), this would refute Newtonian dynamics. The same applies if, say in some distant region, gravitational attraction declined as the cube of the distance. That does not necessarily mean that Newtonian dynamics would be rejected. In Popper's account, refutation is never beyond criticism and does not automatically lead to rejection. And then, of course, there are the Einsteinian predictions which did contradict Newton and led to the rejection of Newton. It didn't seem to bother anyone that this refutation and rejection didn't account for unknown and unspecified non-gravitational forces. So I can't see the force of Huemer's assertion that Newton's theory does not predict the total forces acting on a body.

Duhem understood that laws of nature can never be arrived at by induction. He was a conventionalist; he did not consider major scientific theories, laws of nature, to be literally true or false, but rather unquestioned assumptions or definitions used to guide our thinking, and not subject to empirical proof or disproof. Duhem is part of the intellectual movement, beginning with Kant, that tried to come to terms with Hume's disproof of the possibility of induction by supposing that fundamental physical laws are irresistibly imposed on nature by the human mind. Popper accepts that conventionalism can never be logically refuted. Any theory can always be saved from refutation by holding the theory true by definition. But Popper insists that a theory like Newton's should be treated as testable and therefore possibly false.

Einstein had shown that we could conceive of Newton's theory being false, and we could conceive of Kant's "forms of intuition" as being false (because, among other things, space doesn't have to be Euclidean). Popper therefore embraces a metaphysical and methodological commitment to the view that no physical theory may be decreed immune from attempts to falsify it. Popper believes that without this commitment, science will eventually die, becoming ossified into an apodictic scholasticism.

Huemer presents the Duhem argument as a refutation of the possibility of falsifying a theory by observation, and therefore a refutation of Popper's theory of science. Yet there's surely something strange about Huemer's claim that Duhem's argument shows the impossibility of ever falsifying a theory. For every imaginable conception of how science operates, including whatever conception Huemer would defend, must make some logical link between theory and observations. If no observation could ever contradict a theory, then neither could any observation ever confirm a theory; any logical link between theory and observations would be severed. Any theory of the relation between observation and theory, not just Popperian falsification, would be dismissed by Huemer's employment of the Duhemian argument. Indeed, Duhem saw his argument as specifically refuting Francis Bacon's "inductive" approach to laws of nature. If Duhem's argument disposes of falsificationism, it must equally dispose of any brand of inductivism.

This is all the more relevant because Huemer apparently does accept Popper's claim that a theory ought to be falsifiable (even though Huemer supposes that other criteria are also required for theory selection). According to Huemer:

There really is something important about falsifiability. Intuitively, there is something bad about unfalsifiable theories, and
we have Popper to thank for drawing attention to this.

If falsifiability can be shown to be out of the question, so that all theories
without exception are just not falsifiable, then how could it be the case
that there really is something important about falsifiability and why
would we want to thank Popper for drawing attention to it?

Quine's account is not exactly the same as Duhem's and is more
complex. Since Huemer doesn't go there, neither will I. It's worth pointing out, though, that Quine's argument arrives at the conclusion that no
scientific theory can be tested. Only the whole of science (let's assume
this means physics) can be tested. This would not be compatible with
Huemer's evident view that individual scientific theories can be tested
by some version of Bayesianism.

The Irrelevance of Belief

Huemer's #2 and #6 refer to beliefs (#2 to what someone "thinks" is true).
Popper has no great interest in the philosophy of belief, and the methodology of science does not need to say anything about beliefs. Science is
not about beliefs. We should bear in mind that neither Newton nor Einstein believed their theories to be true—Newton because he could not
accept action at a distance, and Einstein because he felt general relativity
was not complete and would eventually be supplanted by a better theory,
a unified field theory.

Although neither Newton nor Einstein believed their theories to be
true, they did believe their theories were objectively superior to their
predecessors' theories. Any account of scientific discovery has to make
room for the fact that we can prefer one theory to another, we can even
say that one theory is objectively better than another, without believing
the preferred or better theory to be true or likely to be true.

Belief is a subjective feeling of conviction that something is true. It
is a fact about human psychology that people have a need, or at least a
strong tendency, to believe. But we make no appeal to belief when we
try to explain scientific methodology.

We might hit upon a theory which is actually true though we would not be able to demonstrate its truth, since any putative universal law might turn out to have exceptions and thus to be false. For critical rationalists, science is not about subjective feelings but about what can be demonstrated logically, to explain events in the world, in light of the observational evidence.

As a Bayesian, Huemer must be a pure subjectivist, who must suppose that science is all about beliefs, and this no doubt helps to explain why he finds the Popperian theory so hard to fathom. A Gestalt switch is needed to abandon the paradigm of subjective knowledge and embrace the paradigm of objective knowledge.

Now of course, scientists often do believe their theories, and scientific debates often display passionate commitment to beliefs, just as much as religious or political debates. Popper's aim, however, in most of his writing, is not to give a history of science, accounting for all the aspects of science, including the psychological ones, as they actually played out, but to reconstruct the "logic" of scientific research. Similarly, the theory of probability tells us nothing about the emotional states of gamblers, and the subject known as logic ignores what happens psychologically when people make conflicting assertions in debate. If you look at a textbook on decision theory, you will probably not find an index entry for "agony."

Belief as a motivating force is generally ignored in the great majority of Popper's discussion of the logic of empirical science, though it is a perfectly legitimate field of study, no doubt belonging mainly to psychology.

Popper sometimes mentions that he believes such and such a theory to be true (*Realism and the Aim of Science*, pp. 72, 75), but when he does this, his belief is not offered as a reason to accept that theory, and is not logically compelled by the evidence supporting that belief. Such remarks by Popper are informal and illustrative. They do incidentally refute Huemer's assertions that Popper considered all scientific theories to be false. Popper also volunteers that he believes certain propositions, for example realism and indeterminism, but also such theories as "There exists at least one true law of nature," which he classifies as metaphysical and therefore non-scientific; these are claims which can never be empirically tested but which Popper argues for on philosophical lines (*Realism and the Aim of Science*, p. 79).

This brings me to Popper's statement, Huemer's #6, that "belief is never rational." I think I understand what Popper was driving at here, and to that extent I agree with it, but I would never word it that way. For that matter, if we take it with pedantic literalness and ignore context, it is flatly contradicted by what Popper says elsewhere ("But this belief, I assert, is rational." *Realism and the Aim of Science*, p. 57).

Popper's central position is that science is not about belief at all. The relation between a theory and the observational evidence is not a matter of belief, nor is the relation between a theory and other theories. So the 'rationality' of science owes nothing to belief—and belief is therefore non-rational in the sense that it is a psychological phenomenon which intrudes into science from somewhere other than 'scientific rationality'. But in most cases, when people accept that a theory is a good theory, they tend to believe that theory, and that tendency to believe, while not probative in any way, and irrelevant to the validity of scientific reasoning, is usually heavily influenced by what the believer perceives to be the available evidence. As a matter of fact, I agree with Ray Scott Percival (*The Myth of the Closed Mind*) that all belief is rational, but that's a revelation for which I guess most of the world, including Michael Huemer, is not yet quite ready.

I think I have said enough to show that Michael Huemer has misunderstood and mischaracterized Karl Popper. You do not need to be completely out of your mind to agree with Popper and me—though I don't deny that it might help.

References

Cthaeh, The. 2017. Not All Zero Probabilities Are Created Equal <probabilisticworld.com/not-all-zero-probabilities/>.

Duhem, Pierre. 1991 [1906]. *The Aim and Structure of Physical Theory*. Princeton University Press.

Edelstein, Michael R., Richard K. Kujoth, and David Ramsay Steele. 2013. Appendix: Is Psychoanalysis Falsifiable? In *Therapy Breakthrough: Why Some Psychotherapies Work Better than Others*. Open Court.

Feynman, Richard. 2020. Richard Feynman Teaches You the Scientific Method. Farnam Street <https://fs.blog/2009/12/mental-model-scientific-method>.

Gopnik, Alison, 2009. *The Philosophical Baby: What Children's Minds Tell Us about Truth, Love, and the Meaning of Life*. Farrer, Straus, and Giroux.

Gopnik, Alison, and Andrew N. Meltzoff. 1997. *Words, Thoughts, and Theories*. MIT Press.

Gopnik, Alison, Andrew N. Meltzoff, Patricia K. Kuhl. 2001 [1999]. *The Scientist in the Crib: What Early Learning Tells Us about the Mind*. Harper Perennial.

Huemer, Michael. 2020. You Don't Agree with Karl Popper. Fake Nous (25th January).

Hume, David. 1986 [1739]. *A Treatise of Human Nature: Being an Attempt to Introduce the Experimental Method of Reasoning into Moral Subjects*. Penguin.

Miller, David. 1994. *Critical Rationalism: A Restatement and Defence*. Open Court.

Percival, Ray Scott. 2012. *The Myth of the Closed Mind: Understanding Why and How People Are Rational*. Open Court.

Popper, Karl R. 1968 [1962]. *Conjectures and Refutations: The Growth of Scientific Knowledge*. Harper and Row.

———. 1979 [1972]. *Objective Knowledge: An Evolutionary Approach*. Oxford University Press.

———. 1982. *The Open Universe: An Argument for Indeterminism*. Rowman and Littlefield.

———. 1982. *Quantum Theory and the Schism in Physics*. Rowman and Littlefield.

———. 1983. *Realism and the Aim of Science*. Rowman and Littlefield.

———. 2002 [1935]. *The Logic of Scientific Discovery*. Routledge.

Radnitzky, Gerard, and W.W. Bartley III. 1987. *Evolutionary Epistemology, Rationality, and the Theory of Knowledge*. Open Court.

Schilpp, Paul Arthur, ed. 1974. *The Philosophy of Karl Popper*. Two volumes. Open Court.

Siegler, Robert S. 1996. *Emerging Minds: The Process of Change in Children's Thinking*. Oxford University Press.

Stalker, Douglas, ed. 1994. *Grue! The New Riddle of Induction*. Open Court.

3blue1brown. 2020. Why 'Probability of Zero' Does Not Mean 'Impossible'. <www.youtube.com/watch?v=ZA4JkHKZM50&vl=en>.

12

THE STEELE EFFECT:
A NEW EXPLANATION OF THE FLYNN EFFECT

I have a conjecture which, if true, helps to explain a chronic puzzle in psychology, and if it turns out to be untrue, will leave a few loose ends which might be worth picking up.

The Flynn Effect is the rapid rise in measured IQ scores in many countries over the past century or more. Various explanations have been offered but all of them seem less than fully satisfying, so the cause of the Flynn Effect is still something of a mystery.

My conjecture is that the long-term rise in IQ is due to the long-term increase in births by Caesarian section.

IQ is positively correlated with head size. Birthing difficulties are often associated with the head being too large to get easily through the birth canal. Increased recourse to c-section deliveries must cause the average size of live babies' skulls to increase, and this must cause an increased average IQ of babies surviving to adulthood, and thus a higher average IQ of the adult population.

In a distinct and additional process which must also contribute to higher average IQ, more c-sections mean that babies do not incur the same damage to the skull, and therefore to the brain, as occurred with many painful and difficult births before the availability of c-section surgery.

Head size means skull diameter or circumference (in practice usually circumference, because you can trust a nurse to put a tape measure around a baby's skull, while quickly arriving at a measure of diameter would be less reliable). Skull diameter at birth is very closely aligned with brain volume at birth, which correlates with IQ in later life. The correlation coefficient for brain volume and IQ has been calculated at between

0.3 and 0.4, on the weak side but by no means negligible. Some recent studies look at brain volume, directly measured by fMRI imaging. Other measurable brain characteristics are also relevant to intelligence, but only head size, or skull diameter, would be operational in my conjecture.

The rise in IQ which we call the Flynn Effect began in the more industrialized countries and then spread to the less industrialized. This, at least very broadly, aligns with the spread of c-sections. Currently, c-sections account for 32 percent of births in the U.S. and 21 percent worldwide. In some countries, such as Turkey and Brazil, the majority of births are by c-section.

Alternative explanations for the Flynn Effect include improved diet, increased test sophistication, educational changes, the popularization of analytic habits of thought, and the impact of modern technology on occupational training. There is some dissatisfaction with all these explanations.

This is not my field (I don't really have a field; I'm an all-purpose dilettante) and it's entirely possible that someone has proposed what I call "my conjecture" already, and indeed, that it has been discussed and debunked. Although possible, this doesn't seem to be very likely, or I would have come across it in my occasional toe-dips into the relevant literature, and it would certainly be pertinent to the many discussions I have read from time to time on possible causes of the Flynn Effect.

Obstetric Dilemmas

According to the prevailing view, there are competing selective pressures on the mode of human birth, a pressure in favor of bigger heads, presumed to be reproductively profitable because of higher intelligence, and a pressure to keep the birth canal narrow, presumed to be reproductively profitable because of greater physical mobility of the mother. This has traditionally been called "the Obstetric Dilemma." It's generally accepted that this uneasy conflict of selective pressures has arisen because of the transition to bipedalism over six million years ago, followed by increased cranial size much more recently, but certainly very far advanced more than one hundred thousand years ago.

If human pregnancy and birth had been literally designed with an eye to the desirability of high intelligence, then the human body would have been structured very differently, but we are descended from small-brained animals which scampered on all fours. Because of this mammalian heritage which cannot be bypassed by the incremental character of natural selection, the evolution of the birth process has been "cornered"; the pelvic bone structure makes it impossible to move by gradual increments to a birth process that would provide for a much wider birth aperture.

Natural selection is highly inventive, but one thing it can't do, except over millions of years with species extinctions and the emergence of new species, is to wipe the board clean and start afresh (and when it does do this, it can't remember and apply any lessons from earlier experiments). Every evolutionary development within a species has to occur by small incremental departures from an existing design. So natural selection could not give us a new birth aperture higher up the abdomen, skipping the pelvis. But human inventiveness has given us something like that, in the form of the c-section, providing an artificial improvement over the inept natural design of the human body.

Two Independent Mechanisms

Under natural conditions, humans without modern medical aids have an extremely high frequency of "difficult" births, which frequently kill the mother, the baby, or both. This routine tragedy has gone on for over one hundred thousand years, becoming more common with larger baby heads. Birthing mothers usually require direct help from other people, traditionally female close blood-relatives. Although there is some appreciable risk with all mammalian parturition, the really extreme hazard of birth and the resultant reliance of the birthing mother on help from others do not occur with any other primates, nor indeed with any other animals.

According to my conjecture, delivery by c-section would raise population IQ in two independent and very different ways:

#1. A baby with a larger head, who would die without a c-section, and whose mother might die with him, survives birth.

This baby has a probability greater than 0.5 of later having above-average adult IQ. So the average IQ of the population has probably been increased. There is an additional IQ gain, because the mother might have died in childbirth, the c-section may have saved her life too, and she carries the genes for bigger heads and therefore higher IQs, so she can now have more babies, probably also by c-section, with a likelihood that they will have bigger heads and higher IQs than the average (though even if they don't, they will carry the genes for that probability).

This increase is genetically based, and will therefore be cumulative in the population; so we have a cumulative process leading to bigger average head size at birth and the consequent IQ becoming generally higher over generations. The bigger the proportion of births that require c-section because of the large head, the larger the average head size in the next generation, and therefore the bigger the proportion of births calling for c-section. This implies that at each generation, the proportion of births requiring c-section will increase, so that the proportion of vaginal births will fall, pointing to a distant future where all human births are by c-section.

#2. The baby's skull at birth is soft and flexible; the bones at the top of the skull are not yet joined up and are still movable. This adaptation to the Obstetric Dilemma means that the skull, and the brain within it, can be squeezed into a smaller diameter to enable it to get through the process of birth, leaving what in the nineteenth century were sometimes called "womb marks" on the skull. The squeezing of the skull results in a temporary "cone-head" shape. This is why it's traditional to put beanies on new-born babies, to conceal this disconcerting disfigurement, something not usually required for c-section babies (except where the c-section occurred after protracted unsuccessful attempts to accomplish a vaginal birth).

It occasionally happens that a baby born vaginally will have a perfect skull, with no marks and no distorted shape, and then the medical staff in attendance will spontaneously and semi-humorously observe that this vaginally-delivered baby looks just like a c-section baby.

The process of squeezing the soft skull into a smaller diameter presumably damages the brain, if only slightly. Thus, we might expect it to reduce the later adult IQ of babies who undergo it. If the baby can be spared the squeezing of its soft skull through a narrow opening, it seems reasonable to suppose that this will avoid some reduction of subsequent IQ.

Serious cases of brain damage sometimes occur, due to injuries sustained during the difficult transition through the birth canal. They are only detected by later observation of the baby's behavioral abnormalities. It seems reasonable to surmise that less severe brain damage is quite commonplace with vaginal births; this would go undiagnosed, as long as there is no conspicuous dysfunction in the child's behavior, and would reduce adult IQ.

The longer and more painful the labor, the greater the IQ loss, so obviating this lengthy labor would give us babies with higher adult IQs. This however would not be cumulative because it is not genetic. It would be a "one-off" but it might help to account for the historical rapidity of the Flynn Effect; it would defend against IQ loss in a large proportion of babies, including those who might have survived birth at the cost of longer and more painful labor.

Although this is in principle a one-off, in practice there would often be lengthy attempts to go for a vaginal delivery before resorting to c-section, so there would be cases where there was some brain injury even with an ultimate recourse to c-section. Given the increasingly routine nature of c-section over the twentieth century, c-sections would have been implemented more readily with the passage of years, with an increasing number of cases of protracted attempts at vaginal birth skipped, so the reduction in brain damage, and the consequent increase in IQ, could historically have been a more gradual process.

The Rise in IQ

Measured IQ in most countries has risen steadily since at least World War I and, some would argue, since 1900. The increase is quite substantial, even dramatic, sometimes estimated at three IQ points per decade or more.

The Flynn process began in the more industrialized and richer countries, then spread to other countries. This seems likely to correspond, at least very roughly, to the spread of delivery by c-section.

Until around 150 years ago, "still births" (babies born dead) and "death in childbirth" (death of the expectant mother) were extremely common. Various medical advances have changed all that, and both of these occurrences are now much rarer. This is due to several associated advances in medicine and obstetrics, including the use of antibiotics. One of these advances is the gradual improvement of techniques for births by Caesarian section.

Birth Stress in Relation to Head Size

In a vaginal birth, the baby has to get through the vaginal aperture, but even earlier in the process it's a tight squeeze and pelvic contractions will inflict stress on the fetus. The widest part of the fetus is always the head. It's fortunate that, as far as we can tell, the unborn baby does not experience claustrophobia. Birth is the final stage of a hazardous process in which the baby sometimes has to rotate to proceed further.

In most births, and in the most favorable circumstances, the head comes out first, followed by the shoulders. Once the head is out, the baby's body has to rotate somewhat to get the shoulders out, one at a time, and there can be a hitch at this point. Once the head and shoulders are out, the rest is comparatively easy. (Even if the shoulders are the sticking point, there could be correlation between head size and delivery-problematic shoulders, so some selective effect can't be ruled out even there.)

Frequently, birth is only made possible by lacerations in the vagina and adjacent areas, and these tears will generally occur when the head is delivered. (A hundred years ago such tears were helpfully created by surgical intervention, almost as a matter of routine, but research has shown that this procedure, known as episiotomy, is only rarely net-beneficial, so it is now less common, though indicated in a few instances.) The fact that the process of vaginal delivery sometimes actually tears apart the mother's external tissue (most commonly of the peritoneum) is a dramatic and painful sign of the considerable pressure exerted on the mother's anatomy during delivery (tears pronounced one way stimulating tears pronounced the other way). When we're speculating about causation, we shouldn't be too preoccupied with these highly visible ruptures. Natural selection is not in business to make nice to everyone all the time, and the real limit on head size is the bone structure of the birth canal, not the highly observable yet comparatively superficial skin and flesh lacerations. Yet we should bear in mind that the force which can tear apart skin and muscle is the same quantity of force exerted on the soft and incompletely protected baby skull.

A difficult birth may be due to various circumstances, one being a breech birth, where the baby's feet, knees, or buttocks are closer to the vaginal opening than the head, another being twins or triplets, another being unfortunate position of the placenta or umbilical cord. In many cases, perhaps most, a difficult birth would tend to be associated with a large head. If the reason for difficulty, or for having a c-section, is reported as the large size of the baby, this effectively means the larger size of the baby's head, since if the head can get through, the rest of the baby's body can most often get through without much trouble. In all cases, the diameter of the head is wider than that of any other part of the baby's body.

Just as the use of c-sections must increase the incidence of larger heads, it must also increase the incidence of twins, of misplaced placentas, of breech presentations. and of narrower pelvises, insofar as susceptibility to these events is genetically determined.

What proportion of difficult and potentially fatal births are due in whole or in part to larger head size? This is difficult to estimate from easily available data. I looked over various statistical lists of the reasons for difficult births, and they are not easy to map to what's really going on. A common notation is "failure to progress," which leads mothers and the doctors in attendance to favor either a c-section or some artificial inducement of labor, followed by c-section if inducement doesn't work.

But how closely "failure to progress" is associated with large head size is not transparent, at least to me. On general grounds, head size must be decisive in a great many cases, but a precise empirical estimate is not readily available.

Here I should mention a complication, though I don't see that it would nullify the "c-sections increasing IQ" hypothesis. Different populations of humans sometimes have markedly different shapes of the birth canal. This is thought to be due to varying evolutionary influences such as climate. We're dealing here with an equilibration of sorts in which various factors arrive at a balance, two of these factors being the baby's head size and the shape of the birth canal. For this reason, it's now considered over-simple to refer to a single "obstetric dilemma," though instructive as a first approximation.

An End to the Flynn Effect?

The Flynn Effect began in high-income countries and later spread to lower-income countries. It looks reasonable that this might track the incidence of c-sections.

Although the general tendency is for the availability of c-sections to spread from industrialized to less industrialized populations, it doesn't seem likely that the Flynn Effect would always be closely associated with a fully industrialized way of life. Missionaries, philanthropic organizations, the Peace Corps, and others take advanced industrial culture, education, public health measures, and medical procedures to less developed countries. Availability of c-sections can increase significantly in a predominantly pre-industrial, third-world culture.

In those populations with a comparatively long history of rising IQ scores, it's observed that the rate of rise of IQ has recently declined, so that the Flynn Effect might be coming to an end. This would fit my theory, because once comparatively cheap and safe c-sections are equally available to everyone, the selective mechanism of IQ increase by reduced stress to the brain would tend to reach a point where further increase would be slow. (On the other hand, the decline in the rate of IQ increase would also fit many other conjectured causal factors, whose influence would be expected to approach a maximum after a while.) There would continue to be a tendency to indefinite long-term improvement in IQ due to genetic selection, but this would be much slower than the total initial effect of the introduction of c-sections.

Implications

Aside from any connection with IQ, higher incidence of c-sections can be expected to favor the evolution of bigger-diameter skulls, thus increasing the incidence of genes for bigger heads, which will in turn create an increased need for c-sections, so that the tendency will be for c-sections as a proportion of all births to rise (because the riskiness of vaginal birth has risen), the limit being universal birth by c-section. Even if there were no correlation with IQ, we could expect the continued easy availability of c-sections to lead to wider heads, and ultimately to a situation where vaginal birth became altogether ruled out as a practical possibility. If in fact more c-sections lead to higher average IQ, this trend would be associated with cumulative IQ increases.

Extrapolating ahead by thousands of years, we might even reach a point where humans can reproduce only by c-section delivery. After that point, a disaster which eliminated modern obstetrics and other features of modern medicine would incidentally bring the human species to an end.

Unfortunately, we are now at the end of an interglacial, which means (if the recurring pattern of the last sixty million years continues) that at some time in the next few thousand years, most land areas now populated by humans will be covered in ice more than a kilometer thick, and this sorry state of affairs will then last for over one hundred thousand years. It is not inconceivable that we could reduce the human population by more than 98 percent and keep the smaller population maintained at a high income, or even a continually growing income per head. But it's easy to see possible obstacles to this scenario, the most obvious being destructive wars over the shrinking habitable land space due to global freezing. So there is the distinct possibility that luxuries like modern hospitals offering c-sections may not survive the next few thousand years, in which case any speculation about what would have happened with long-term easy availability of c-sections becomes moot.

Why Was the Influence of
C-Sections on IQ Overlooked?

Several people before Flynn remarked on the rise in IQ, but his work drew more attention to it. "The Flynn Effect" was a term coined by Her-rnstein and Murray in their excellent and widely read book, *The Bell Curve*, and so the term has stuck. Flynn himself subsequently wrote a major work on the subject, *What Is Intelligence?*

Flynn's book presents his own theory (or rather the theory developed jointly by Flynn and W.T. Dickens) to account for the Flynn Effect. It would take me too far afield to expound this theory here, and I'm not sure I fully understand it, but it acknowledges a bigger role for culture without denying the preponderant role for genes indicated most starkly by twin studies. It contains the lemma that the proportionate genetic causation of differences within a group need not imply the same proportionate genetic causation of differences between groups, whether contemporaneous or chronologically successive.

We live in a culture which is uncomfortable with the notion that people's individual abilities and accomplishments are to a considerable extent governed by heredity. So one general response to the Flynn Effect is to conclude that it casts doubt on a large role for heredity.

At the same time, a statistical analysis of the data on identical twins raised apart, and other genetic studies, yields the finding that IQ is over 70 percent due to heredity in people of advanced years (the older you get, the more closely your IQ is predicted by your genes). and only 30 percent non-heredity. I say "non-heredity," because Judith Rich Harris has taught us that the main alternative to heredity is *certainly not* "nurture," and even the term "environment" doesn't really do justice to the non-genetic influences.

In giving his reasons for arriving at the Dickens-Flynn theory, Flynn discusses several genetic and environmental factors, specifying his reasons for dismissing them. One possible genetic mechanism might be that higher-IQ people could have more babies than lower-IQ people, but in fact the reverse is observably the case (pp. 100–01). This is often noted, as is the corollary, that there should consequently be a steady fall in average population IQ (*The Bell Curve*, Chapter 15, and the movie, *Idiocracy*).

It has therefore long been a familiar idea that the Flynn Effect is masking an underlying decline in IQ, which we might expect to eventually assert itself more visibly.

Flynn asserts, "That leaves hybrid vigor" (p. 101). Hybrid vigor is the only alternative hypothesis, that Flynn could think of, to explain the Flynn Effect genetically. Hybrid vigor signifies that prior to the twentieth century national populations were somewhat inbred and would become more intelligent as a result of more exogamous mating patterns. Flynn convincingly explains why this theory doesn't work, and then goes on to consider the dietary hypothesis.

But Flynn here overlooks one genetic and one non-genetic possibility. The overlooked genetic hypothesis is that c-sections have altered the terms of the trade-off in the Obstetric Dilemma, allowing the birth of more babies with wider heads. The overlooked non-genetic hypothesis is that c-sections have saved babies from brain injury during birth.

Early in his major work, *On Fertile Ground*, Peter Ellison describes the birth of his own child by c-section, and almost seems to imply that since this tricky birth had a happy outcome, the genes for larger head size must have increased in the population:

> Because of the intervention of a C-section, Sam's genes live, perhaps among them genes for a large fetal head size or a narrow maternal pelvis. Dramas like this, repeated countless billions of times in our evolutionary history, have endowed us with our physiological capacities and limitations and shape us still. (pp. 7–8)

Exactly! *And then?* When I read that, it was like the proverbial loaded gun which is shown to the audience in Act I and which we all know must therefore be fired in Act III. But Ellison misses the opportunity to fire it. It's very well-known that head size correlates with IQ, but Ellison doesn't even unloose the safety catch.

A Bad-Tempered Aside about Recent Developments

There was a huge explosion in the number of c-sections beginning in the 1970s, but we shouldn't necessarily expect this to be more powerful an influence than earlier, smaller increases, simply because even an increase of c-sections from zero to five percent of births, would take care of the most extremely difficult and dangerous births and could therefore have a bigger impact on population IQ than subsequent, larger increases.

Currently, one in three births in the U.S. is by c-section. The consensus of medical opinion is that this is too high. A substantial proportion of expectant mothers now opt for c-section without any recorded risk factor, presumably partly because they don't want the pain, the bother, and the lost time of labor. In support of the view that this is a bad thing, you often see it pointed out that the mortality from c-section birth is several times the mortality from vaginal birth. This is misleading because virtually all the most difficult and risky births now automatically get c-sections, thus the two populations are not comparable, and even those who choose elective c-section are not strictly comparable with the two-thirds of the birthing population who give birth vaginally; the former may be older, for example, or they may already have had a c-section birth.

The opinions of doctors don't rule, as long as patients are paying customers. With socialized medicine, the tendency would be to enforce the opinions of doctors, and thus we would expect to see women who want c-sections being ruled ineligible for them.

As we know from the work of Gerd Gigerenzer, the opinions of doctors (that is, people with M.D. degrees) and even surgeons are typically woefully ignorant and scientifically ill-educated. What doctors tell patients about risks is very often wildly inaccurate because the doctors are innumerate and don't, for example, understand the meaning of percentage risks. Doctors should present their opinions to patients, if patients choose to hear them, and then patients alone should decide what medical procedures they want to purchase.

In recent decades there have been indications that the Flynn Effect might be slowing down or halting, and even more recently, there are indications that average IQ in some industrialized countries (but not the U.S.) has started to fall. This fall was observed in Scandinavia in the 1990s; possibly that was explicable by massive immigration. Even more recent declines might be due to brain damage from the Covid "vaccines." But, as pointed out, an eventual reversal of the rise in IQ has been more or less expected, because low-IQ people reproduce faster than high-IQ people.

Corroborators and Falsifiers

The most direct and simple way to test my conjecture would be to collect and compare data on the adult IQs of those born vaginally and those born by c-section.

The test would have to control for income, education, and social class, since even today these might be positively associated with choice of c-section (or perhaps, in Berkeley, California, or Portland, Oregon, negatively associated).

My theory predicts increased adult IQ for those delivered by c-section. A positive finding would not be full corroboration of the whole mechanism, but it would at least align with the main component of the theory. A positive finding which was publicized would increase still further the patient demand for c-section delivery.

There are several ways in which my conjecture might turn out to be provably incorrect, and I will mention a few of them.

> 1. The only report I could find of a scientific study closely related to my conjecture is the study done by Tamas Horvath's team in 2012. This widely reported study suggested that c-section delivery "may" have harmful effects on the baby's health including cognitive development.
>
> The study was on mice. It was found that when baby mice were delivered by c-section, production of the protein UCP2 was "impaired," presumably a negative value-laden term for "reduced." UCP2 is thought to be necessary for optimal brain development, and the idea is that enhanced production of UCP2 by the mother is an adaptation to birth stress. Then, when production of this protein was prevented altogether (not merely reduced), the baby mice grew up to be less successful in a maze test designed to measure their memory and cognition. It's noteworthy that the researchers apparently didn't just look at the maze performance of their c-section-born

baby mice. Horvath is quoted as warning about the "previously unsuspected lasting effect on brain development and function in humans as well" arising from "the increasing prevalence of C-sections, driven by convenience rather than medical necessity." The fashionably propagandistic tone of this wording is embarrassingly evident, but not at all unusual in medical and "scientific" references to c-sections.

We don't know whether production of UCP2 is reduced by c-sections in the case of human babies, and we don't know whether this would have any deleterious effects. We also don't know whether the survivability of babies with large heads might more than compensate for any such effects. Mice, of course, don't have the problem of difficult births due to large heads of their babies.

This whole issue could be greatly clarified by direct comparison of c-section births in humans in relation to subsequent adult IQ. Results which might be insufficient to fully corroborate my conjecture might be sufficient to refute Horvath's conjecture.

2. The crucial link, correlation of head size with IQ, might be challenged. The correlation of adult head size with adult IQ is so abundantly documented as to be practically beyond revision, but the correlation of natal head size with subsequent adult IQ looks a bit less safely supported. The point here is that head size grows dramatically in the first eighteen months after birth (this postponement of brain growth until after birth is itself an adaptive response to the Obstetric Dilemma) and continues to grow more slowly for a few years after that. It is in principle possible that any correlation of adult head size with adult IQ might be more due to this postnatal expansion of the skull rather than to head size at birth (though some studies do seem to contradict that).

If, however, any correlation between natal head size and adult IQ were to be rejected, this would face us with a new challenge: how to explain the apparently tremendous selective pressure for bigger natal head size, only in humans and their immediate ancestors.

3. Supposing nutrition to be an important contributor to IQ differences, this might give a misleading association, because better nutrition might be correlated with both bigger head size at birth and subsequent IQ. In that case, even though head size would correlate with IQ, nutrition rather than genetically determined head size at birth would be the decisive variable. (Another conjecture, those mothers who were chain smokers and had tiny babies might not have been as unambiguously dysfunctional as we might suppose. Their bad habit might occasionally have saved their lives and even their babies' lives too.)

The clearest known case where nutrition plays a role is iodine deficiency. This deficiency undoubtedly lowers IQ, and can be completely prevented by, for instance, the use of iodized salt. One possible way to refute this mechanism as an explanation of the Flynn Effect would be to find a country which never had a high incidence of iodine deficiency (perhaps deducible from an absence of historical records of goiters) yet which still showed the same Flynn Effect. If other nutritional deficiencies of consequence are discovered, or other influences linking a more industrially-influenced culture with higher IQ, this might at least render my conjecture redundant.

A hypothesis involving nutrition has been found attractive, because the twentieth century saw a steady and substantial increase in adult height, and it's difficult to think of anything other than nutrition which could account for that. On the other hand, the increase in average IQ seems to have continued after the increase in average height had plateaued, and all likely dietary deficiencies terminated.

4. It might be that the terrific pummeling the baby's brain sometimes gets during vaginal birth would not affect later brain functioning adversely, or even that it would be beneficial

(like some trees that only reproduce well when they are all but consumed by forest fires), but this seems dubious on its face. We should not extrapolate from what might happen with exogenous shocks to a delicate piece of machinery such as clockwork to what might happen with such shocks to a fetal brain, which is very un-clockwork-like. Yet an absence of damage, let alone an improved functioning, does not look likely. Still, this causal link is mostly intuitive and would have to be tested by appropriate research. Again, testing for any correlation between c-sections and IQ would be highly informative. (There has been plenty of testing for head size in relation to IQ, but as far as I know, no testing linking IQ specifically to c-sections.)

It's conceivable that the c-section theory might represent one of several interacting influences leading to the Flynn Effect, another factor being nutrition, yet another being some role for culture of the Dickens-Flynn sort. I feel a bit of a wimp saying this, but I can't think of any good reason not to say it.

The Most Vulnerable Point

The most vulnerable point in my theory is the question of how closely availability of c-sections tracks the rise in IQ, and the most vulnerable aspect of this is the earliest period of onset of the Flynn Effect. What attracted attention in the 1940s was that the measured IQ of soldiers in World War II substantially exceeded the measured IQ of soldiers in World War I. From a U.S. point of view, the relevant dates would be 1918 and 1941, so we can assume that the most relevant birth dates would be roughly 1898 and 1921. What happened to c-sections in that period? Presumably their incidence increased fairly rapidly, but just how rapidly, and from what quantitative starting point? We'd also have to check that the persons tested in 1918 were comparable, as to variables like age, social class, and general health, with those tested in 1941.

From what I have read, the indications are that c-section had become a completely accepted, though no doubt still very rare, procedure by the

1880s. Its high mortality rate ensured that its use was confined to the few most extremely dangerous pregnancies. After that, the procedure was improved in stages and employed more widely. This is compatible with my conjecture, though close empirical work could conceivably show that c-sections were too infrequent from 1898 to 1921 to have sufficient impact to account for much of the Flynn Effect.

A Patchy Bibliography

Antoine, Clarel, and Bruce K. Young. 2020. Cesarean Section One Hundred Years 1920–2020: The Good, the Bad, and the Ugly. *Journal of Perinatal Medicine* 49:1.

Broekman, Birit F.P., Yiong-Huak Chan, Yap-Seng Chong, Swee-Chye Quek, Daniel Fung, Yen-Ling Low, Yoon-Phaik Ooi, Peter D Gluckman, Michael J. Meaney, Tien-Yin Wong, Seang-Mei Saw. 2009. The Influence of Birth Size on Intelligence in Healthy Children. *Pediatrics* (June).

Deary, Ian J., Simon R. Cox, and W. David Hill. 2022. Genetic Variation, Brain, and Intelligence Differences. *Molecular Psychiatry* 27:1. <https://psycnet.apa.org/record/2021-14607-001>.

Ellison, Peter T. 2001. *On Fertile Ground: A Natural History of Human Reproduction.* Harvard University Press.

Flynn, James R. 1984. The Mean IQ of Americans: Massive Gains 1932 to 1978. *Psychological Bulletin* 95.

———. 2009 [2007]. *What Is Intelligence? Beyond the Flynn Effect.* Cambridge University Press.

———. 2018. Reflections about Intelligence Over 40 Years. *Intelligence* <https://scottbarrykaufman.com/wp-content/uploads/2018/08/1-s2.0-S0160289618300904-main.pdf>.

Gigerenzer, Gerd. 2003. *Calculated Risks: How to Know when Numbers Deceive You.* Simon and Schuster.

———. 2014. *Risk Savvy: How to Make Good Decisions.* Penguin.

Harris, Judith Rich. 2009 [1998]. *The Nurture Assumption: Why Children Turn Out the Way They Do.* Simon and Schuster.

———. 2007 [2006]. *No Two Alike: Human Nature and Human Individuality*. Norton.

Herrnstein, Richard J., and Charles Murray. 1994. *The Bell Curve: Intelligence and Class Structure in American Life*. Free Press.

Jaekel, Julia, Christian Sorg, Josef Baeuml, Peter Bartmann, and Dieter Wolke. 2018. Head Growth and Intelligence from Birth to Adulthood in Very Preterm and Term Born Individuals. *Journal of the International Neuropsychological Society* 25:1. <https://pubmed.ncbi.nlm.nih.gov/30426909>.

Johnson, F.W. 1991. Biological Factors and Psychometric Intelligence: A Review. *Genetic, Social, and General Psychology Monographs* 117:3 (August).

Kirkegaard, Helene, Sören Möller, Chunsen Wu, Jonas Häggström, Sjurdur Frodi Olsen, Jørn Olsen, and Ellen Aagaard Nohr. 2020. Associations of Birth Size, Infancy, and Childhood Growth with Intelligence Quotient at 5 Years of Age: A Danish Cohort Study. *American Journal of Clinical Nutrition* 112:1 (July).

Koch, Christoff. 2016. Does Brain Size Matter? *Scientific American*. <www.scientificamerican.com/article/does-brain-size-matter1>.

Neisser, Ulric, ed. 1998. *The Rising Curve: Long Term Gains in IQ and Related Measures*. American Psychological Association.

Qian, Li, F. Gao, B. Yan, L. Yang, W. Wang, L. Bai, X. Ma, J. Yang. 2021. Mendelian Randomization Suggests that Head Circumference, but Not Birth Weight and Length, Associates with Intelligence. *Brain and Behavior* 11.

Rettner, Rachael. 2012. C-Sections May Not Provide the Brain Benefits of Vaginal Birth. Yahoo! News (August 8th) <www.yahoo.com/news/c-sections-may-not-brain-benefits-vaginal-birth-210423334.html>.

Rosenberg, Karen R. 1992. The Evolution of Modern Human Childbirth. *Yearbook of Physical Anthropology* 35.

Rosenberg, Karen R., and Wenda R. Trevathan. 1996. Bipedalism and Human Birth: The Obstetrical Dilemma Revisited. *Evolutionary Anthropology* 4:5.

————. 2001. The Evolution of Human Birth. *Scientific American* (November).

Simon-Areces, J., M.O. Dietrich, G. Hermes, L.M. Garcia-Segura, M-A. Arevalo, and Tamas L. Horvath. 2012. UCP2 Induced by Natural Birth Regulates Neuronal Differentiation of the Hippocampus and Related Adult Behavior. *PLOS One* 7:8 <https://journals.plos.org/plosone/article?id=10.1371/journal.pone.0042911>.

Trevathan, Wenda R. 1987. *Human Birth: An Evolutionary Perspective*. Aldine de Gruyter.

Tuddenham, Reed D. 1948. Soldier Intelligence in World Wars I and II. *American Psychologist* 3.

World Health Organization. 2021. Caesarean Section Rates Continue to Rise Amid Growing Inequalities in Access. <www.who.int/news/item/16-06-2021-caesarean-section-rates-continue-to-rise-amid-growing-inequalities-in-access>.

13

WHY DO WE SEE LYSENKO-TYPE MASS DELUSIONS IN WESTERN DEMOCRACIES?

Lysenkoism was an intellectual movement, a system of ideas. Its adherents and political supporters murdered thousands of people and indirectly caused the deaths of hundreds of thousands. Lysenkoism committed these terrible crimes in the name of rationality, progress, antiimperialism, and . . . wait for it . . . science.

Trofim Lysenko (pronounced Lee-syen-ka) was a Soviet agronomist—an agricultural scientist—who came to prominence in the late 1920s. This was the period of the First Five-Year Plan. The USSR was excitedly preparing to be catapulted into paradise at warp speed. Anyone who voiced a note of caution might be sent to Siberia or shot as a saboteur.

Lysenko won the favor of Comrade Stalin, a jovial kind of guy who could be extremely persuasive, and in 1935 Lysenko became the unassailable boss of Soviet agricultural technology. He proposed methods for changing the inherited qualities of living things by subjecting them to special treatment. It had long been known that plant growth can be stimulated or retarded by the way the seeds are treated. For example, if the seeds of some plants are subjected to low temperatures, this leads to more vigorous growth. This process, called "vernalization," was generalized by Lysenko into a theory that promised hugely increased agricultural yields. Later he proposed new approaches to hybridization.

Lysenko's theory resonated with the Communist notion that environment could over-ride heredity. Lysenkoism seemed to harmonize with the view that humans, like winter wheat, are products of their environments, and that therefore socialism could produce a "new man." Lysenko denied the existence of genes and branded genetics as a pseudoscientific product of the bourgeois West. Anyone advocating this decadent Western science risked being fired, then imprisoned or killed. Lysenko didn't know much about science, but more than made up for it by his down-to-earth peasant wisdom, inaccurate reporting of his results, and identification of his methods with the world-conquering worldview of Marxism-Leninism-Stalinism.

From 1935 until 1965, Lysenko ruled Soviet agricultural science. Farmers throughout the USSR were compelled to adopt his methods, or at least to pay lip service to them and keep away from the right-wing bourgeois theory known as genetics. The campaign against genetics intensified, and teaching the subject was completely outlawed in 1948.

Lysenko's methods failed to yield any net benefits for food production; the application of these methods wasted resources and contributed to the chronic failure of Soviet agriculture. Acceptance of the Lysenko theory was binding on members of Communist Parties throughout the world, all funded and controlled by Moscow, which could be a little awkward in some cases because this was a time when it was cool among Western intellectuals to sympathize with Communism, and some left-leaning Western biologists found they had a conflict.

Lysenko, and therefore the international Communist movement, not only opposed genetics; they also opposed vital elements of Darwinian evolution, because they rejected the possibility of competition among individuals within a species as an evolutionary driving force.

The repeated failure of Lysenkoism in practice was concealed from view, because the general public didn't know enough to question the official line and had no democratic recourse for organizing any kind of public counter-argument, while the relevant scientists were barred from publicly questioning Lysenkoism. Skeptics or people who considered that there might be something in the Western science of genetics, were silenced ("canceled," as we would now say), vilified, and fired from their jobs for (as we would now say) peddling dangerous right-wing misinformation. Lysenko was adroit at repeatedly turning to new projects promising big increases in output, distracting attention from examination of what precisely had been the fate of his earlier projects.

In 1953 Stalin died and the double helix structure of DNA was published, strongly corroborating genetics. Yet Lysenko remained powerful because he was favored by Comrade Khruschev, another people person with a persuasive manner. Lysenko's theories got crazier and crazier; he maintained that cuckoos could be changed into thrushes and wheat into rye, by means of early conditioning—and no one dared to publicly contradict him. He was not finally deprived of authority until Khrushchev's loss of power in 1965. Personally, Lysenko then became an obscure figure, and died with little attention in 1976.

Lysenkoism Resurrects Under Democracy

When Lysenkoism prevailed, most people who heard about it in the West attributed it to the undemocratic character of the Soviet political system. Absence of democracy was associated with absence of open debate. The Party Line could not be criticized. In such a situation, Westerners reasoned, the Party bosses could not be given powerful feedback challenging their ideological assumptions and enthusiasms. Thus, someone like Stalin, prone to paranoid delusion, could not be stopped when he gave his support to someone like Lysenko, a transparent mountebank and charlatan. It was confidently assumed that Western science was simply immune from anything like this.

There's some truth in this account, but it overlooks the fact that similar mechanisms can operate within a democratic political system, if it is one in which the government intervenes a lot in people's lives and in which the government provides most of the financing for scientific research. The West has suffered successive ideological tsunamis, with the characteristics of Lysenkoism, and we should expect many more and worse to come, unless certain reforms are put in place.

I will briefly mention three of these bouts of ideological enthusiasm, very much akin to Lysenkoism, which have managed to capture political power in Western democracies. These are: 1) The Low-Fat Diet; 2) Global Warming Catastrophism; 3) The Covid Ideology which produced those two successive and related Crimes against Humanity: first the "lockdowns" and then the "vaccines."

In these cases, pseudoscience masquerades as science while real science, or even just naively asking questions, is persecuted as dangerous pseudoscience and right-wing conspiracy theory.

The Low-Fat Diet unnecessarily caused the deaths of millions. The Covid Lockdowns unnecessarily caused the deaths of millions. The Covid "vaccines" unnecessarily caused the deaths of millions. When I say "caused deaths," I mean, "negatively impacted people's health so that they died earlier than they otherwise would." Even Global Warming Catastrophism cannot be acquitted on the charge of causing millions of unnecessary deaths because, in a world where there are still some remaining pockets of extreme poverty, anything that substantially raises the price of energy will lead to mass deaths of third-world babies.

These cases all have strikingly similar features. People who question or contradict the official line are discriminated against in various ways; they lose their jobs and their research funding, they are unable to publish in prestigious venues, nasty stories are made up about them and disseminated with lavish financial backing from mysterious sources.

So far, in the democratic West, they are mostly not imprisoned without trial or shot, but I have no confidence this sentimental afterglow of classical liberal norms will last much longer. Meanwhile mediocrities or outright incompetents in the relevant fields find a way to gain a competitive career advantage by loudly proclaiming the official story, while advertising their super-orthodox credentials by screaming abuse at the more thoughtful and more competent critics of the official view.

One symptom of the progression of neo-Lysenkoism is that the champions of the orthodox view have no interest in publicly discussing the merits or demerits of their theoretical position; in fact the vast majority of them don't know enough to even attempt this (try asking Greta Thunberg about the Stefan-Boltzmann equation—no, wait, try asking her about the first law of thermodynamics), and they exert considerable efforts to suppressing any such public discussion. They are only concerned to silence the critics and, failing that, to discredit them by smearing them and shutting down any platforms that might be available to them. They sense that the big danger to their power and privilege is open debate, and this must be stamped out at all costs.

A related observation is that if you talk to experts in the relevant fields, you frequently find that they will disclose in hushed tones: "Between you and me, what these critics are saying has some merit, but I don't dare to say that publicly. I have a family to feed."

1. The Low-Fat Diet

In the 1950s there was a wave of public alarm concerning the incidence of heart disease, especially among middle-aged males. Various hypotheses were proposed to account for this but the one which won out for the next half-century was the theory linking intake of fat, or saturated fat, with heart disease.

Nina Teicholz has meticulously laid bare the chain of events which led to the acceptance by the government of this theory, though there was never any good evidence in its favor. Teicholz describes the limitations of every important study, and the ways in which contrary evidence was ignored or even in some cases suppressed.

Epidemiological or observational studies are inherently inconclusive, especially when the correlations they turn up are small, because they can only show association, and two things can be associated for any number of irrelevant reasons. The more conclusive, and usually more expensive, randomized controlled studies have always been consistent with the view that you need plenty of fat for optimal health and that fat consumption does not clog your blood vessels, while excessive carbohydrate consumption is implicated in causing heart disease, as well as diabetes and obesity.

The diet-heart hypothesis, blaming fat and especially saturated fat for heart disease, was energetically promoted by Ancel Keys, the Lysenko of the Low-Fat Diet. Keys, like Lysenko, vilified and discredited individuals who opposed his theory, so that they were either silenced or removed from any possibility of influence. Proponents of the diet-heart hypothesis such as the American Heart Association were wooed with large cash donations from the manufacturers of vegetable oils. This troika of dogmatic academics, authoritarian government, and opportunistic business interests crushed all opposition, in a manner that has become increasingly familiar in the democratic West.

Keys launched his famous Seven-Country Study in 1956; it covered the years 1958–1964. The study showed a strong correlation between high consumption of saturated fat and heart disease. Seven countries sounds like a big study, but actually only small and idiosyncratic numbers from each of the countries were looked at, and countries like France,

Switzerland, Germany, Norway, and Sweden, which consumed high quantities of saturated fats accompanied by low rates of heart disease, were purposely excluded. Keys was looking for subjects which would be likely to confirm his hypothesis rather than test it.

This was a purely epidemiological or observational study, unable to show causation. The subjects were all middle-aged men. The many problems with the data were concealed and Keys systematically vilified and discredited critics. In Keys's follow-up study of the same populations in 1984, the crucial correlations all disappeared, but by this time the Low-Fat Diet had become entrenched orthodoxy, and this new data was not so lavishly publicized.

The Low-Fat Diet has gradually been abandoned, because all the recent high-quality research shows it to be baseless, but its abandonment has not been attended with the same fanfare with which it was promoted, so that echoes of it are all around us. In your supermarket, you will often see products labeled "low fat" or "fat free," as though this were some kind of recommendation, when it ought to be a warning sign. For optimal health, you need to consume plenty of fat, including saturated fat, and cut down on carbohydrates, especially sugar.

The Low-Fat Diet hugely impacted the actual American diet. The evidence we have is consistent with the view that the Low-Fat Diet is responsible for the three great epidemics—obesity, diabetes, and Alzheimer's dementia—that have engulfed the American population since the 1970s. (Thus, in a kind of strange, baroque twist, many of the deaths attributed to Covid are actually the result of the Low-Fat Diet.) In any case, the Low-Fat Diet is responsible for the premature deaths of many millions, past, present, and future.

The Low-Fat Diet now differs from Global Warming Catastrophism and the government's Covid narrative in that it has already been officially abandoned. While official sources will not openly denounce the Low-Fat Diet as a monumental blunder, public health disaster, and (insofar as it was implemented coercively in government policy) Crime against Humanity, recommendations to reduce fat consumption have been quietly dropped from various official dietary guidelines (though there are a few holdouts). Orthodox officialdom is sullenly acquiescing in the acknowledgment, borne out by high-quality studies, that we need fat for optimal health, and restricting fat intake shortens lives.

We can't say by what exact process Global Warming Catastrophism and the Lockdown/"Vaccines" belief systems will be abandoned, but the actual abandonment of the Low-Fat Diet provides a clue as to how other such belief systems might meet their demise: a slow, grudging acceptance that the old belief system is altogether untenable, transmitted at different rates to different segments of the population, so that recognition that the consensus of accredited experts has been frantically disseminating a lot of dangerous untruths is indefinitely postponed. The implicit strategy seems to be to get people gradually used to the absence of the old pseudoscientific cult, so that no one ever has to admit that our rulers and their pet experts screwed up culpably and their heads ought to roll. Fifty years in the future people will write books digging up these by-then-forgotten ideological panics and marveling that anyone could ever have been so gullible as to entertain them for two seconds.

2. Global Warming Catastrophism

In the history of climate, cycles of warming and cooling go on all the time. For the last sixty million years, the Earth has been in an ice age, in which periods of glaciation alternate with periods of comparative warming, known as interglacials. Interglacials last for somewhat over ten thousand years, whereas periods of glaciation, called glacials, last for somewhat over one hundred thousand years.

There are cycles within cycles, or rather, since some of the events don't show much regularity, recurring fluctuations within recurring fluctuations. Within each interglacial there are many alternating periods of warming and cooling, lasting a few decades or a few centuries. The present warming began in 1850 (before the human-caused rise in CO_2, which according to current models only became large enough to appreciably affect global temperature after World War II). So this warming immediately followed the Little Ice Age, from 1450 to 1850, the coldest episode in several thousand years. The earlier period of Medieval Warming (950 to 1250) was warmer than today, the even earlier Roman period (250 B.C.E. to 400 C.E.) was warmer still, and before that the Minoan period (1200 to 700 B.C.E.) was yet warmer. In other words, if there had been no human-caused increase in CO_2 emissions, and no enthusiastic Greenist ideologues bent on abolishing industrial civilization as the first step in abolishing humankind itself, there would have been nothing in the present warming trend which would have struck anyone as requiring a special explanation. (These successive warming periods, within the interglacial, get progressively cooler as we slide into the next glacial, popularly known as an ice age; technically, we are already in an ice age).

There is nothing distinctive or unusual about the present warming. It is what we might very well expect, in line with repeated cycles of warming and cooling since the end of the last glaciation, 13,000 years ago. Climate always changes, and the notion that it ought to stay the same has no serious rationale. Of course, we might expect the very tiny recent increase in carbon dioxide, from 300 to 420 parts per million (restoring this number to what it was a few million years ago), to produce a very tiny warming, but it seems just as likely that the climate system's homeostatic character would largely cancel this out. Instead, the catastrophists speculate that the climate system will amplify the warming, in a runaway process, though this did not happen in Medieval, or Roman, or Minoan times.

Global warming catastrophism may be criticized in two ways: by criticizing the currently dominant theory of global warming, reliant on computer models, or by pointing out that even the dominant theory does not predict catastrophe. Although I favor an alternative to the dominant theory, namely the theory of solar influences expounded by Henrik Svensmark and Nir Shaviv (which assumes a much bigger role for solar variations and therefore a much smaller role for CO_2), it is simpler to point out that the economic impact of a likely rise in global temperatures, according to accepted models, will be minimal. The stated official view of the IPCC, based on the standard climate models along with respectable econometric studies which look at the impact of warming as predicted by those models, suggests that warming will be a minor factor in determining future economic growth (Koonin, *Unsettled*, pp. 177–182). This means that the human impact of warming (assuming it occurs as predicted, which you shouldn't bet on) will be far less than the impact of wars, or economic recessions, or changes in government regulation of business.

It is therefore false, according to the most respectable of officially recognized experts, to describe global warming as an "existential threat," just as it would be false to describe it as no problem at all. The standard view, among econometricians who completely accept the official "science" of the IPCC, is that the problem can be taken care of by a modest tax on CO_2 emissions.

Here we encounter a curious feature of both the global warming pseudoscience and the Covid pseudoscience (perhaps this is to become a feature common to all future outbreaks of neo-Lysenkoism). The official view of the experts contradicts the more popular view of the media promoters of the official doctrine, so that you can be canceled or otherwise punished for repeating elements of the official story to a popular audience. But this persecution will be done in the name of "science," as purportedly represented by those very same experts.

Thus, the "official" account of "climate change," as endorsed by the IPCC, flatly contradicts the popular claim that "climate change" is an "existential threat," but to point this out in a venue that might be accessed by the common rabble will get you canceled and vilified. Similarly, at the height of the "pandemic" frenzy, you could be penalized for purveying "disinformation" simply by repeating official statistics to a popular audience.

3. The Covid Crimes

The craziness of the official response to the Covid epidemic was what stimulated Mattias Desmet to speak out in opposition, and to thereby become a leading figure among opponents of the Covid Crimes. Desmet, a statistician as well as a psychologist, was struck by the fact that unprecedented and unorthodox lockdown procedures were suddenly adopted on the basis of enormously exaggerated projections of likely contagion and likely deaths. These projections were quickly corrected, but the lockdown policies were continued, unaffected by the new data.

Everything was then done to maintain the exaggeration of the scale of the emergency. Hospitals were given generous incentives to falsely classify deaths as due to Covid, with the result that reported Covid deaths were from seven to ten times the real numbers. Widespread testing with the faulty PCR tests yielded inflated numbers of "cases" of people who were not sick. A minor outbreak comparable to the routine annual flu was misrepresented as a catastrophic "pandemic." There were wild prophecies of bodies in the streets and overwhelmed health facilities, which were entirely unfounded and never even remotely fulfilled.

Now that the lockdowns and the "vaccination" campaigns have died down—though with visible reluctance on the part of government bureaucrats and authoritarian politicians, who can't wait to find another excuse to put us all through the same pointless and destructive misery again—there is general agreement among those who have studied the subject that these measures did far more harm than good. If governments had done absolutely nothing in response to Covid, the outcome for aggregate human well-being would have been hugely more favorable. This is especially true of the irresponsible "vaccinations," whose devastating "adverse events" will be a scourge of public health for generations to come.

The mRNA "vaccinations" are strictly not vaccinations, but gene therapy, something that, before the Covid epidemic, everyone agreed could easily be performed but was so little understood that incurring the risks would be unthinkable irresponsibility. Indeed, one of the many indirect costs of the imposition of Covid "vaccines," and the public health havoc it has caused, is that many people will now be too suspicious of real vaccines with a proven record of considerable net benefit.

Eminent virologists and epidemiologists warned at the outset that putting these "vaccines" on the market, and then striving to make them compulsory, was fraught with danger. They pointed out that these "vaccines" would suppress the immune system, and precipitate the selection of new strains of virus against which the "vaccinated" (but not the "unvaccinated") would be defenseless. They also pointed out that, because of the characteristics of the spike protein, it would get into organs such as the brain, liver, kidneys, and ovaries. The coerced "vaccination" of healthy children and pregnant women, and the associated closing of schools, was a particularly vile crime by the authorities.

The ruling ideology was that nothing should be allowed to interfere with "vaccines" as the only solution. The coercive measures included those who had already had Covid. If you have had Covid, you have natural immunity, and then the "vaccine" is more likely to shorten your life than to cure you of anything, and you will only get the jab if you are seriously misinformed or coerced. Thousands of healthcare workers, who had acquired natural immunity by treating patients, were fired for refusing to get "vaccinated," though "vaccination" could do them or their patients no good whatsoever.

Any mention of treatment of the disease—by vitamin D, a low-carb diet, hydroxychloroquine, or ivermectin, led to abuse being hurled, and cancelation on social media. The fact that acquired immunity from having been infected is highly protective was suppressed, along with the fact that the "vaccines" provided no protection at all against infection. The one treatment that was approved, for a while, was remdesivir, distinguished from those other treatments because they were all out of patent and therefore cheap whereas remdesivir was under patent and therefore expensive, providing yet more billions in monopoly profits to the pharma company which had patented it. The corruption is that naked.

Remdesivir had far less evidence for its effectiveness or safety than hydroxychloroquine or ivermectin, but it had been validated by a recent study conducted, of course, by the company that was to market the drug. These pharma studies are full of tricks designed to create bogus evidence for effectiveness and safety (*Turtles All the Way Down*). An elementary reform would be to have all tests of new treatments conducted by a completely independent body, its members well rewarded, appointed for life, and prohibited from receiving any benefits from pharma companies for the rest of their lives, *with full results of the entire research made public immediately.*

Probably a simpler and more effective policy solution would be to simply abolish patents for medical treatments. This would greatly reduce the rate of discovery of new drugs, but most new drugs yield only the tiniest of net benefit, accompanied by incompletely quantifiable harms, while de-monopolization would lead to reduced emphasis on one-size-fits-all chemical cures, more emphasis on using existing knowledge flexibly for the individually focused benefit of patients.

The coercive use of these "vaccines" contravenes the Nuremberg Code, formulated to address Nazi experiments on humans. It is contrary to the Nuremberg Code to give experimental drugs or other experimental treatments to people without disclosing the risks and allowing them a free choice as to whether to accept the treatment. In the case of Covid "vaccines," the politicians and their abject defenders denied the risks and went to some trouble to hide them. They denied the myocarditis, the neurodegenerative processes, the immunosuppressive impact, and the reproductive effects which they, at the very least, had every reason to suspect would be caused by these "vaccinations."

New drugs and vaccines are exceptionally profitable because they are under patent. Were it not for patents, temporary grants of monopoly privilege, competition would automatically ensure that the profit on these new treatments would be the same regular rate of return as prevails in normal business enterprises. New treatments would be no more profitable than old treatments, including repurposed treatments. Because of patents the rate of return on new treatments is vastly higher.

The original idea behind medical patents was to encourage new treatment innovations. The pharma companies can spend a lot on research because they can recoup these outlays through the monopoly profits they make when they find a new treatment that is approved. But this has the unintended consequence that it provides an incentive to market new treatments rather than old treatments, and to realize this monopoly profit quickly because the patent will expire within twenty years.

So we see the drug companies claiming that the new treatments are better than the old, and discouraging use of the old. Most treatments, even when they show a net benefit for some groups of people, are net harmful for other groups, and here we see the companies denying this and trying to get everyone to take the treatment. If they have any chance of using political coercion to *compel* people to take the treatment, that is, from their financial point of view, a godsend. Adam Smith's invisible hand, which in normal competitive conditions confers colossal benefits on people, in cases of monopoly privilege can lead to colossal harms to the population.

To secure a patent, a company has to show that the product works, and in the case of a medical treatment, that it has benefits which outweigh the risks. Studies are conducted for new medical treatments, but, amazingly, these studies are carried out by the companies which will make huge gains if the patent is awarded, and the detailed results of these studies are kept secret! Naturally, the companies routinely distort and misrepresent the studies, to downplay the risks and magnify the benefits.

Sometimes these dishonest results come out, and there is a public scandal. The companies have to pay damages, but the damages do not cancel out the monopoly profits, let alone impose a further deduction. The damages should be calculated high enough to turn a huge monopoly profit into a huge loss, but this is not the standard practice. Instead, the companies come out ahead financially, even on those treatments which have become tardily recognized as unacceptably harmful. In the Covid episode, this bounty for the merchants of poison was ramped up to an inspiring new level: they were guaranteed immunity against any liability, so that even if the scandalous harm of the "vaccines" were to be proved beyond all doubt, the surviving victims would not even be able to claim the paltry compensation heretofore considered normal.

The obsession with "vaccination" as the sacred panacea led to the most amazing excesses, which future historians will find hard to believe. Healthy young kids were forcibly "vaccinated." People were "vaccinated" who already had natural immunity, vastly superior to any immunity conferred by a vaccine, even a genuine one. Some healthcare professionals would "vaccinate" patients *who had just recovered from severe Covid symptoms.* People who did this should have been prosecuted for attempted murder.

Many parents, sadly, didn't hesitate to sacrifice their children to this insatiable Moloch. Healthy children don't get sick with Covid, and if infected, they almost never infect adults. In any case "vaccination" doesn't stop them catching Covid, or make it any less likely that they will become infected (without getting sick) or less likely that they will pass the virus on to others, while it does give them a heightened probability of myocarditis, cancer, and other potentially fatal conditions later in life. The only easily discernable motivation to "vaccinate" them is to be obedient to the thinking of the herd, thereby giving yet more billions to the pharma companies, at the cost of the health of these defenseless "vaccinated" victims. Politicians get their cut from this grisly traffic in the form of donations from the pharma companies, and so the cycle of lucrative killing of innocents is perpetuated.

Theories defending the low-fat diet, global warming catastrophism, and Covid lockdowns and vaccines, were all *untrue*, and the people who objected to these official stories were *telling the truth*, or at least, raising questions about the falsehoods. So it's worth making the point that the techniques of cancellation, censorship, and smearing would still be wrong even if the official doctrine were true, and even if its critics were doing harm by encouraging alternative thinking. There is no such thing as a magical guarantee of truth, and truth when it is found is often surprising. In the long run, truth will tend to emerge more quickly and more dependably if there is free and open debate, despite some cases where acceptance of the truth is delayed. Science itself absolutely depends on free and open debate; science dies if debate dies. The same applies to public discussion of policy within a democracy.

Understanding Collective Political Craziness

What explains the growth of these ideological tsunamis, in which a belief system acquires the power to persecute and silence those who disagree, and then often moves to causing the deaths of millions of innocents?

I can identify six relevant influences:

1. The inherent quality of belief systems which causes them to become bigoted. When a group of people adhere to a distinctive set of beliefs, there is always quite naturally a tendency to dogmatism and cultishness. Open debate or other external influences can limit this tendency, but it's always there.

2. Ideological currents which favor any development that complies with fashionable ideology. After World War II, most of the Left switched from being pro-growth and pro-wealth to being against material well-being itself and therefore against economic growth. The "progressives" turned against progress. This new, consciously anti-human ideology seeks to destroy modern industry and return to a more primitive economy (the most advanced thinkers see this as the step before

abolishing humankind completely), and constantly looks for marketable ways to proclaim that modern industry and its conjoined organism, the free-market economy, are about to destroy the world.

3. The expansion of government financial support for science. Government funding for science means that bureaucrats have billions of dollars to disburse, and they are inclined to give this bounty to research projects which are "relevant," meaning that they confirm the fashionable prejudices of politicians or comply with the interests of political donors. Once the great majority of science funding comes from the government, a chain of events is set in motion that tends to lead to the abolition of science. By some such route, we might arrive at Ayn Rand's "Seventeen Illustrious Inventors of the Candle."

Terence Kealey has made a solid case that government funding of science is less effective at producing scientific knowledge and technological benefits than private funding, which is crowded out by government funding. Thus, there is a clear indication that we should terminate government funding of science, even for purely economic reasons.

But more broadly, today's dangerous religions all take the form of "science," so any government policy favoring one scientific opinion over another should be viewed as contravening the First Amendment. There must be a wall of separation between government and science.

4. Political dynamics which favor the emergence of a single belief system excluding others. For example, once a type of policy begins to be accepted as something that can easily be sold to the voters as urgently required, politicians are stampeded by their mutual competition into taking up more and more extreme versions of that policy.

5. Economic interests which benefit from measures implied by the belief system. Once the government is in the position

of disbursing vast quantities of money, special interests move in and influence politicians and thus "science." The many examples given in Teicholz's book (for example the rapid development and marketing of hydrogenated oils, chemicals unlike any ever encountered in previous human nutrition, and, we now know, seriously harmful to health) would have been unthinkable without the political framework derived from government domination of research funding.

6. Psychological traits which favor certain kinds of totalist beliefs. It is an irresistible conclusion that, when we witness a spectacle like the movement for compulsory "vaccination" in 2021–22, we're observing some kind of collective insanity. The craziness of the government pronouncements, following each other in an illogical and contradictory torrent of untruths (many of them silently dropped a few weeks or months later, usually with no explicit recognition that there had been any mistake), is only exceeded by the demented docility of the poor saps who swallow this propaganda, and rush to get "vaccinated," thus ensuring millions of subsequent early deaths from cardiological, neurodegenerative, immune-compromised, and other "adverse events."

We're dealing here with a historically recurring pattern of behavior, variously labeled "mass hysteria," "psychogenic epidemic," or "moral panic." A genetically determined pattern of conformist group behavior which was adaptive when humans lived in comparatively small packs can become more hazardous in a world of huge states, huge populations, and preternaturally potent technologies.

Mattias Desmet's Theory

When something like the Covid belief system seizes all the most powerful institutions in the culture, people of a more skeptical disposition are faced with what looks like an amazing spectacle of mass insanity. There is something baffling about the apparent stupidity of the reigning doctrine, with its conspicuous elements of nonsense, incoherence, and blatant fallacy, along with the fanatical commitment to this doctrine by all kinds of people, ranging from the comprehensively ignorant (Rachel Maddow) to those bedecked with the trappings of expertise (Anthony Fauci). In the case of Covid, the puzzlement was intensified because of the monthly and weekly changes in the doctrine, including some 180-degree reversals, all absorbed into the doctrine instantly, with no let-up in fanatical zeal and determination to stamp out all dissent.

When this puzzling spectacle was at its height, with growing skeptical pushback against the official story, something unexpected occurred: the appearance and instant popularity of a theory which offered to explain the whole mass insanity phenomenon, and to do so in a way that seemed at first blush to cover all the angles. And this "right-wing" diagnosis came from just the kind of source most respected by the Wokish left (who had fallen in like zombie troops behind the official doctrine), a handsome psychology professor with a cute foreign accent, who would occasionally betray his indebtedness to Michel Foucault and Jacques Lacan.

One Covid skeptic after another was apparently converted to the whole Desmet package, including Peter McCullough, Robert Malone, Tucker Carlson, Bret Weinstein and Heather Heying, and dozens of lesser lights.

Desmet deserves high praise for seeing that something was terribly wrong and giving us a theory of what was going on, a theory which seemed to explain a lot and to offer hope for a comparatively benign outcome. Like other public dissenters from the Covid orthodoxy, Desmet displayed marvelous courage in speaking out, incurring the personal and occupational penalties which fall upon those who dare to contradict the official line.

Currently, Mattias Desmet's theory of "mass formation" is widely accepted among opponents of the Covid Crimes. While Desmet has done a much-needed job in at least alerting the public to the necessity for some comprehensive theory of such outbreaks of collective madness, I believe Desmet's theory is untenable in some of its components. It has serious flaws, some of them going back to Gustave Le Bon, upon whom Desmet draws heavily.

I have given my own explanation above, but I see that as a more or less obvious preliminary listing of the relevant factors, not a truly deep and satisfying explanation. It does immediately point to a deficiency in Desmet's theory, his almost exclusive focus on mass psychology, neglecting the role of political and economic processes. Criticizing the Desmet theory may help us to arrive eventually at a more complete explanation.

Mass Formation

Desmet says that the preconditions for mass formation (from the German *Massenbildung*, often translated as "crowd formation") begin with a sense of individual atomization, or lack of social bonds. People have also lost any sense of purpose in life, as shown by the high percentage of people who describe their occupations as "bullshit jobs." These mental states lead to free-floating anxiety, anxiety which is not attached to any definite object, and this in turn generates a feeling of unfocused fear.

Once these conditions prevail, the people in this state of mind are prepared to accept the preaching of leaders who offer a belief system which focuses on a single problem, a single enemy. Many people eagerly embrace this message. They find that acceptance of this message gives them a bond with the collective of believers. The adherents of this belief system tend to overlook critical problems with it because, unconsciously, they are not so much interested in the truth as they are in the renewed sense of a bond, even though this is not a genuine bond with other individuals, but only a vicarious bond with the movement and its official doctrines.

Desmet suggests that often the followers of the movement will cling to the doctrine the more fiercely, the more absurd it becomes (an observation that will evoke a spontaneous gasp of recognition from those of us who lived through the often comical behavior of the gullible herd, including such droll spectacles as a person driving around alone in his car, wearing a mask). Repetition of the required beliefs serves as a ritual of self-sacrifice. The obvious absurdity of the beliefs may add to the sense of commitment and bonding with the abstract collective.

Desmet proposes that about 30 percent of the population actually believe in the doctrinal system. Another 60 to 65 percent are not inwardly convinced, but decide not to say anything critical, saving themselves the inconvenience of going against what has become the publicly approved and official story. Only 5 to 10 percent seriously question the official story, and this small minority are suppressed, canceled, persecuted, and vilified in numerous ways. (These numbers have varied somewhat on different occasions.) Their reputations are besmirched by concerted campaigns and their livelihoods are threatened. If they are working scientists, they suddenly lose all research funding. Although they include some of the most distinguished experts, even these individuals find themselves treated, and presented to the public, as though they were no more than unqualified cranks.

The final stage is for these critics and their supporters to become the chief enemies of the system, the only things that stand in the way of a perfectly marvelous outcome. At this point, the critics must be literally exterminated, as began to occur in the USSR in 1930 and the Third Reich in 1935.

Here Desmet strikes an optimistic note. The final stage of extermination, he says, will only occur if the critics abandon their public opposition. As long as the critics keep on speaking out publicly, the final stage will be prevented. But if the critics stop their public protests, as happened in the USSR in 1930 and Germany in 1935, the final stage, the holocaust, will ensue.

Finally, Desmet claims that the underlying reason for the initial conditions leading to mass formation is the prevalence of what he calls a mechanistic, rationalist, and technocratic worldview, which sees the universe as fully understandable by the methods of science and logic, whereas what we need, according to Desmet, is a less rational, more intuitive (he doesn't use the word "mystical" but it springs to mind) approach of "resonance" with nature.

Although I'm going to explain why I believe Desmet's theory is untenable, this is not to deny that Desmet's presentations are filled with accurate and provocative insights. Discussing the complementary roles of leaders and mass followers, for instance, he says that totalitarianism results from what Arendt calls a "diabolical pact" between the leaders and the mass. Desmet observes that while the leaders generally don't believe in all the specific narratives by which the reigning doctrine is transmitted to the masses, they generally do passionately believe in the basic core of the official ideology.

Some Problems with Desmet's Theory

Two names frequently figure in Desmet's account of his theory: Gustave Le Bon and Hannah Arendt. Le Bon's 1895 work, *The Psychology of Crowds* (most English editions title it *The Crowd*) has been continually in print in many languages for over a century. The book influenced Freud, Lenin, Hitler, Vilfredo Pareto, Émile Durkheim, and many others. Le Bon concealed his indebtedness to earlier writers such as Gabriel Tarde, in what amounts to plagiarism. The best general account of the idea of mass formation in this early stage is still the indispensable book by Jaap van Ginneken.

Le Bon's work has been frequently criticized and has sparked numerous reactions from many different points of view. Desmet occasionally makes remarks showing his awareness of these post-Le Bon currents of thought, but perhaps wisely in the context of the Covid controversies, he decided to keep it simple, and just present what he took from Le Bon, supplemented by Arendt, as his essential message.

Le Bon was a member of the scholarly bourgeois elite, suspicious of the new democracy, and he always saw any ideological movements stirring among the common people as dangerous. He was alarmed that the masses were prone to irrationality and not controlled by elite persons like himself and his friends. Later discussion of these problems converged on the view that the elites should take the initiative in creating the belief systems which can be used to lead the masses by the nose into approving whatever the elite decides is rational.

We should be aware that social psychologists and sociologists now definitely reject some of Le Bon's ideas. For example, the theory that in crowds individuals lose their identity and become mere parts of the crowd is now understood, on the basis of much detailed study of the actual behavior of crowds, to be mistaken. We should also be aware that the phenomenon of "mass hysteria" has been given a number of explanations quite different to that of Le Bon and Desmet. For example, William Sargant's popular book of 1957, *Battle for the Mind*, offers a Pavlovian explanation in terms of a purely physiological response to stress. Sargant's book was as popular in the Sixties as Desmet's is today. (Sargant is more concerned with the persuasion of individuals and small groups—in the 1950s there was much fascination with the "brainwashing" of prisoners of war—but the analysis is equally applicable to the broader public.)

I will follow Desmet in eschewing intellectual history for its own sake (but see my bibliography for a few pointers), and will not consider alternative theories, except my own rough preliminary approach outlined above. I will simply point out some difficulties that arise with respect to Desmet's theory as he has presented it.

Some of Desmet's bold assertions cry out for an empirical test, and I suspect that any such empirical test would falsify them. Take, for instance, Desmet's claim that lack of social bonds is one of the key predictors of mass formation. This suggests that if we could measure the magnitude of social bonds, we would find a correlation between low social bonds and susceptibility to mass formation. I assume that carefully crafted question-naires could provide a metric of people's available social bonds.

This work has not been done, as far as I know, but we should heed the results of the research into happiness or "subjective well-being." Tra-ditionally, most intellectuals, under the influence of the *fin de siècle* anti-progress ideology, have held that the masses are unhappy, that people in pre-industrial cultures are happier than people in industrialized cultures, and that money can't buy you happiness. Actual research into subjective well-being clearly indicates that the great majority of people in indus-trialized cultures are happy, that people in industrialized cultures are hap-pier than people in pre-industrial cultures, and that happiness is robustly correlated with income, so money can indeed buy you happiness. (After Covid, it would be useful to repeat some of this research. We might ex-pect that the lockdowns would reduce happiness, but Desmet's theory would presumably predict diminished happiness before the lockdowns, and an increase in happiness once lockdowns had begun.)

Subjective well-being is not the same as social bonds, but I predict that if we do the research, we'll find that people's preferred amount of so-cial bonds is correlated with their subjective wellbeing. And here we must remember that there can be too much in the way of social bonds; millions of people living in villages throughout the third world are tearing their hair out, living for the day when they can escape to the sweet anonymity of city life, with its blessed emancipation from oppressive social bonds ("If you've never been to Kumasi, you've never been to Heaven").

As for bullshit jobs, I think the typical medieval peasant would regard his work as nothing but bullshit (on occasion, literally), though he might be less vocal about it than workers today, because he was not suffering from the "first world" malady of unbounded dissatisfaction created by immense affluence combined with immense ignorance.

Desmet's picture of the individual suffering from a lack of social bonds and then finding a substitute for these in bonds with the collective has the weakness of all psychoanalytic-style explanations: it attributes to people motivations of which they are unaware and which cannot be independently corroborated, confirms the worldview of the *fin de siècle* intellectual, and ignores a far simpler explanation: in this case, that most people, from an early age, probably for mainly genetic reasons, are unconcerned about objective truth outside a narrow range of everyday practical living. Outside that narrow range, they simply desire to assent to the cultural approved propositions, which they are able to detect by listening to what "everyone" endowed with authority is telling them.

In other words, people's readiness to swallow the absurdities of the official Covid narrative was not necessarily due to a weird and exceptional state of mind caused by something mysterious, but could be simply the normal state of mind of most people. The unusual feature is not that the masses revere manifest stupidities as beyond doubt—this is the case in all times and places—but that the precise specifics of the stupidities are rapidly changing (and, not having been winnowed by the passage of time, are even more defiantly stupid).

Desmet accepts that the phenomenon of mass formation is as old as humankind, and he instances the witch hunts, the Crusades, and the French revolution, reaching a climax with Communism and National Socialism. He considers that the frequency of mass formation has increased in recent centuries because of the meaninglessness of life, caused in turn by the increase in the rationalist, technocratic view of life. To test this, we would have to see whether, for example, people's lives in Massachusetts were felt to be less meaningful during the Salem witch trials (1692–93) than before or after that period. This could be done, of course, but I doubt that even Desmet would be confident of a positive finding. Purely on common-sense grounds plus a basic knowledge of the historical circumstances, we would be likely to say that seventeenth-century

Massachusetts was a culture with an intense sensitivity to the spiritual (Cotton Mather's "invisible world"), and a resistance to rationalism or skepticism—the exact reverse of what Desmet's theory would predict.

Looking at the broad sweep of history, we don't see much of a correlation of mass formation with rationalism. The pre-Christian Greeks were comparatively rationalistic, and don't give many actual examples of mass formation. The descent from Alexandrian Hellenism into the gloomy darkness of Christendom seems to have favored the rise of mass formations. Naturally, these are broad-brush evaluations and a closer look might upset them. I merely point out that Desmet's claim that excessive rationalism leads to more mass formations has not really been investigated closely, and it is one of several dubious and uncorroborated historical claims which Desmet's theory commits him to.

There is a much simpler explanation of the fact that episodes of mass formation have become more common in recent historical times: the fact that the means of communication have become so much more rapid and inclusive of almost the entire population. As recently as the seventeenth century, most Europeans did not even have access to newspapers.

Another problem with Desmet's theory about the rationalist, mechanistic, technocratic outlook being the stimulus for mass formation is that, by almost any standard you can think of, the cultural norm today is immensely less rationalistic, mechanistic, or technocratic than it was a century ago, while Desmet sees it as reaching new heights, accounting for episodes like the Covid Crimes. When you read Desmet's account of rationalism, mechanism, and technocracy, you immediately think of a certain kind of "scientific" ideology which prevailed until about 1900, but then began to decline. Partly because of the impact of relativity and quantum mechanics, that ideology has largely disappeared. Scientists today are far more modest about what they can achieve—even while their actual achievements are impressive. In popular culture, the "occult underground" has become the "occult establishment," and woo-hoo New Ageism enjoys considerable sway. Whatever else may explain the gibbering lunacy of the official Covid lockdowns and "vaccines," it can hardly be a recent excessive growth of rationalism or mechanistic thinking.

As to Desmet's statements about "free-floating anxiety," I take the view that there is no such thing. While it's true that people will go to therapy reporting general anxiety with no distinct object, Rational Emotive Behavior Therapy (REBT) predicts that when the therapist questions the client about her "free-floating anxiety," it's possible to pinpoint the specific source of the anxiety, which is never free-floating. (Often a key question is, "What were you thinking about immediately before your most recent attack of anxiety?") Desmet does not produce evidence that the presentation of free-floating anxiety has become more common.

Desmet claims that in both Stalin's Russia and Hitler's Germany critics stopped speaking out, in Russia in 1930, in Germany in 1935, and this caused the ruling ideology to move into the phase of physically destroying its critics and others seen as enemies. Therefore, we should always continue to "speak out" against government crimes, because this is necessary to prevent mass murder. But surely a more likely (and less optimistic) interpretation is that in both countries, people stopped speaking out because it was becoming increasingly costly to do so. If the likely penalty for speaking out becomes internment in a camp or even immediate execution, this may be something of a disincentive, and after a short while, those who persist in speaking out just won't be around any more.[*]

Bibliography

Arendt, Hannah. 1973 [1951]. *The Origins of Totalitarianism*. Harcourt, Brace.

Astrup, Arne, et. al. 2020. Saturated Fats and Health: A Reassessment and Proposal for Food-Based Recommendations. *Journal of the American College of Cardiology* (August).

Bernays, Edward. 2005 [1928]. *Propaganda*. Ig.

Billington, James H. 1980. *Fire in the Minds of Men: Origins of the Revolutionary Faith*. Basic Books.

* Thanks to Sandra Woien for criticisms of an early draft of this chapter.
  I do not attempt to quantify the estimated number of deaths resulting from the Covid Crimes, because these numbers are continually being revised upward by new findings. In a few years, no doubt, someone will publish a definitive study giving a good estimate. Meanwhile, there are some basically sound treatments of the essential points, like Saxon, Viglione, and Thorp 2023.

Bartley, William Warren, III. 1990. *Unfathomed Knowledge, Unmeasured Wealth: On Universities and the Wealth of Nations.* Open Court.

Benatar, David. 2006. *Better Never to Have Been: The Harm of Coming into Existence.* Oxford University Press.

Berenson, Alex. 2021. *Pandemia: How Coronavirus Hysteria Took Over Our Government, Rights, and Lives.* Regnery.

Canetti, Elias. 1984 [1960]. *Crowds and Power.* Farrar, Straus, and Giroux.

Chakhotin, Sergei. 1971 [1939]. *The Rape of the Masses: The Psychology of Totalitarian Political Propaganda.* Haskell House.

Courtois, Stéphane, et al. 1999. *The Black Book of Communism: Crimes, Terror, Repression.* Harvard University Press.

Desmet, Mattias. 2022. *The Psychology of Totalitarianism.* Chelsea Green.

Diener, Ed, and Eunkook M. Suh, eds. 2000. *Culture and Subjective Well-Being.* MIT Press.

Easterbrook, Don J. 2019. *The Solar Magnetic Cause of Climate Changes and Origin of the Ice Ages.* Independent.

Edelstein, Michael R., and David Ramsay Steele. 2019 [1997]. *Three Minute Therapy: Change Your Thinking, Change Your Life.* Lulu.

Ellis, Albert, and Debbie Joffe Ellis. 2019. *Rational Emotive Behavior Therapy.* Second edition. American Psychological Association.

Epstein, Alex. 2022. *Fossil Future: Why Global Human Flourishing Requires More Oil, Coal, and Natural Gas—Not Less.* Penguin.

Ginneken, Jaap van. 1992. *Crowds, Psychology, and Politics, 1871–1889.* Cambridge University Press.

Gøtzsche, Peter C. 2017 [2013]. *Deadly Medicines and Organized Crime: How Big Pharma Has Corrupted Healthcare.* CRC Press.

Hayek, F.A. 1944. *The Road to Serfdom.* Routledge.

Hsiang, Solomon, Robert Kopp, Amir Jina, James Rising, et al. 2017. Estimating Economic Damage from Climate Change in the United States. *Science* (June 30th) <https://science.sciencemag.org/content/356/6345/1362.full>.

Joravsky, David. 1970. *The Lysenko Affair*. University of Chicago Press.

Kealey, Terence. 1996. *The Economic Laws of Scientific Research*. Macmillan.

Kendrick, Malcolm. 2021. *The Clot Thickens: The Enduring Mystery of Heart Disease*. Columbus.

Kennedy, Robert F., Jr. 2021. *The Real Anthony Fauci: Bill Gates, Big Pharma, and the Global War on Democracy and Public Health*. Skyhorse.

Knight, Les. 2020. Experience: I Campaign for the Extinction of the Human Race. *The Guardian* (January 10th).

Koonin, Steven E. 2021. *Unsettled: What Climate Science Tells Us, What It Doesn't, and Why It Matters*. BenBella.

Kory, Pierre. 2023. *The War on Ivermectin: The Medicine that Saved Millions and Could Have Ended the Pandemic*. Skyhorse.

Kucharski, Adam. 2020. *The Rules of Contagion: Why Things Spread—and Why They Stop*. Basic Books.

Le Bon, Gustave. 2002 [1895] *The Crowd: A Study of the Popular Mind*. Dover.

Lindzen, Richard S. 2012. Climate Science: Is It Currently Designed to Answer Questions? *Euresis Journal* 2 (Winter).

Lippmann, Walter. 2012 [1922]. *Public Opinion*. Martino.

Malhotra, Aseem. 2022. Curing the Pandemic of Misinformation on COVID-19 mRNA Vaccines through Real Evidence-Based Medicine. *Journal of Insulin Deficiency*.

Malone, Robert W. 2022. *Lies My Gov't Told Me: And the Better Future Coming*. Skyhorse.

McPhail, Clark. 1991. *The Myth of the Madding Crowd*. Aldine de Gruyter.

Medvedev, Zhores A. 1969. *The Rise and Fall of T. D. Lysenko*. Columbia University Press.

Mises, Ludwig von. 1969 [1944]. *Omnipotent Government: The Rise of the Total State and Total War*. Arlington House.

Noakes, Tim, and Marika Sboros. 2019 [2017]. *Real Food on Trial: How the Diet Dictators Tried to Destroy a Top Scientist*. Columbus.

Noakes, Tim, et al., eds. 2023. *Ketogenic: The Science of Therapeutic Carbohydrate Restriction in Human Health*. Academic Press.

Nye, R.A. 1975. *The Origins of Crowd Psychology: Gustave Le Bon and the Crisis of Mass Democracy in the Third Republic*. Sage.

O'Toole, Zoey, and Mary Holland, eds. Authorship anonymous. *Turtles All the Way Down: Vaccine Science and Myth*. The Turtles Team.

Palmer, Michael, Sucharit Bhakdi, et al. 2023. *mRNA Vaccine Toxicity*. Doctors for Covid Ethics <https://d4ce.org/mRNA-vaccine-toxicity>.

Peters, E. Kirsten. 2012. *The Whole Story of Climate: What Science Reveals about the Nature of Endless Change*. Prometheus.

Rand, Ayn. 1996 [1938]. *Anthem*. Signet.

Rushworth, Sebastian. 2021. *Covid: Why Most of What You Know Is Wrong*. Karneval.

Sargant, William. 1959 [1957]. *Battle for the Mind: A Physiology of Conversion and Brainwashing*. Pan.

Saxon, Sally, Deborah Viglione, and James A. Thorp. 2023. *The Covid-19 Fallacies and Beyond: What the Medical Industrial Complex Is Not Telling Us*. Invitation to Destiny.

Shellenberger, Michael. 2020. *Apocalypse Never: Why Environmental Alarmism Hurts Us All*. HarperCollins.

Smith, George H. 2013. *The System of Liberty: Themes in the History of Classical Liberalism*. Cambridge University Press.

Soyfer, Valery N. 1994. *Lysenko and the Tragedy of Soviet Science*. Rutgers University Press.

Steele, David Ramsay. 2017. *Orwell Your Orwell: A Worldview on the Slab*. St. Augustine's Press.

———. 2019. *The Mystery of Fascism: David Ramsay Steele's Greatest Hits*. St. Augustine's Press.

Taubes, Gary. 1993. *Bad Science: The Short Life and Weird Times of Cold Fusion*. Random House.

———. 2007. *Good Calories, Bad Calories: Fats, Carbs, and the Controversial Science of Diet and Health*. Knopf.

Teicholz, Nina. 2015 [2014]. *The Big Fat Surprise: Why Butter, Meat, and Cheese Belong in a Healthy Diet*. Simon and Schuster.

———. 2023. A Short History of Saturated Fat: The Making and Unmaking of a Scientific Consensus. *Current Opinion in Endocrinology, Diabetes, and Obesity* 30:1 (February).

Trotter, Wilfred. 1919 [1916]. *Instincts of the Herd in Peace and War*. Fisher Unwin.

Webb, James. 1974 [1971]. *The Occult Underground*. Open Court.

Widener, Alice. 1979. *Gustave Le Bon: The Man and His Works*. Liberty.

14
THE MOST EVIL MAN IN HISTORY

There are notable parallels between the Ayn Rand movement, launched in the 1960s, and the Jordan Peterson movement, commencing fifty years later.

Both movements were intellectual revolts against prevailing orthodoxies. Both movements came to be viewed as right-wing. Both movements appealed chiefly to "young men," though the Petersonian recruits were a bit older than their Randian counterparts of half a century before. Both movements were headed by their prophets, Rand and Peterson, who betrayed considerable ignorance of some of the subjects on which they confidently laid down the law.

Both movements had a noticeable cult-like quality, Rand's much more than Peterson's because Rand encouraged the cultish aspects and Peterson didn't. Both movements were vitally connected with two extraordinary best-selling books by the prophet—in Rand's case, the novels *The Fountainhead* (1943) and *Atlas Shrugged* (1957), in Peterson's case, the self-help manuals *12 Rules for Life: An Antidote to Disorder* (2018) and *Beyond Order: 12 More Rules for Life* (2021).

There's another similarity between the recruits to the two movements. Both sets of recruits became adherents of a doctrinal system which required specific views on highly intellectual topics, yet both sets of recruits typically had no previous acquaintance with these topics. For example, the young man who joined Rand's "Objectivist" movement would accept that Dostoevsky and Hugo were the greatest writers of fiction while Kafka and Joyce were despicable trash, but such a young man typically had no prior knowledge of, or interest in, any of these four writers, and only adopted the Objectivist line on them (and in some cases started to read them) because he had joined the movement. The Peterson recruit swallowed the view that Nietzsche and Jung were profound thinkers with essential insights into how to give our lives meaning and purpose, and typically this was the first time such a person had taken particular note of either thinker.

Most recruits to both systems of belief were not converted from a different set of opinions on the relevant topics, but from no opinions at all. If holding a decided opinion on such matters makes you an intellectual, then recruitment to the movement made intellectuals out of non-intellectuals. Because the recruits were amateurs drawn into a non-establishment movement, they had a most excellent disdain for established ways of thinking, which sometimes made up for the gaps in their knowledge. But not always.

The Rand movement and the Peterson movement are very different as regards the content of their beliefs. Their views on ethics, epistemology, metaphysics, and esthetics are dissimilar, and their views on economic policy and practical living are alike only in that they both reject equalitarianism and socialism, and both put an emphasis on self-development. Rand was a proponent of laissez-faire capitalism, Peterson certainly not. In fact, if we could move Peterson with all his opinions back in time to the 1960s, he would be in the center of the political spectrum, perhaps slightly to the left, not especially right-wing.

And yet, the Rand movement has impacted the Peterson movement in one specific area. Rand held that Immanuel Kant, the most influential of modern philosophers, was "the most evil man in mankind's history" ("Brief Summary"). If you know anything about the history of philosophy, this may strike you as a rather idiosyncratic take, but it went along with many other curious doctrines of the Rand movement: that a photograph cannot be a work of art, that smoking cigarettes is a noble practice, even a sacrament, that Bach and Beethoven were bad composers because of their "malevolent sense of life," while Tchaikovsky and Rachmaninov were the greatest of all musical creators, that to be anti-abortion is seriously immoral, and yet that women are unsuited to high political office. This is the kind of assortment you get when you accord scriptural status to the strong opinions of a talented popular writer who is a bit of a muddlehead.

One of Rand's latter-day disciples, Stephen R.C. Hicks, published a book in 2004, *Explaining Postmodernism*, recycling Rand's view of Kant as the prince of evil, responsible for the horrors of twentieth-century totalitarianism. Hicks updates and expands Rand's doctrine by applying it to postmodernism, which Hicks depicts as the culmination of Kantianism.

It appears that Hicks's book appealed strongly to Jordan Peterson, who has long had it in for the postmodernists. Peterson warmly recommended Hicks's book and occasionally made pronouncements on philosophy that seem to be indebted to Hicks. Sales of Hicks's book, which had been devolving into obscurity, marvelously revived, and the book is now selling very well, mainly because of the Peterson imprimatur.

In this odd way, the Rand movement has helped to determine the doctrinal content of the Peterson movement half a century later. Peterson and his followers now share with Rand and her followers certain unconventional judgments about the history of philosophy, an area with which both Rand and Peterson were not well acquainted. Hicks, on the other hand, has taught philosophy for a living, is comparatively knowledgeable about philosophy's history, and yet preaches the Randist interpretation of Kant—the familiar pattern of the disciple who is more erudite than the prophet, yet manages to remain a slavish exponent of the ill-informed prophet's message.

I'm going to look at the claim made by Miss Rand, devoutly reproduced by her followers like Dr. Hicks, and perhaps endorsed by Dr. Peterson, that Immanuel Kant is in some way responsible for the Gulag and the Holocaust.

Why would anybody think such a thing? Rand's explanation is nowhere given a systematic or even a coherent exposition. But we can put together, from numerous scattered remarks, a broad outline.[1] According to Rand, Kant teaches that we cannot gain knowledge of reality. Once people have been convinced of this, Rand thinks they will be inclined to favor collectivism rather than individualism. That seems to be a key step in Rand's argument.

1   Perhaps the simplest way to pick up the thread of Rand's narrative is to go through Peikoff's *The Ominous Parallels* and look up each Index entry for "Kant" in succession. Peikoff's book was written under Rand's years-long continual close scrutiny and may be considered canonical Rand.

Most of the time Rand refers to Kant in the *Critique*, but occasionally she mentions Kant's ethical theory. Rand is an egoist, a believer in selfishness as the correct foundation of morality. She maintains that Kant's ethical theory is based on self-sacrifice, the opposite of selfishness and therefore the epitome of moral badness. We can understand why Rand might think that someone who believed in self-sacrifice as a moral principle would favor collectivism rather than individualism. Yet, as we'll see, it's demonstrably untrue that Kant advocated self-sacrifice as a moral principle.

I will criticize the Rand-Hicks narrative in two ways. First I'm going to show that Kant did not hold the views Rand and Hicks attribute to him. Kant did not believe that we can have no knowledge of reality and he did not preach a morality of self-sacrifice. This argument may not be conclusive, since influential thinkers are often misunderstood and Kant may have had an influence he didn't intend. So I will also argue that the heritage of Kant's ideas doesn't account for the rise of collectivist or anti-individualist ideologies. The facts of intellectual history can't be reconciled with the Rand-Hicks narrative.

In the course of this demonstration, I also hope to convey a little of the excitement and fascination of the brilliant Enlightenment and libertarian thinker, Immanuel Kant.

Two Facile Misrepresentations

Before I get down to the real meat of this, I want to clear away a couple of superficial misconceptions, both of them commonly encountered and both of them warmed over and served up by Stephen Hicks.

Kant's greatest work is his *Critique of Pure Reason*, published in 1781. If you know nothing except the title, you might conclude that Kant is in some way against reason, and Hicks does indeed tumble into this very elementary blunder (*Explaining Postmodernism*, pp. 28, 47, et ad nauseum).

Now, if you've read a bit of Kant, you instantly perceive that there's something wrong here. Kant's writing is just packed with continual recognition of the indispensability and immense importance of reason. So why did Kant have a bone to pick with "pure reason"?

Kant was a critic of rationalism, the philosophical approach of René Descartes, Benedict Spinoza, and Gottfried Leibniz, which attempts to derive a whole theory of the universe, a complete system of metaphysics, by reasoning from a few supposedly self-evident truths.

When Kant uses the phrase "pure reason," or as he sometimes calls it, "speculative reason," he means reason detached from "experience," and by "experience" he means the evidence of our senses, including especially observation of the physical world. Kant argues for the use of reason in the scientific manner, as practiced by Galileo and Newton, and not in the "pure" sense, as practiced by Descartes, Spinoza, and Leibniz. It's a simple blunder to take Kant's criticisms of "pure reason" and try to suggest that this phrase shows that Kant is in any way against reason. Yet Hicks repeatedly claims that Kant is against reason, without qualification. This alone demonstrates that Hicks has yet to begin any serious reading of Kant.

The other superficial misunderstanding is Hicks's use of a quotation from Kant which is often cited out of context.

> Thus I had to deny knowledge in order to make room for faith. (Kant 1998, p. 117)

The dead give-away here is that little word "thus" (German *also*; in some translations, "therefore"). You'd think Hicks might be curious as to what this word points back to in the preceding sentence. When we look, we find that denying knowledge means depriving "speculative reason" of its "pretension to extravagant insights." The pretended extravagant insights arise because pure reason deals with entities unrelated to any possible experience.

So it's not *all* knowledge which Kant is denying but a narrowly defined subset of alleged knowledge. Within this subset, Kant claims to have gotten rid of knowledge by demonstrating it to be out of the question, while allowing the possibility of belief. Kant takes the position that belief in a spiritual world, or any other kind of physically undetectable world, is allowable, but unprovable by reference to observation, and therefore not supportable by natural science. And so, in his terminology, it doesn't qualify as "knowledge."

Torn out of context, the quotation can be misrepresented to imply that Kant means that he denies *all* knowledge, and therefore that Kant thinks that knowledge is impossible! This makes Kant say the opposite of what he really means. If you read Kant, you can't ignore the fact—you just keep bumping into it—that he firmly holds that our possession of genuine knowledge of objective reality is a demonstrable and indisputable fact. Kant is a firm believer in the existence of a hugely important body of real knowledge of the world, or as philosophers like to say, of "the external world" meaning the universe out there, as opposed to the representation of that universe inside our minds. Most conspicuously, he holds that Newtonian physics is knowledge of physical reality external to us, and is just as certainly true as the two times table.

Hicks also says that Kant's chief motive for writing the *Critique* is to defend religion (Hicks, p. 29). Kant was not an orthodox Christian, but rather a rational Deist (see his argument with Hamann in the *Correspondence*) who looked forward to the eventual demise of organized religion. His clear goals were to refute rationalism while avoiding empiricism and skepticism, by providing a good logical framework for accepting the existence of a world of physical objects explorable by science.

While there's no doubt that Kant was a sincere believer in a deity, and meant this quoted statement to apply to religious faith (in other contexts the word *Glaube* can equally well refer to ordinary, everyday "belief"), we should recall that in the eighteenth century, writers had to watch their step when asserting anything about religion. It was not safe to publicly say anything contrary to the official interpretation of Christianity (in Prussia this was Protestantism, with some tension between Lutheranism and Calvinism). In the *Critique*, Kant provides convincing refutations of the standard proofs of the existence of God (pp. 563–589), seriously risking accusations of atheism, which could have meant personal ruin. In 1794 Kant was given a warning by the King (Friedrich Wilhelm II), because of the offensive nature of his writings on religion. To avoid possible serious consequences, Kant had to promise not to write any more about religion (a promise he viewed as voided when this king died three years later).

Kant's Revolutionary Philosophy

Kant reacted against two schools of philosophy influential in his day: rationalism and empiricism. Rationalists took the view that, since our senses are notoriously fallible, a philosophical theory of the nature of reality could best be worked out from a few self-evident principles, by pure reason. Empiricists, by contrast, maintained that the ultimate source of evidence for any claim to knowledge must lie in what's given to us by our senses. What we perceive, especially what we see, must be the foundation of any science.

Kant was educated in the rationalist approach, as propounded by a now largely forgotten philosopher named Christian Wolff (who put the fragmentary and controversial thoughts of Leibniz into a presentable textbook form). Kant's early philosophical works are within the rationalist framework of Wolff. Kant was also fully up to speed with natural science, and but for slight accidents of his career might easily have become a physicist or a mathematician. Kant was one of the earliest to see that the nebulas, those faint, tiny, misty-looking patches in the night sky, are galaxies, like our own Milky Way, each made up of billions of stars, and Kant himself was the very first to propose the theory of the origin of galaxies now accepted by astrophysicists.

In his mid-forties, Kant was suddenly convinced, upon reading David Hume, that there was something seriously wrong with rationalism. Kant later said that Hume woke him up from his "dogmatic slumber." Kant also couldn't accept empiricism. Nor could he accept Hume's skepticism. And so he formulated a new kind of philosophy, his "critical" philosophy. He worked on this for several years, and then presented his conclusions in the *Critique of Pure Reason*, published when he was aged fifty-seven. He went on to write several more outstanding works of philosophy, but the breakthrough was the *Critique of Pure Reason*. Two of these later works also have the title *Critique*, so the *Critique of Pure Reason* is often referred to as "the first *Critique*." I will refer to it here as just "the *Critique*." Ayn Rand and her followers barely allude to any of Kant's many other writings.

When the *Critique* came out, many people familiar with recent philosophical writing would have known what its title meant: Kant was challenging the rationalist view that a system of metaphysics could be worked out by logical deduction alone from a few self-evident truths. Kant insists that knowledge has to be based on "experience," meaning observation of the world using our senses. What Kant finds lacking in rationalism is that it tries to construct a philosophical system cut loose from any possible experience, that is, from empirical observations and empirically testable theory. At the same time, Kant could not accept empiricism, because he held that a person could not arrive at knowledge of the world by relying on nothing but sensations or logical inferences from sensations.

The rationalist approach was what Kant called "pure reason." He often also called it "dogmatism," and the *Critique* could easily have been titled *Critique of Dogmatism*. It could not have been called *Critique of Rationalism*, because that terminology had not yet become settled, but in retrospect that would now be accurate (*Critique of the Rationalist Method* would be even closer to what Kant was driving at). When Kant writes of "pure reason," he means the approach to metaphysics characteristic of the rationalism of Descartes, Spinoza, Leibniz, and Wolff, and whenever he criticizes "pure reason," he's criticizing the distinctive approach of rationalism, never reason itself.

Kant was also among the earliest to employ the word "critique" (in German, *Kritik*). This word has come into common English usage fairly recently, and is now often used to mean a wholly negative criticism, even a debunking. This is not the meaning Kant gave to the term. A critique is an examination of a system of thought in order to show its inadequacies and then reconstitute that system as a different and better system of thought. So, even as regards "pure reason," reason detached from experience, Kant does not entirely dismiss it. He wants to rethink it, curtail it, and give it a limited role within a system of thought that will be chiefly governed by empirical observation.

Tabula Rasa

Ayn Rand makes two claims, both echoed by Hicks: 1) Kant says that reality is unknowable, and 2) The belief that reality is unknowable, and therefore the writings of Kant, automatically lead (though only after several generations) to all the horrors of totalitarian collectivism. I contend that both of these claims are false.

The interpretation of Kant as holding that reality is unknowable, or that what we take for reality is illusory, is an elementary misunderstanding of Kant, but it's nothing new; it's a misunderstanding that plagued Kant from the first publication of the *Critique*. It caused Kant to make a revised edition of the *Critique*, which appeared in 1787. It also provoked him to write the *Prolegomena*, published in 1785, explaining his metaphysical system more simply and briefly, and asserting even more forcefully something that he had always maintained quite unequivocally, that his system fully acknowledges the existence of a world of physical objects, which exist independently of us, and about which we acquire knowledge through our senses.

Kant believed he had accomplished an intellectual revolution with *Critique of Pure Reason*. It certainly presents a new way of looking at the world, which, if correct, puts metaphysics and epistemology on a new basis. Is it correct? In my opinion it's partly correct and partly incorrect.

Kant's first, crucial step is to claim that when we use our senses to perceive the physical world, we're not mere recipients of impressions, as the empiricists believed that we were, and as, later, Rand apparently believed that we were. Here's Ayn Rand:

> At birth, a child's mind is tabula rasa; he has the potential of awareness—the mechanism of a human consciousness—but no content. Speaking metaphorically, he has a camera with an extremely sensitive, unexposed film (his conscious mind), and an extremely complex computer waiting to be programmed (his subconscious). Both are blank. He knows nothing of the external world. He faces an immense chaos which he must learn to perceive by means of the complex mechanism which he must learn to operate. (*Return of the Primitive*, p. 54)

This looks like a slightly confused restatement of the empiricism of Locke and Hume. Confronted with this Rand quotation, Kant would ask, in a heartbeat (as soon as we had explained to him the meaning of "camera," "computer," and "program"), *How can a conscious and a subconscious, both blank, turn sensations into perceptions? How can an extremely complex computer lack an operating system, which would influence what it can look for and how what it finds can be interpreted? Why assume the mind starts by knowing nothing? (Everything we have learned about child development tells us that the mind starts with a lot of built-in knowledge.) Oh, and by the way, why do you assume there exists a person, a decision maker, independent of that person's conscious and subconscious minds?*

This statement by Rand (and a similar strong endorsement of tabula rasa in "The Objectivist Ethics," p. 30) may appear to contradict the opening sentence of her *Introduction to Objectivist Epistemology*, where she says that "consciousness" is not passive but "an active process" (p. 5). She seems to have supposed that it's possible to actively seek without any presuppositional structure to one's seeking. She thinks you can have an empty mind and still seek. I say that if there is a structure to your seeking, then the most evil man in history was right, at least on this one crucial point. If there is no structure to your seeking, then "seeking" is indistinguishable from passive reception. (It may be pointed out that Kant also occasionally made statements emphasizing passive receptivity. Kant wanted to make clear that the mind's contribution to perception, while crucial, is effortless and automatic.)

Kant rejects empiricism because he rejects the theory of the blank slate. Kant says that there's more to perception than sensation; there's more to vision than photography. As Günter Wächtershäuser says (though he's making a somewhat different point), there's more to vision than meets the eye. Kant asserts that humans are, from the get-go, armed with an innate, ready-made interpretation which they impose upon sensory impressions as they receive them. The newborn baby doesn't have an open mind. According to Alison Gopnick and her associates, researchers into child development, "Babies are born with powerful programs already booted up and ready to run" (*The Scientist in the Crib*, p. 142).

For instance, we're programmed to interpret our visual impressions in the context of three-dimensional space. We do not first experience sense impressions and then deduce from them a conceptual model of three-dimensional space (as Locke, Hume, and—at least in the above quotation—Rand would have it). We're equipped with that conceptual model (or with the propensity to easily develop that model) before we receive the impressions, and the impressions immediately activate the model. We're pre-programmed (by our genes, though Kant knew nothing of genes) to see the world in three dimensions.

To put Kant's insight in very un-Kantian language, our perceptions embody theories about the world; they are theory-laden, and if they weren't theory-laden, we couldn't perceive anything. We could have sensations, the way a limpet has sensations, but we couldn't perceive things without an "intuition," a sort of defining notion of what those things are. It takes a theory to see a tree. It takes a theory to see your mother's face.

Philosophers before Kant had argued for "innate ideas," going back to Plato with his theory of the "forms," but Kant clarifies and transforms the discussion. The ideas are not literally innate in the sense that a human holds these ideas before birth. Rather, the human's brain is programmed so that, when activated by experience, a certain mode of understanding occurs automatically.

Plato thought that humans were born with knowledge of the "forms." Plato was responding to the fact that reality as we experience it is messy and disorderly, while our theories about it, even the informal theories we reflexively employ in infancy to make sense of it, are comparatively tidy and elegant—some such thought occurs to everyone who learns geometry. Plato really was onto something, but he concluded that the forms (basic models of the world) are the true reality, and what we perceive with our senses is a sadly imperfect copy of the true reality. Kant reverses this: what we perceive with our senses is the true reality and the "forms" arise from innate theoretical preconceptions which, spontaneously and automatically, we impose upon reality in order to comprehend it.

My view is that this first step in Kant's thinking, his reason for rejecting empiricism, is correct and vitally important. We do not learn about the world by absorbing unprocessed sensory data and then making inferences from those data. As we absorb the data, we instantly process it—we could not truly absorb it without processing it—and *what we subjectively experience is only the already processed data.* Before we begin to observe things, we "know" a vast amount about the world, in the sense that this knowledge was already pre-programmed in us when we were embryos. (Kant's insight isn't denied if we assume that this genetic pre-programming kicks in at successive stages of development.)

Reading the above you might think that Kant is advancing an argument about human psychology. Kant firmly denied that he was doing empirical psychology—in the eighteenth century, empirical psychology means psychology by introspection. Yet, as Popper argued in 1930–1933, Kant is not rigorous in distinguishing between an introspective conviction and a logical necessity, and so he classifies some of the former along with the latter (Popper 2009, pp. 97–107). Kant sometimes thinks he's doing metaphysics when he's actually doing psychology—this is putting it anachronistically, because in Kant's time psychology had not yet become a subject separate from philosophy. Taken as psychology, Kant's insight has been abundantly corroborated by modern research. Tabula rasa (the blank slate) is an erroneous way of understanding human learning: in light of the findings of psychology, linguistics, and neuroscience, tabula rasa is untenable (Gopnik et al., *The Scientist in the Crib*; more broadly, Pinker, *The Blank Slate*).

Waiting for Darwin

The next big step in Kant's argument is, I believe, an error, though an error that would have been difficult for him to have avoided given the inherited assumptions of eighteenth-century thought. Kant moved from the accurate and wonderful insight that our acquisition of knowledge involves imposing "what we already know" upon nature to the mistaken conclusion that "what we already know" has to be true, and not just true, but necessarily true.

For instance, the three-dimensional model of space which we impose upon the world is assumed by Kant to be true, and guaranteed to be true. Hence, he supposes that Euclidean geometry must be true. Euclidean geometry is part of the Newtonian theory of space, which is also, Kant supposes, necessarily true.

Once having set foot on this path, Kant becomes preoccupied with bolstering his position by finding numerous examples of "synthetic a priori" propositions, statements which are self-evidently true and yet not true by definition. A favorite in the eighteenth century was "Every event has a cause." Since there is no contradiction in asserting that some event happened without any cause, the statement cannot be analytic (true by definition). But Kant wants to say it is still necessarily true. What could that mean, except for the claim that what I find impossible to imagine to be false must be true? That would be an inadequate standard, if only because physics sometimes upsets our prejudices about the imaginable.

The contrary view is that a statement can only be necessarily true when its denial would imply a contradiction—when it is "analytic." Kant's preoccupation with necessarily true yet non-analytic statements is an error which led him astray. This is my view; it's called "logicism"; it's not universally accepted; there are some people prepared to claim, for example, that mathematics cannot be reduced to logic, and therefore mathematical truths are not analytic. However, even those who take this position would now agree that most of the statements which Kant took to be necessarily true are actually open to question, and indeed, some of them (like Euclid's axioms) have been found to be false.[2]

Be that as it may, we can take the view that as infants we're programmed to experience the world in terms of inbuilt expectations, which Kant calls "forms of intuition" and "categories," and also, contrary to Kant, accept the possibility that we can, as the years go by, come to criticize and modify those inbuilt expectations, or at least, their formal elaboration. We're capable of intellectually rejecting principles which in infancy we were irresistibly impelled to accept as beyond question, including things which were indispensable to our learning enough so that we could be in a position to intellectually reject them later. We now believe that Euclidean geometry, while true in the sense that the theorems follow from the axioms, is not an accurate model of reality; the axioms don't fit the world. Real cosmic space is not Euclidean. Because of the

2   Rand rejects the analytic-synthetic distinction, and maintains that all truths are necessary truths (*Introduction to Objectivist Epistemology*, pp. 108–09). Evidently she doesn't see any logical difference between "This house is red" and "This house is a house." I won't pursue issues like this because I'm not here primarily concerned to evaluate the merit of Rand's philosophical positions, or of Kant's, but more modestly to show that the Rand-Hicks interpretation of what Kant wrote is seriously inaccurate.

curvature of spacetime, the shortest distance between two points is not a straight line, though that's often a good approximation for short distances.

Kant summed up his metaphysics in the pithy epigram, "Thoughts without content are empty. Intuitions without concepts are blind" (pp. 193–94). This is stated, with slight variations in wording, about half a dozen times in the *Critique*. "Thoughts without content" refers to the inadequacy of rationalism, or over-reliance on "pure reason," while "intuitions without concepts" refers to the inadequacy of empiricism, mistakenly taking our sensations to give us our concepts of physical objects.

"Thoughts without content" are thoughts which don't refer to empirical observations (even hypothetical ones). Kant uses the word translated as "intuition" as a technical term to refer to what happens when we perceive something. (The German word, *Anschauung*, most normally means "view.") The instant we see an object, we grasp the kind of thing we take it to be. We don't, for example, experience ourselves as sensing a patch of color with a shape and calculate from this that we're seeing a solid object; we have the immediate experience of seeing a solid object, an experience which we can, upon subsequent contemplation, correctly analyze as the result of our reflexively processing a patch of color with a shape.

Things in Themselves

The position I have here attributed to Kant is mostly commonplace and not seriously controversial among people who have read Kant (though of course you can quibble about nuances of my precise phrasing), but I will now move to a topic where there are controversial interpretations of Kant, some of them closer to Hicks's interpretation than to mine. This is the issue of "things in themselves."

Kant draws a distinction between "appearances," objects as we become aware of them through our experience and "things in themselves" and says that we can "know" nothing about things in themselves (though we can speculate about them and talk meaningfully about them). Many readers of Kant have taken this to mean that "things in themselves" are things as they really are, the objectively real things, rather than "appearances," which are imperfect copies of the objectively real things. We might then conclude, as many have and as Hicks does, that Kant is claiming that we can know nothing about ultimate reality but only about how it appears to us.

The conclusion doesn't follow, because maybe the appearances and the things in themselves are both real, and so we would be able to know about one kind of reality but not about another kind. After all, an imperfect copy may still tell you something about the original. As far as it goes, that's correct. However, I accept a different interpretation of Kant on this point. According to this interpretation, "things in themselves" is a way of referring to those possible attributes of things which cannot even hypothetically be known by observation. So, the thing in itself is not the thing as it really is. The appearance represents the thing as it really is and gives us a lot of information about the thing as it really is. The thing in itself is a highly technical and abstract construction which only people doing metaphysics have any reason to think about: it is whatever is true of the object that we have no way of getting to know about by any conceivable observation or scientific theorizing.

Kant holds that the "appearance" and the "thing in itself" are *the same object*, thought about in two different ways. Among Kant scholars this is known as the "one object, two aspects" interpretation of Kant and I think it's clearly correct.[3] "Thing in itself" is short for "thing considered as it is in itself" (*Ding an sich selbst betrachtet*), independently of our experience of it. So even if, in some sense, Kant supposed that the thing in itself is more "real" than the thing we observe (which I deny), it would remain true that we may know a great deal about the object we sometimes think of as a thing in itself.

Theological Intermezzo

It seems unlikely that Kant would never have thought, in this connection, about the doctrine of the Real Presence, an article of faith to both

---

3   I make no pretension to being a Kant scholar. I'm just doing a quick Cleanup on Aisle Five of the libertarian movement. But for what it's worth, my impression is that the one object, two aspects view has been gaining ground, in part because of the work of Gerold Prauss.

Catholics and Lutherans (the major point on which Luther differed from the other Reformers such as Calvin). This is the claim that at some point (in the Catholic view, when the bread and wine are consecrated by a priest) the bread and wine become the body and blood of Christ.

According to Catholics and Lutherans, the bread and wine really do become the body and blood of Christ. This is not to be taken figuratively, but with absolute literalness. If you say it's a metaphor, as the heretic Calvin does, Catholics may, in all love and compassion, decide to burn you at the stake. At the same time, Catholic teaching insists, there is no way, by any physical test, to detect a difference between the bread and the wine before and after consecration. You can't find any hemoglobin in consecrated wine and you can easily become inebriated on it (Don't ask me how I know). Or as the Church puts it, "the appearances remain the same," the appearances meaning all physical and chemical properties. So it would also be a heresy to say that the bread and wine are physically transmuted, though the Church probably wouldn't come after you for that. We might think of the body and blood of Christ as the things in themselves, unavailable to perception, while the bread and the wine would correspond with Kant's "appearances."

Today, by contrast, we tend to assume that when we know everything about the appearances of an object, including instrumental measurements, and including any theories needed to account for the appearances, we know everything we can possibly know about any object, *and that is precisely Kant's view*. This metaphysical viewpoint, which has become part of our common sense, was not yet taken for granted in the eighteenth century.

What are we to make of the claim that bread and wine have become human flesh and blood, while this is undetectable by any empirical investigation? We might be tempted to say: "There's nothing beyond the appearances and what can be inferred from the appearances." The Catholic or Lutheran theologian might respond: "How can you possibly know that? Why couldn't there be something to these objects that we can't detect by those methods?"

We might be baffled, but Immanuel Kant would have a quick comeback. "Yes, you're right that there could be that undetectable something, but since it would be undetectable, there's no way you could *know* about it." And the theologian might happily reply: "In the scientific sense that's quite true, but we can *believe* in things we don't scientifically *know*. That's why we have faith." No doubt Kant was thinking more about Leibniz's monads than about Christ's flesh.[4]

To most people today, it seems puzzling that the Catholic Church could ever have entertained the doctrine of transubstantiation, in which the essential nature of things can be changed without any alteration in their observable properties, and that we can know this. How were they unable to see that this is almost tantamount to nonsense? We instinctively tend to suppose that everything we can know about a material object must be derived from observation, including scientific theories tested by observation, and this is Kant's view. A full answer to this puzzle would have to go back to Aristotle's argument, taken over by Aquinas, that sensory observations inform us only of "accidents," counterposed to "substance," a view which could be taken to imply that our senses can tell us nothing definite about "substance."

Subjective and Objective

Now suppose that everything I've said about Kant's position is wrong. Let's give Kant the most "subjectivist" theory imaginable. Let's suppose for a moment that "things in themselves" means the way things really are, and we are condemned to complete ignorance of those things. Let's assume that all we can know are "appearances," and appearances are molded by mentally determined "forms of intuition." Then what?

We'd still be left with Kant's clear and consistent statements, that these appearances are caused by objects which exist independently of us,

---

4   I was first put on the track of my present understanding of Kant when I read Popper's claim (in effect) that Kant was a realist (Popper 1968b, p. 179). (Throughout this lecture, I use the term "realism" to refer to realism with respect to mind-independent physical entities in the external world.) Later I read Campbell's article "Evolutionary Epistemology," which among other accomplishments lays out the history of the view that Kant's synthetic a priori is a theory of psychology which can be elucidated by Darwinian adaptation. Especially impressive is the remarkable essay on Kant by the biologist Konrad Lorenz.

outside of us, and that all perceived aspects of those objects, other than what Kant calls the "forms of intuition" and the "categories," represent something in those objects, not just in our minds. So, the fact that we can't help but experience the Sun and the Moon as located in space and time is one thing. That the Sun is hotter and bigger than the Moon, that the light of the Moon is the reflected light of the Sun, these are, in Kant's system, objectively true factual statements, discoveries we have made about real objects in the external world, ascertainable facts which exist independently of our minds. Therefore it would still be misleading to claim without qualification, as Hicks and others do, that Kant holds that we cannot "know reality." It's fair to say that Kant holds that we cannot acquire *perfectly complete* knowledge of reality, there are limits to what we can possibly know, but I assume no one's going to dispute that.

I suppose that a minimal formulation which would be good enough for most readers of Kant is that our ideas about the world outside us are an amalgam of information we get through our senses and ordering or structuring principles which are imposed upon that information by our innate mental capacities. That loose formulation has varying possible de-tailed elaborations, which I won't go into here.

Philosophers have debated whether the color of an object is in the object or in the human perceptual apparatus (currently the predominant view is that it is the former), but those who take the latter view would accept that color does tell us something about the object; at the very least it's a fact about the object that some property causes us to experience a specific color sensation. We surely wouldn't say that someone who took this view was saying that eyesight can tell us nothing about reality. The argument I have just stated, by the way, is taken directly from Kant, in the "Prolegomena" (p. 84), where he uses this point about color explicitly to rebut the accusation that he doubts the existence of physical objects external to human perception.

The charge of denying any knowledge of mind-independent reality can more credibly be laid against Johann Fichte, who influenced the much more famous Georg Hegel. Kant died too early to be aware of Hegel, but he knew Fichte and vigorously denounced Fichte on precisely this point. In an example of Hicks's motivated selectivity, he cites Kant's early friendliness towards the young Fichte (pp. 112–13), but omits to mention Kant's later bitter hostility to Fichte's idealism. Kant took the extraordinary step of issuing "A Public Declaration concerning Fichte" (*Correspondence*, pp. 559–561) vigorously dissociating himself from Fichte's idealist system.

If we're considering Kant's *influence*, rather than the soundness of his philosophy, we should also be aware that some philosophers have taken the following view: Kant believed in an objectively real world external to our minds, and believed we know a lot about it, but Kant's arguments for this position ("the objective deduction") just don't work very well. Therefore, although Kant was not an idealist but a realist, the influence of his theory might have been, contrary to his intention, to encourage support for idealism.

Hicks quotes Bertrand Russell (with a detectable tone of disapproval) as saying that we can't "prove that there is an external world" (p. 72). He doesn't mention that Rand agreed with Russell on this point (*Introduction*, p. 55). Rand says we have to accept "existence," including the existence of the external world, as an unprovable "axiom." Kant, by contrast, believed he could prove the existence of the external world, and he made an ambitious attempt to do so. His attempt in the first edition was more or less completely scrapped and replaced for the second edition. If there had been a third edition, it might have been scrapped and replaced again. Here I agree with both Russell and Rand, though I think we can do better than an "axiom."

The key point, to my mind, is that there are meaningful metaphysical positions which cannot be proved or disproved, either logically or empirically. Contrary to Kant, the existence or non-existence of the external world are equally unprovable. These alternatives have to be evaluated by arguments which do not possess the character of proofs (Popper, *Realism*, pp. 80–102, 131–158).

Does Kant Deny Knowledge of Reality?

Hicks repeats umpteen times that Kant denies all knowledge of reality (pp. 28, 34, 52, 57, 78, et ad nauseum). To buttress this conclusion he rips quotations out of context and mangles their meaning. Let's watch the way Hicks pulls off these unworthy tricks.

Hicks presents a summary of what he takes to be "Kant's Essential Argument," in a section with that title (pp. 32–36). Hicks first quotes a passage where Kant argues that there are two ways in which a connection can hold between a person's mental representation of an object and the object. Either the object makes the representation possible or the representation makes the object possible. At this point, Kant says that the representation makes the object possible. Hicks concludes that Kant is thereby abandoning objectivity for subjectivity.

Hicks has made an error here, but this is only the enabling step for a more serious error to follow. The initial error is to claim, or at least to leave his readers with the impression, that according to Kant the representation completely determines the perception of the object. But in this passage, Kant is specifically talking about the a priori aspects of the object. This seven-page section in the *Critique* is headed "On the Deduction of the Pure Concepts of the Understanding" (pp. 219–226). Kant holds that the pure concepts of the understanding, the a priori rules which are not derived from experience but are logically prior to experience, are imposed on objects by the subject (the perceiver), while the sensory qualities of the perceived object, such as redness or brightness or heaviness, are given to the subject by the object perceived.

Kant's view is that when we perceive an object, we get information through our senses, and this information is ordered or structured in a certain way by our mind, by our understanding. In this section he is focusing only on that ordering or structuring. He acknowledges that all the purely sensory information (color, smell, feel, weight, sound, temperature, dimension, impenetrability, and so on) comes from the object, not from our mind ("Prolegomena," p. 84).

Kant is asking where the a priori aspects of the representation come from, aspects such as substance and location in space, aspects which Kant quite correctly says cannot be strictly deduced from sensations alone. Kant is arguing that these aspects do not come from the object itself but from the representation, in other words they are contributed by the "subject," whereas all other aspects of the object do indeed come from the object itself. On the next page Kant explains how the empiricists Locke and Hume went wrong by assuming that everything they found in experience is given by pure sensation.

Kant sees space and time, not as physical entities in the world, but as a kind of mental filing system which we require in order to make sense of the physical world. As an alternative metaphor, Kant may be read as holding that perception, like language, requires a grammar to make sense of it. Humans used language for many thousands of years before they noticed that their language was organized by an elaborate system of grammatical rules. Kant sees space, time, and the "categories" as like grammatical rules which we impose upon the objects we perceive. The objects and their perceptible properties are really there, in the external world outside our minds, not so the rules.

As Kant points out here, the very fact that we're aware that the object exists is not due to the a priori aspects but to the other, purely sensual, aspects. Our representation of the object does not cause it to come into existence! It exists independently of us, with all its perceptible qualities, before we perceive it (Kant, p. 224).

Now to Hicks's more serious error. Here is what Hicks writes:

> The objects that science explores exist "only in our brain," so we can never come to know the world outside it. (Hicks, p. 35)

Oh dear, what a disaster. Poor Hicks. Here he has jumped to a completely different place in the *Critique*, in order to pull out the rather alarming phrase, "only in our brain."[5] Well now, that sounds pretty damning, right? The birds and the bees, the Moon and the stars, have no existence except inside my skull!

However, Kant is here talking s*pecifically about objects which he holds that natural science cannot explore*, "transcendental objects" which cannot be perceived—exactly the opposite of the way Hicks characterizes Kant's argument. A little earlier, Kant contrasts these with the objects of natural science, "objects that are given to us independently of our concepts, to which, therefore, the key lies not in us and in our pure thinking, but outside us" (Kant 1998, p. 505).

So, Kant's actual position is, quite clearly and unambiguously, that real physical objects do not exist only in our brains but in external reality,

---

5   Literally, *bloss in eurem Gehirne* (Kant 2020, p. 134), "simply in your brain."

independent of our brains, while transcendental objects, products of pure reason, exist only in our brains. That's why they can become a problem for metaphysics, in Kant's view. If I say "Horses exist outside your brain, and can be studied by natural science, whereas unicorns exist only in your brain, and can't be studied by natural science," the Hicks type of misunderstanding presumably won't arise. This isn't difficult; you just have to pay attention.

The above is concerned with Section IV of Kant's Antinomy. The Antinomy is a section fairly late in the *Critique*, consisting of four "antinomies." What Kant is trying to do here is to show that, if we confine ourselves to pure reason, without any constraint from the evidence of our senses or from tested scientific theory, we are able to prove both one conclusion and its opposite. For instance, we can, Kant claims, prove both that the universe has always existed and that it had a beginning in time, both that space is infinite and that space is bounded, and so on. Kant calls these contradictions "antinomies of pure reason," meaning contradictions resulting from the rationalist, non-empirical approach. Kant's view is that reason works well when it's constrained by empirical reality. Kant does not for a moment accept that reason, when it deals with empirical matters of fact, can ever lead to contradictions. But when reason is applied to entities of which we have no experience, such as all of time, all of space, or the entire universe, absurdities can easily result.

Hicks interprets Kant's antinomies as trying to show that *reason itself* leads to contradictions (p. 47). This is a grotesque and risible blunder, severe attention deficit on Hicks's part. He repeats it numerous times, though it is an elementary error. My surmise is that Hicks believed what Rand told him about Kant and eagerly glanced over Kant looking for phrases which could be snatched and twisted to confirm what Rand had told him. He should bear in mind the trick of evangelical preachers: if you want to use a biblical verse as a text, be sure to read the verse before it and the verse after, just in case.

The next and final step in Hicks's summary of "Kant's Essential Argument" relies on a quotation in which Kant says that "everything intuited in space and time, and therefore all objects of experience possible to us, are nothing but appearances, that is mere representations, which in the manner in which they are represented, as extended beings or as series of alterations, have no independent existence outside our thoughts" (Hicks, p. 35; Kant, p. 511). This is Kant's familiar position, that we impose our intuitions of space and time onto the world we perceive. The things outside us have no independent existence outside our thoughts *in the manner in which they are represented*, the clear implication being that they do exist outside our thoughts *apart from the manner in which they are represented*.

Kant immediately goes on to talk about how his position might be misinterpreted. Here, as so often, Kant points out that it would be a misunderstanding to interpret what he is saying the way Hicks will interpret it 250 years later:

> One would do us an injustice if one tried to ascribe to us that long-decried empirical idealism that, while assuming the proper reality of space, denies the existence of extended beings in it, or at least finds this existence doubtful, and so in this respect admits no satisfactorily provable distinction between dreams and truth. (Kant, p. 511)

Kant's position is that we perceive things in the world using both our senses and our understanding. The objects we perceive are real objects which exist outside us and independently of us, and we get to find out about them using our senses and the methods of science. In order to perceive them, we automatically structure our perception of the world using the formal principles of space and time. Space and time are not objects in the world; they are ordering principles or techniques we require to make any sense of our impressions and thus be aware of objects in the world. Kant, as we have seen, claims to be able to prove that the objects we perceive do exist in the world independently of our minds.

At this point you might wonder why people misinterpret Kant in just this way. Is this suspicious? Even Kant's attempts to explain that this is not his view might be taken as evidence that he knows he will be misinterpreted like this, and "there's no smoke without fire." The explanation is that Kant's theory was utterly new in the history of philosophy, and in some ways quite subtle, therefore many people found it baffling. The middle-aged Kant was like the young Hume, in that almost no one around at the time had the IQ or the patience to follow his arguments properly. Consequently, people in the eighteenth century were liable to pigeonhole Kant as something already known to them, a follower of George Berkeley, whose theory was familiar and notorious. Berkeley was believed to have held that solid objects are completely illusory. Some Berkeley scholars energetically dispute that this was Berkeley's position, but it was then and is now most commonly assumed that this was his position, and Kant shared this supposition. Kant consistently protests that he is no Berkeleyan and that objects in the external world are real, not in the least bit illusory.[6]

The "Diaphanous" Argument

Again following Rand (*Introduction*, p. 80), Hicks attributes to Kant a very strange argument which Kant in fact never deployed. It goes like this: the human sensory apparatus has a specific nature, an identity of its own; this specific nature must (according to Rand's view of the way Kant argues) be a barrier between the world and the human observer. Contrast this with a situation where there is nothing between the world and the perceiver, then perception would be direct and "diaphanous," nothing would get in the way. Therefore, since our senses in fact do have a structure (a specific nature or identity), we cannot know about the world (Hicks, pp. 36–38).

This argument was never advanced by Kant (nor, I'm guessing, by anyone in the modern period; it's much easier to attribute the silliest arguments to people you don't like than to pay attention to what they say). From Kant's point of view, this argument would be absurd, for he appears to hold that the way our sensory apparatus is constructed (not in minor matters like whether we use vision or echolocation, but in the relations

6 "Prolegomena," p. 84. "Berkeley" is pronounced "Barklee." Those damned Brits. Despite this, the city of Berkeley, California, was named after him. As well as being a bishop in the Church of Ireland and a visitor to the American colonies, Berkeley wrote poetry, and after his death one of his lines became famous as the motto of Manifest Destiny: "Westward the course of empire takes its way." It was therefore natural to give Berkeley's name to a town in the far West, mispronouncing it in the process.

between sensations, perceptions, and concepts) is the only way the sensory apparatus of a rational creature could be constructed, and that precisely because it's constructed that way, it can give us accurate information about external reality.

The card-carrying Objectivist the late George V. Walsh went to the trouble of paying attention to what Kant says, and, in *The Journal of Ayn Rand Studies*, no less, Walsh analyzes relevant statements by Kant and concludes, with respect to this "diaphanous" argument, that "Kant never said this, and, in fact, no evidence has ever been presented that he did" (Walsh, p. 91). I may have missed it, but I'm not aware of any attempt, by Hicks (who personally knew Walsh; they both taught at Rockford College) or any other Randist, to refute Walsh's exegesis of Kant on this point. The diaphanous argument was just made up by Rand (or made up by someone she relied on) and uncritically copied by her devout disciple Hicks.

In claiming that Kant denies knowledge of reality, Hicks is not alone. Several passably bright philosophers who have read Kant have concluded that his arguments imply (whether or not Kant embraced this conclusion himself) that we can have no knowledge of reality. As far as I know, all the writers who reached this conclusion based it to a major extent on their misreading of "things in themselves." Obviously, I think they're mistaken. However, there's another angle to this.

Most philosophers are not at all disposed to accept that we can know nothing of reality, and so if they believe that Kant's theory leads to that conclusion, they infer that Kant must be wrong on that point. As examples, see the works of H.A. Prichard and P.F. Strawson. Such philosophers usually say that there is some value in parts of Kant's analysis, but sadly, major parts have to be rejected because they lead to the conclusion that we can't know reality. This is what philosophers call a *reductio*: proving that a theory must be wrong by showing that an absurdity logically follows from it. Since this is preponderantly the philosophers' response, then, even if Kant did deny any knowledge of reality, *this would not support the contention that Kant has persuaded philosophers to believe that we can know nothing of reality*, which looks to be essential for Rand's claim that Kant is the most evil man in history.

Kant is quite explicit that the reason, or at least the main reason, we can never come to know things in themselves is that all perception is relational. The impossibility does not arise because our senses have a specific nature, but because all perception, whatever its nature, necessarily involves a relation between the perceptual apparatus, including the mind, and the object perceived. So what we learn about objects can never be what is purely intrinsic to them.

As against this, it might be possible to take metaphorical cross-bearings, and so we might eliminate, or at least reduce, the relational aspect and arrive at some arbitrarily closer approximation to the intrinsic. The room left for a thing in itself can thus be narrowed. Popper gives the example of our natural tendency to interpret some features of color (such as the fact that there cannot be a reddish shade of green) to be a priori truths about the world around us. We are not, however, trapped in this outlook; we have quite easily been able to determine that this apparent property of color is nothing but a feature of the way that the physiology of human color sense is set up. It tells us absolutely nothing about color as a quality of objects in the real world. A similar point applies to well-known optical illusions (*Realism*, pp. 153–54).

At the same time we have to admit that we have no guarantee that these cross-bearings will correct our knowledge of reality *perfectly*; there may be some aspects that slip through the cracks, perhaps even some aspects that must always slip through the cracks. It would be colossal presumption to deny that human knowledge has impassable limits (though we don't know exactly where those limits are, and that is itself one component of those limits).

From Metaphysics to Politics

Kant did not hold the philosophical views attributed to him by Ayn Rand and Stephen Hicks. But supposing that he did, how could the influence of Kant's ideas have given rise to the horrors of modern collectivism, the Gulag and the Holocaust? There are two aspects to this question.

First, why would the ideas attributed to Kant make people who accepted those ideas become collectivists rather than classical liberals, or conservatives, or hermits (advocates of complete withdrawal from social life)? Why would someone who thought he couldn't know reality turn to economic or political collectivism? I have never seen this explained by Rand or any Rand disciple, though it's crucial to the Rand narrative. Certainly Hicks makes no attempt to explain it. This is a gaping hole in the story.

Second, is it true, as a matter of historical fact, that people who accepted Kant's ideas had a tendency to become political collectivists? Can we show historical examples of any such causation?

Kant was a classical liberal. His broad views on political matters were similar to those of Rand, Hicks, and me. Rand didn't call herself a classical liberal or a libertarian, but her strictly political and economic views (not her philosophical views) are the same as those of classical liberals like Herbert Spencer, Ludwig von Mises, or Milton Friedman. Rand added nothing to the political or economic theory of classical liberalism, which she appropriated in its entirety from earlier writers.

Hicks insinuates that Kant wasn't a classical liberal (p. 107), but his arguments on this point are just as unfounded as his interpretations of the *Critique*. Still, Objectivists usually do acknowledge that there is some individualism in Kant, and Peikoff comments that people may hold philosophical views without noticing their political implications (*Ominous Parallels*, p. 33). So Kant couldn't see the political implications of his metaphysical ideas, and neither can I, but others who came after Kant did see them, though neither Rand nor Hicks has disclosed how we get from the metaphysics to the politics.

Instead of explaining what the intellectual process is that leads someone who accepts that we can't know reality to conclude that he has to embrace collectivism, Hicks does something quite different. In effect, he makes a list of evil ideological positions (disagreeing with Rand) and a list of righteous ideological positions (agreeing with Rand) and then works hard to associate these with various individuals in history. This is the procedure of a KGB dossier, cooking up a case that one putatively evil person has "links" with another axiomatically evil person.

Look at the way Hicks treats Kant in relation to Jean-Jacques Rousseau. Kant was an admirer of Rousseau's writing and was influenced in his ethics and political theory by Rousseau. I guess Rousseau, who died before the *Critique* came out, never heard of Kant. Hicks spends several pages describing the baleful influence of Rousseau on Kant, on the French revolution, and on subsequent events.

You see the problem? Hicks wants us to believe that Rousseau and Kant were thoroughly bad guys who exerted a thoroughly bad influence. Now, if Rousseau had bad political ideas which influenced Kant's political ideas, this fits with the notion that these were two very, very bad guys who together had a very, very bad influence. But it does nothing to support what should be the narrative. Rather it, shall we say, disconfirms that narrative. For, according to Hicks, Rousseau independently developed some terribly bad and influential political ideas without ever becoming convinced by Kant that we can't know reality. Oops.

What Hicks has to show (if he wants to defend Rand's claims about Kant) is that bad political ideas derive from collectivism, which derives from denial of knowledge of reality. What he purports to show instead, in this passage, is that Rousseau came up with some bad and influential political ideas without any help from Kant. It follows that *totalitarian political ideas didn't need and don't need Kant's metaphysics*, thus undermining Rand's key contention.

Whereby Everyone Can Be Free

There's also the point that to make this whole Rousseau-Kant thing sound even remotely credible, we have to believe that Rousseau is a "socialist"—as the very subtitle of Hicks's book tells us. Surely this is a little less than strictly accurate. Rousseau was a proponent of natural rights, private property, and democracy.

It's true that his theory of the General Will has been argued by some to be a kind of presaging of "totalitarian democracy." Yet the totalitarian democracy thesis does not really help Rand's argument, inasmuch as it gives a rival account of the rise of totalitarian thinking which dispenses with the denial of knowledge of reality. An alternative, non-totalitarian interpretation of Rousseau's General Will is that it means the rule of law, the law being discovered and formulated by a government embodying popular sovereignty (Cranston, pp. 27–43).

Hicks tries to present Kant as a nasty authoritarian by quoting Kant's ominous-sounding statement that "Man . . . requires a master who will break his self-will and force him to obey a universally valid will" (Hicks, p. 108). But, hold on a sec, the resourceful Professor Hicks has sneakily omitted Kant's next five words, "whereby everyone can be free" (Kant 1983, p. 33).

Kant's argument here is that, since humans are fallible, and prone to unjustly transgress upon each other's freedom, there has to be a government. (This is surely quite commonplace—I do recall that a minor American popular novelist of Russian origin said the same thing.) The best form of government, says Kant, is one which, by enforcing justice, provides for the individual members of society the greatest possible freedom. The outstanding problem is that the persons empowered to compel everyone to obey the law and thus preserve everyone's freedom, may themselves be inclined to act unjustly and thus limit people's freedom.

Since it may be hazardous to your teaching career in the Kingdom of Prussia to advocate a republic, Kant speaks of a single office-holder but adds in passing that the "guarantor" of justice might be a single person or "a group of several selected for the role." The person or persons who require their will to be broken, so that everyone can be free, are the persons who hold political office. Kant has no definite solution: he holds that the problem of finding the best political constitution is not perfectly soluble, and we can only hope to approximate it (pp. 33–34). It's in this context, finding a way to constitutionally check political office-holders in order to safeguard individual liberty, that Kant pens his famous, gloomy statement: "from such warped wood as man is made, nothing straight can be fashioned" (p. 34).

You've read my mind. Immanuel Kant was a really good guy. In fact, a great guy, a terrific guy!

Kant's Ethics

Kant has a well-known theory of ethics, and you might expect people like Rand and Hicks to spend a lot of time on it, but actually they spend far more time on Kant's metaphysics and epistemology. Kant's ethics is all about each individual respecting the autonomy of other rational individuals, which is highly congenial to classical liberalism.

When Randists do mention Kant's ethics, the main claim they make about it is demonstrably false. Rand advocates "the virtue of selfishness," rational egoism. Her fundamental ethical rule is the pursuit of self-interest. It's never wrong to pursue your self-interest. In arguing for this unusual position, she assumes that the only alternative to her advocacy of untrammeled self-interest is the ethical rule of always sacrificing your self-interest. Very few people, and certainly no eminent philosophers, have ever taken that view (the only arguable example I can think of is Auguste Comte, not a significant figure in the field of ethics, and even he didn't value self-sacrifice *per se*).

The more prevalent position, common to a very wide range of ethical theories, is that pursuing your self-interest will sometimes be morally right, sometimes wrong, sometimes morally neutral. People who hold to this position will often assume that there's no problem about getting folks to do what's in their self-interest, and will therefore sometimes focus on the more difficult cases where the morally right thing is contrary to self-interest. This doesn't mean they're assuming the standpoint that being contrary to self-interest is what makes something morally right.

Rand attempts to attribute the virtue of self-sacrifice to all those who reject the virtue of selfishness, including Kant. In fact Kant holds, like most philosophers of ethics, that, while ethics sometimes requires sacrifice of self-interest, sacrifice of self-interest is no guarantee of ethical rectitude. And so, part of the twisting the Randists do is to misrepresent Kant as holding that there is ethical merit in self-sacrifice itself.

As has often been spelled out (for example by William Vallicella and by George H. Smith), this was not Kant's view at all. Kant holds that it's right to obey the moral law, respecting the autonomy of others; he does not think there's any special merit in going against your own inclinations, or sacrificing your own interests, for the sake of it. In Kant's words:

> No one can compel me ... to be happy after his fashion: instead, every person may seek happiness in the way that seems best to him, if only he does not violate the freedom of others to strive toward such similar ends as are compatible with everyone's freedom under a possible universal law ... (Kant 1983, p. 72)

Whatever you think of this as ethical theory, applied as a legal principle it becomes pure classical liberalism.

Collectivism Didn't Come from Kant

Did Kant's metaphysics lead to the rise of socialism? There are puzzles here. Why did this process take several decades (four, if we count from the *Critique* to *A New View of Society*, six if we give it till *The Doctrine of Saint-Simon*)? Why were the founders of modern socialism not adherents of Kant's philosophy, but of quite different philosophies? Why do we not find the founding thinkers of socialism expressing any doubts about our ability to acquire knowledge of reality?

One of the most conspicuous objections to the Randist narrative is the example of Marxist-Leninist philosophy. The great totalitarian monster of the twentieth century, directly responsible for ninety million innocent deaths, held strictly to a philosophical position that was completely "objectivist," rejecting all supernaturalism or subjectivism and denouncing Kant as a "bourgeois idealist." Why does the biggest, the worst, and the most influential form of collectivism insist so rigidly on similar metaphysical tenets to those of Rand and Hicks?

As young men, Marx and Engels were Young Hegelians, but then they were abruptly converted to the atheism and materialism of Ludwig Feuerbach and David Friedrich Strauss, rejecting Hegel but, as Marx puts it, "coquetting" with some of Hegel's turns of phrase. Marx soon soured on Feuerbach but he didn't go back to idealism. The Marxist philosophy which eventually culminated in such works as Lenin's *Materialism and Empirio-Criticism* (though it re-introduced elements of Hegelianism) has noticeable similarities to the philosophy of Ayn Rand, and not just in the bad-tempered prose. It's a seductive surmise that Rand, before she left Russia at the age of twenty, might have had conversations with Communists and accepted their atheism and materialism, as well as their cartoonish account of the bourgeois idealist Kant. Pursuing this conjecture thirty years later, in another country, Rand would claim that these views she had picked up from Communism were essential to defend capitalism. (This is just one speculation. I don't know where Rand got her ideas of Kant from, except that it most certainly was not from Kant.)

Contrary instances to Rand's narrative keep cropping up. To mention just one example, Hicks attributes the intellectual defeat of socialism after World War II to the work of Mises, Hayek, and Friedman (p. 87). Mises and Hayek were both out-and-out Kantians or, if you want to stretch a point, neo-Kantians. Friedman and the entire Chicago School rarely made any philosophical pronouncement, but were most like logical empiricists, a philosophical approach which Hicks views as reprehensible because it incorporates the analytic-synthetic dichotomy (pp. 72–77), though we still await an explanation of why this is such a disaster for humankind. Examples like these could be multiplied throughout the history of thought; what we find, when we look at the data, is that Kantians tend to be classical liberals, respectful of individual rights.

There have of course been some socialists who favored Kantian ethics, but these were usually members of the social democratic movement dissatisfied with the prevailing Marxist distaste for ethics, who turned back to the best-known ethical theory in the German-speaking world. Politically, they were usually the more moderate and tolerant wing of social democracy, the wing which evolved to acceptance of capitalism in practice. (That shouldn't be relevant, but I'm trying to answer Hicks in a Hicksian spirit.)

Aside from looking for traces of Kant in the early socialists, another approach is to read the early socialists and see what arguments they actually advance. As we might expect, early socialists don't argue that we need socialism because we can't know reality. In fact, early socialist writers seem pretty confident, not only that knowledge of reality is possible, but also that they have acquired it. Socialists and communists have always claimed that commercial society is both unfair and inefficient, and presented specific arguments for these judgments. I think these arguments are wrong; however, holding a different opinion than mine on some aspects of reality is not the same as denying that knowledge of reality is possible. Perhaps Rand had trouble seeing the distinction.

The Strange Contradiction in Hicks's Story

And now we come to a strange twist in Hicks's story, really a double contradiction.

Hicks explains the origins of postmodernism in the 1960s as follows (Chapters 5 and 6 of *Explaining Postmodernism*). After World War II, liberal Western capitalism was so dramatically successful, and Communism such a catastrophic failure, that reality was telling the Left they should renounce socialism. But they were so attached to socialism that they decided instead to ignore reality, give up reason, and embrace the irrational, hence postmodernism was concocted for their benefit.

Aside from the question of whether anything like this really happened, there are two odd features of this account. According to Rand's thesis, which Hicks gives every appearance of accepting, Kant poisoned the minds of Western thinkers by denying we could know reality, thus leading to collectivism, and thence to the Gulag and the Holocaust. So, before the 1930s, Western thinkers, especially those who became socialists, must have been convinced that reason can't be trusted and we can't know reality. But after all that had happened, from World War II until the 1950s, Hicks's story has all socialists, Communist and non-Communist alike, trusting reason and believing they could know reality. With the economic success of Western capitalism in the 1950s and Khrushchev's 1956 admission of the vast atrocities committed under Stalin, reality was now telling socialists that socialism was a failure. That's why, according to Hicks, postmodernism had to be invented, combining socialism with irrationalism. But then, how did those deniers of the possibility of knowing reality who perpetrated the Gulag and the Holocaust in the 1930s morph into those scientific-minded people, acutely sensitive to objective reality, in the 1950s?

Hicks opens his Chapter 4 by saying that where there is skepticism about reason, followed by subjectivism, and relativism, "we would expect to find that postmodernists represent a roughly random distribution of commitments across the political spectrum" (p. 84). Exactly, but why wouldn't the same question apply to those Kant-influenced people in the period from 1871 to the 1920s, who supposedly ended up with Bolshevism and National Socialism? Why wouldn't they have been equally likely to become classical liberals, conservatives, or hermits?

In fact, Hicks points out, we find that the postmodernists are nearly all leftist and mostly extreme leftist. He goes on to say that "Leftist thought has dominated political thought among twentieth-century intellectuals, particularly among academic intellectuals." But this, he says, leaves a puzzle because socialism had traditionally been defended on "the modernist grounds of reason and science" (p. 85). To Hicks, modernism is a good word, as opposed to postmodernism, a bad word. So then Hicks offers his solution to the puzzle: socialists were able to remain socialists by becoming irrationalists and deniers of reality because postmodernism had come along to bail them out. Postmodernism provided socialists with a way to retain socialism by rejecting reason—Hicks equates rejection of reason with denial of the possibility of knowing reality.

It follows that, nearly two centuries after the *Critique*, and two or three decades after Stalin's purges and Hitler's Holocaust, *socialists, including Communists, remained convinced that we can acquire knowledge of reality*. Apparently without Hicks noticing it, this flatly contradicts Rand's narrative. How could Kant persuade everyone to reject reason, causing the Gulag and the Holocaust, if acceptance of reason were still the characteristic leftist doctrine long after the Gulag and the Holocaust, so that postmodernism had to be engineered to afford the socialists an off-ramp from reality?

A Defeat for Socialism?

There are some large stretches of Hicks's book which are both substantially true and valuable; these are the places where he forgets his Randist crusade against Kant. For example, Chapter 5 is a good and persuasive narrative and I tend to agree with nearly all of it. It deals with the response of Marxism and Western liberalism to historical developments such as the 1930s depression, World War II, and the collapse of the Soviet Union. The word "Kant" does not appear in these thirty-nine pages, and no element of Kant's philosophy is referred to, not once.

I don't see a unique puzzle in the events. It has been a fixed fact since the 1930s that people studying humanities subjects are overwhelmingly leftist. Whatever the explanation for this, it can't have much to do with Kant or with postmodernism. A 1970s student in the humanities might indeed be *reacting randomly to his or her reference group* (rather than to the wider population) by becoming a leftist. Add to that the enormous expansion of the universities, which ineluctably means a steep decline in the average IQ of students and faculty. The whole development can be explained without supposing any special link between metaphysics (or epistemology) and politics. The hypothesis that some leftists were attracted to postmodernism because it enabled them to ignore dangerous criticism is not something I would dismiss out of hand, but we don't seem to need that hypothesis to explain the emergence of postmodernism.

No doubt we have much to learn about the way these currents of thought developed and will develop in the future. However, postmodernist leftists in the 1960s and later did not really preserve the main gist of the socialism of earlier times. The leftism of the postmodern neo-Marxists, when it comes to actual policies, is fuzzier and feebler than old-fashioned leftism, which still survives to some extent alongside postmodern leftism. A leftist from the 1930s might look at today's postmodern neo-Marxists and judge that they have discarded the very essence of what it is to be "left."

Socialism was primarily an economic theory with political implications. As the socialist George Orwell put it in 1941, socialism is a system in which "the State, representing the whole nation, owns everything, and everyone is a state employee" (*Complete Works*, XII, p. 410). Orwell added democracy and approximate income equality to his definition of socialism. It's not clear that today's Wokish postmodern neo-Marxists would accept this definition as embodying the kind of social order they want.

Western capitalist success contrasted with the Communist fiasco may have prompted many leftists to change the subject, from central economic planning to areas like sex and ethnicity. To many of us, this might not seem like much of an improvement but, taking a long view, it may turn out to be all part of the terminal decline of collectivist belief. One of the lessons we ought to have learned from Karl Marx is: don't evaluate an institution, or even an entire culture, by what it says about itself, but by what it actually does.

A momentous reality of our time is that China, ruled by a body calling itself the Communist Party, has made itself rich and successful by becoming thoroughly capitalist. India, Russia, and many other countries are now unequivocally capitalist, and right now there is no serious movement to reverse these outcomes. With a very few wretched exceptions, such as North Korea and Venezuela, all countries in the world are now run by governments which in practice accept the necessity for their economies to be predominantly capitalist. The scale and scope of the global triumph of capitalism is breathtaking and, until fairly recently, unexpected (Sachs, "Twentieth-Century Political Economy").

Traditional leftism survives, though its following has shrunk, and it sharply criticizes postmodern neo-Marxism. Sundry leftists unsmitten by Derrida have shrewdly made the point that academic postmodernism is a convenient career enhancer—a way of sounding terribly radical without thereby incurring any handicap. Traditional Marxists, being scientific materialists, would have to oppose postmodernism; as one example, we get the criticism by Alex Callinicos. Leftists who can't be classified as traditional Marxists and who vigorously attack postmodernism have included Noam Chomsky, David Detmer, Terry Eagleton, and Alan Sokal. Capable people on the Left were debunking postmodernism before most on the Right had noticed its existence.

Postmodernism versus Idealism

There's one point on which Hicks's readers new to philosophy are liable to be confused, and it may help to clear this confusion out of the way. Hicks talks a lot about postmodernism, and in discussing philosophy before postmodernism, he talks a lot about idealism. He claims, falsely in my view, though this is a common opinion, that Kant was the founder of nineteenth-century idealism. And, separately from this, he claims that postmodernism was "the culmination of Kant."

We ought to be clear that *postmodernists are not idealists*. Postmodernism is incompatible with idealism, at least in any form that was important in the history of philosophy.

In the late nineteenth century, "absolute idealism" was a well-established, well-worked-out metaphysical system, which today has almost no adherents. Idealism may be briefly characterized by saying that everything we can talk about is a construction of our minds. In saying this, the idealists most definitely did *not* mean that we can believe anything we like. The mental constructions are assumed to be involuntary and inescapable. Idealists did not suppose that, because, for instance, our idea of the solar system is a mental construction, we could change it at will or pick and choose which theory of the solar system to accept, according to our fancy. Just like realists, idealists held that there is precisely one correct conception of the solar system, it's the job of science to find it, and it's the same for idealists as it is for realists. (For precisely this reason, the logical empiricist Rudolf Carnap concluded—wrongly, in my view—that there's no significant difference between realism and idealism.)

Idealism did not grant license to any individual or group to throw aside scientific evidence. Any notion that the traditional Navajo or Yoruba story of the origin of the world might be a serious alternative to that of modern astrophysics would have been viewed by Hegel, or Royce, or Bradley as just as idiotic as it would have been viewed by Moore, or Quine, or Searle. This kind of extreme-relativistic notion, however, is seriously entertained by postmodernists. But then, as we shall see, contrary to the impression left by Hicks's account, postmodernists are almost never philosophers and philosophers are almost never postmodernists.

Idealism dominated British and American philosophy in the 1890s and was then quite suddenly abandoned. In 1890, all the most outstanding philosophers in the English-speaking world were Hegelians or "Absolute Idealists." By around 1920, none of them were. How did that doctrinal cataclysm come about? Mainly because of the super-genius Bertrand Russell and, to a lesser extent, G.E. Moore. Absolute idealism had been accepted because of specific arguments, the most important being what would later retrospectively be called the argument from "internal relations." Those arguments were faulty and were refuted, a refutation favored by the abandonment of defective Aristotelian logic and its replacement by modern logic.

A consequence of that intellectual revolution, around the year 1903, is that 120 years later, ninety percent of today's anglophone philosophers repudiate all forms of relativism and subjectivism. (I can say this with more confidence because of the survey of the views of thousands of philosophers conducted by Bourget and Chalmers.)

Philosophers Are Not Postmodernists. Postmodernists Are Not Philosophers

Hicks's book is focused on postmodernism. Why? Hicks encourages his reader to suppose that postmodernism is a major force, or at least a more than negligible force, in philosophy. In truth, postmodernism has had very little impact on philosophy. Very few academic philosophers are post-modernists, or have any interest in or sympathy with postmodernism. In fact, not only are the vast majority of philosophers not postmodernists, they are decidedly averse to any form of relativism or subjectivism.

People not normally familiar with philosophy hear that there is a brand of French philosophy which is now very influential in American universities. They naturally conclude that this brand of philosophy be-came dominant in French philosophy and then spread to American phi-losophy and became dominant there. *Nothing even remotely like that has occurred.*

What really happened was that in France in the 1960s a coterie of philosophers began to adhere to a cluster of ideas that later came to be called postmodernism. At the time it was called post-structuralism or deconstruction. Most French philosophers were unaffected by these ideas, but they began to be picked up by American academics in subjects other than philosophy, principally literary studies, *and had almost no im-pact on American philosophy.* (We can see a marvelous satirical response to the impact of these ideas in literary theory in *Postmodern Pooh* by Fred-erick Crews.) Then, these ideas spread into other American humanities disciplines, such as history and sociology, *but not philosophy.*

While this was going on, various leftist writers, such as Judith Butler, Kimberlé Crenshaw, Robin DiAngelo, and Gyatri Spivak, none of them philosophers, were combining postmodernism with neo-Marxism. Post-modern neo-Marxism came to completely dominate the new, rapidly expanding bogus disciplines like Women's Studies, Gender Studies, Africana Studies, Culture Studies, Queer Studies, and the like. The abysmal level of intellectual rigor in these new, fake disciplines is all too familiar. Postmodern neo-Marxism also became an appreciable presence, but not quite so dominant, in more traditional humanities subjects like literature, history, and sociology.

Most academic philosophers were unaffected by this, except that they observed the growth of these ideas in humanities disciplines other than philosophy and, if they had any interest at all, beyond fleeting an-noyance, reacted by deploring this sloppy thinking, and occasionally pub-lishing criticisms of it.

Hicks mentions the late Richard Rorty as a postmodernist and the innocent reader might assume that Rorty must be a representative figure in American philosophy, or at least representative of a major tendency. But Rorty is an outlier, an anomalous figure, often described as American philosophy's "bad boy." Looking back in around 1999, Rorty himself recalled that those American scholars who had taken any interest in what he called "the Hegel-Nietzsche-Heidegger-Derrida sequence" in the early 1980s were all in literature, not philosophy; he makes clear that he was the only exception, or almost the only exception, among philosophers ("Response to Jacques Bouveresse," p. 152). This has remained largely true. Those few American philosophers who paid any sustained attention to Rorty mostly found his key ideas unacceptable.

Postmodernists are very thin on the ground in philosophy departments, whereas they're very thick in literary and "culture" disciplines. In 2006, a little book by Paul Boghossian came out, *Fear of Knowledge*, straightforwardly debunking "relativism and constructivism" (postmodernism) from a very conventional, more or less standard, analytical philosophy standpoint.

Boghossian points out that "anti-objectivist conceptions of truth and rationality" are generally rejected within academic philosophy, and as a result, there has been "a growing alienation of academic philosophy from the rest of the humanities and social sciences, leading to levels of acrimony and tension on American campuses that have prompted the label 'Science Wars'" (p. 8). From Hicks's account, you would never guess that within the universities, philosophy is visibly estranged from other humanities disciplines, precisely because the philosophers just won't go along with anything smacking of postmodernism, whereas the other departments are full of it.

The truth is that contemporary philosophy is overwhelmingly realist and philosophers suffer because of their opposition to the fashionable anti-realism prevalent in other humanities disciplines. Hicks leaves the impression that mainstream academic philosophers must be responsible for the non-realism of these non-philosophers, a story which is ludicrously false. Hicks omits to divulge that in deprecating postmodernism he has more than ninety-five percent of philosophers on his side, giving his more innocent readers the impression that in this respect he is one of a few lone voices crying in the wilderness.

The allegation of Randists like Hicks is that postmodernism derives its anti-realism from Hume and Kant and in general from skepticism about perception. But if you look at the arguments proponents of postmodernism offer for their anti-realism, you find that they appeal to cultural relativism and social constructivism, not to skepticism about perception, and if you look at current mainstream criticisms of postmodernism, you find that they rarely if ever mention skepticism about perception.

The French Connection

Postmodernism is one of a succession of French philosophical tendencies, beginning with existentialism in the 1940s, which came into anglophone, mainly American, literary theory and from there into more popular discussion, bypassing anglophone philosophy. These tendencies had proportionately far more support from American non-philosophers than from American philosophers or even from French philosophers. Most French philosophers, like nearly all anglophone philosophers, were never existentialists and never postmodernists.

The recurring pattern is that a trendy but distinctly minority coterie within French philosophy is transmitted into American literary and "culture" disciplines, gets media attention, is swallowed by media pundits, educational bureaucrats, and other ignoramuses, and is resoundingly rejected by American and British philosophers, who then occasionally offer criticisms of that tendency. (Perhaps even before World War II, Bergsonism might have followed a roughly similar pattern.)

Naturally, Hicks could retort that what professional philosophers think doesn't matter much, and that postmodernist ideas have seeped into the general culture. This is true. But then, his "whirlwind tour" (p. 80) specifically of philosophy would be even more misleading, as well as pointless.

Hicks's book is aimed at readers who haven't read much philosophy, and these are the people who are most likely to be seriously misled by what Hicks tells them. Perhaps the worst kind of misunderstanding arises from Hicks's garlic-crucifix-and-holy-water approach to ideas he apparently perceives as akin to unclean spirits which require to be driven out.

Philosophy is too valuable to be appropriated as the heraldic device of an ideological squadron, right or left, though this sad and deplorable event has occurred several times in history, and will no doubt happen again.*

Bibliography

Allison, Henry E. 2004 [1983]. *Kant's Transcendental Idealism: An Interpretation and Defense.* Yale University Press.

Bird, Graham. 2006. *The Revolutionary Kant: A Commentary on the Critique of Pure Reason.* Open Court.

Boghossian, Paul. 2006. *Fear of Knowledge: Against Relativism and Constructivism.* Oxford University Press.

Bourget, David, and David J. Chalmers. 2014. What Do Philosophers Believe? *Philosophical Studies* 170.

Brandom, Robert B., ed. 2000. *Rorty and His Critics.* Blackwell.

Callinicos, Alex. 1991. *Against Postmodernism: A Marxist Critique.* Polity.

Campbell, Donald T. 1974. Evolutionary Epistemology. In Schilpp 1974. Reprinted in Radnitzky and Bartley 1987.

Chomsky, Noam. 1995. Noam Chomsky on Postmodernism. <http://bactra.org/chomsky-on-postmodernism.html>.

Courtois, Stéphane, et. al. 1999. *The Black Book of Communism: Crimes, Terror, Repression.* Harvard University Press.

Cranston, Maurice. 1968. Introduction. In Rousseau 1968.

Crews, Frederick. 2001. *Postmodern Pooh.* Farrar, Straus, and Giroux.

Detmer, David. 2003. *Challenging Postmodernism: Philosophy and the Politics of Truth.* Prometheus.

---

* I thank David Gordon for valuable criticisms of drafts of this chapter.
   This volume was almost in press when David Gordon drew my attention to the recently published "Symposium: Ayn Rand and the Metaphysics of Kant," including an essay by Stephen Hicks, "Kant at the Masked Ball" (*Reason Papers* 43:1). While this symposium is very much worth reading, nothing in it requires me to retract anything in the above chapter.

Eagleton, Terry. 1996. *The Illusions of Postmodernism*. Blackwell.

Ewing, A.C. 1934. *Idealism: A Critical Survey*. Methuen.

Gopnik, Alison, and Andrew N. Meltzoff. 1997. *Words, Thoughts, and Theories*. MIT Press.

Gopnik, Alison, Andrew N. Meltzoff, and Patricia K. Kuhl. 1999. *The Scientist in the Crib: What Early Learning Tells Us about the Mind*. Morrow.

Gordon, David, and Ying Tang. 2021. What Jordan Peterson Should Have Said about Marxism. In Sandra Woien, ed., *Jordan Peterson: Critical Responses*. Open Universe.

Guyer, Paul. 1987. *Kant and the Claims of Knowledge*. Cambridge University Press.

Hicks, Stephen R.C. 2018 [2004]. *Explaining Postmodernism: Skepticism and Socialism from Rousseau to Foucault*. Ockham's Razor.

Hume, David. 1988 [1738–1740]. *A Treatise of Human Nature: Being an Attempt to Introduce the Experimental Method of Reasoning into Moral Subjects*. Oxford University Press.

Hylton, Peter. 1990. *Russell, Idealism, and the Emergence of Analytic Philosophy*. Oxford University Press.

Iggers, Georg, translator. 1972 [1958]. *The Doctrine of Saint-Simon: An Exposition, First Year 1828–1829*. Beacon.

Johnson, Kent, and Wayne Wright. 2006. Colors as Properties of the Special Sciences. *Erkenntnis* 64.

Kant, Immanuel. 1983. *Perpetual Peace and Other Essays on Politics, History, and Morals*. Hackett.

———. 1998 [1781]. *Critique of Pure Reason*. Cambridge University Press.

———. 1999. *Correspondence*. Cambridge University Press.

———. 1999 [1799]. Public Declaration concerning Fichte's Wissenschaftslehre, August 7, 1799. In Kant, *Correspondence*.

———. 2002. *Theoretical Philosophy after 1781*. Cambridge University Press.

———. 2002 [1785]. Prolegomena to Any Future Metaphysics that Will Be Able to Come Forward as Science. In Kant, *Theoretical Philosophy after 1781.*

———. 2020 [1781]. *Kritik der reinen Vernunft.* Hyperborea Classica.

Langton, Rae. 1998. *Kantian Humility: Our Ignorance of Things in Themselves.* Oxford University Press.

Lenin, V.I. 1927 [1908]. *Materialism and Empirio-Criticism: Critical Comments on a Reactionary Philosophy.* In Lenin, *Collected Works,* Volume 13. International.

Lorenz, Konrad. 1962 [1941]. Kant's Doctrine of the A Priori in the Light of Modern Biology. In L. von Bertalanffy and A Rapoport, eds., *General Systems.* Society for General Systems Research.

Nelson, Quee. 2007. *The Slightest Philosophy.* Dog Ear.

Orwell, George. 2000 [1941]. The Lion and the Unicorn: Socialism and the English Genius. *The Complete Works of George Orwell,* Volume XII. Secker and Warburg.

Owen, Robert. 1991 [1813]. *A New View of Society and Other Writings.* Penguin.

Peikoff, Leonard. 1982. *The Ominous Parallels: The End of Freedom in America.* New American Library.

Peterson, Jordan B. 2018. *12 Rules for Life: An Antidote to Chaos.* Random House Canada.

———. 2021. *Beyond Order: 12 More Rules for Life.* Penguin.

Pinker, Steven. 2003 [2002]. *The Blank Slate: The Modern Denial of Human Nature.* Penguin.

Popper, Karl R. 1968 [1962]. *Conjectures and Refutations: The Growth of Scientific Knowledge.* Harper.

———. 1968 [1954]. Kant's Critique and Cosmology. In Popper, *Conjectures and Refutations.*

———. 1979 [1972]. *Objective Knowledge: An Evolutionary Approach.* Oxford University Press.

———. 1983. *Realism and the Aim of Science.* Rowman and Littlefield.

———. 2009 [1930–33]. *The Two Fundamental Problems of the Theory of Knowledge*. Routledge.

Prauss, Gerold. 1974. *Kant und das Problem der Ding an sich*. Bouvier.

Prichard, H.A. 1909. *Kant's Theory of Knowledge*. Clarendon.

Radnitsky, Gerard, and William Warren Bartley III. 1987. *Evolutionary Epistemology, Rationality, and the Sociology of Knowledge*. Open Court.

Rand, Ayn. 1964 [1962]. *The Virtue of Selfishness: A New Concept of Egoism*. Signet.

———. 1964. The Objectivist Ethics. In Rand, *The Virtue of Selfishness*.

———. 1968 [1943]. *The Fountainhead*. Bobbs-Merrill.

———. 1971. Brief Summary. *The Objectivist* (September).

———. 1984 [1982]. *Philosophy: Who Needs It*. Signet.

———. 1999 [1971]. *Return of the Primitive: The Anti-Industrial Revolution*. Penguin.

———. 1990 [1966–67]. *Introduction to Objectivist Epistemology*. Penguin.

———. 2005 [1957]. *Atlas Shrugged*. Dutton.

Rothbard, Murray N. 1972. The Sociology of the Ayn Rand Cult. <www.lewrockwell.com/1970/01/murray-n-rothbard/understanding-ayn-randianism>.

Rorty, Richard. 2000. Response to Jacques Bouveresse. In Brandom 2000.

Rousseau, Jean-Jacques. 1968 [1762]. *The Social Contract*. Penguin.

Sachs, Jeffrey D. 1999. Twentieth-Century Political Economy: A Brief History of Global Capitalism. *Oxford Review of Economic Policy* 15:4 (December).

Schilpp, Paul A., ed. 1974. *The Philosophy of Karl Popper*. Two volumes. Open Court.

Siegel, Harvey. 2007. Review of Paul Boghossian, *Fear of Knowledge: Against Relativism and Constructivism*. *Notre Dame Philosophical Review*.

Smith, George H. 1991. *Atheism, Ayn Rand, and Other Heresies.* Prometheus.

———. 2013. *The System of Liberty: Themes in the History of Classical Liberalism.* Cambridge University Press.

Smith, George H. 2016. Ayn Rand and the History of Philosophy. First in a series of thirteen articles <www.libertarianism.org/columns/ayn-rand-history-philosophy>.

———. 2016. A Few Kind Words about the Most Evil Man in Mankind's History. Sixth in a series of thirteen articles <www.libertarianism.org/columns/few-kind-words-about-most-evil-man-mankinds-history>.

Sokal, Alan, and Jean Bricmont. 1999. *Intellectual Impostures: Post-Modern Philosophers' Abuse of Science.* Profile.

Steele, David Ramsay. 1987. Alice in Wonderland. *Free Life: Journal of the Libertarian Alliance* 5:1–2. Reprinted in Steele, *The Mystery of Fascism.*

———. 2002. Ayn Rand and the Curse of Kant. *Liberty* (August).

———. 2018. Is Naive Realism the Cure for Postmodernism? Review of Quee Nelson, *The Slightest Philosophy.* The London Libertarian. <https://la-articles.org.uk/la_blog.html>.

———. 2019. *The Mystery of Fascism: David Ramsay Steele's Greatest Hits.* St. Augustine's Press.

Strawson, P.F. 1966. *The Bounds of Sense: An Essay on Kant's Critique of Pure Reason.* Methuen.

Talmon, J.L. 1961. *The Origins of Totalitarian Democracy.* Praeger.

Vallicella, William F. 2016. A Note on Ayn Rand's Misunderstanding of Kant. Maverick Philosopher <https://maverickphilosopher.typepad.com/maverick_philosopher/2016/12/a-note-on-ayn-rands-misunderstanding-of-kant.html>.

Wächtershäuser, Günter. 1987. Light and Life: On the Nutritional Origins of Sensory Perception. In Radnitsky and Bartley 1987.

Walker, Jeff. 1999. *The Ayn Rand Cult.* Open Court.

Walsh, George V. 2000. Ayn Rand and the Metaphysics of Kant. *Journal of Ayn Rand Studies* 2:1 (Fall).

Origins of These Chapters

1. "The Conquistador with His Pants Down." I have given many talks to small groups of libertarians and others about the inferiority of psychodynamic therapy, and its Freudian roots. This piece appeared in 2013 as a chapter in the book *Therapy Breakthrough: Why Some Psychotherapies Work Better than Others*, which I wrote jointly with Michael R. Edelstein and Richard K. Kujoth. This is one of the chapters I wrote alone, though its content and its inclusion in the book were approved by my two co-authors.

2. "An Inconceivably Humble Defense of the Inconceivably Holy Book." This little piece is set around 110,000 years in the future. The world has awakened from more than 100,000 years of glaciation, the ice has melted, and civilization has begun again. The established religion has come to be based on an ancient book, believed to be handed down from before the world was frozen.

3. "Dexter the Busy Bee." A previously published piece in which I draw upon the TV show *Dexter* to explain something about Bernard Mandeville and his *Fable of the Bees*. This essay appeared as a chapter in *Dexter and Philosophy: Mind over Spatter* (2011), edited by Richard Greene, George A. Reisch, and Rachel Robison-Greene. After I wrote it, the *Dexter* seasons declined in quality, though still worth watching. Years later, in 2022, a final season of *Dexter* was produced. Although this started out quite well, the final episode was an artistic atrocity, with the characters all behaving wildly out of character in order to produce a particular ending which was required by the claustrophobic standards of ideological rectitude. No creative person, but only a studio executive, dictated that appalling ending. If by chance I ever meet up with that wretched apparatchik, his body parts will be consigned to six black Hefty bags.

4. "Some Second Thoughts on Atheism." I presented my arguments for atheism in *Atheism Explained: From Folly to Philosophy* (2008). This piece gives a few of my more recent reflections. I think of myself as a "naturally regular materialist," by contrast with the laxative implications of "eliminative materialism." I'm a pretty standard kind of Critical Rationalist, but I think Popper's biggest mistake is his mind-body dualism.

5. "Cold Comfort for Pacifists" (2018). A short review for *Reason* magazine of the book, *The Duty to Stand Aside*, about the 1942 dispute between George Orwell and Alex Comfort on whether to support Britain's war against Germany.

6. "Is It a Fact that Facts Don't Matter?" This is a previously published piece in which I criticize Scott Adams's claim that "facts don't matter" and that humans are ill-equipped to find the truth, with some attention to the rise of Donald Trump. It was written shortly before I arrived at the view that Trump, though admittedly not quite perfect, has to be supported by libertarians and by decent people, as the only political force willing and able to fight the psychotic Left and the pedophile ruling class. This piece appeared in *Scott Adams and Philosophy: A Hole in the Fabric of Reality* (2018), edited by Daniel Yim, Galen Foresman, and Robert Arp.

7. "Dr. Peterson! Clean Up Your Theory!" is addressed to the prophet of "Clean Up Your Room!" It appeared in the 2022 volume, *Jordan Peterson: Critical Responses*, edited by Sandra Woien, with the title, "Clean Up Your Theory!" It's the culmination of several talks and discussions. An early, very muddled approach is "Good and Bad in Jordan Peterson," still available on YouTube.

8. "Sam Harris and How to Spot Dangerous Ideas." Continuing my Old Atheist attack on the bigoted New Atheists, here I criticize Sam Harris on a number of points, most notably his claim that there is something inherent in Islam which causes it to promote suicide terrorism. I gave a version of this as a talk at the College of Complexes ("Good and Bad in Sam Harris"), available on YouTube. The piece as reprinted here appeared

in *Sam Harris: Critical Responses* (2023), edited by Sandra Woien, with the title, "Spotting Dangerous Ideas."

9. "Here's Why There Can Never Be a Marxist Revolution" (2021). In 1970 I was a convinced and dedicated believer in Marxian communism (which at that time I called "socialism"). I was suddenly confronted with the argument of Ludwig von Mises showing "socialism" to be "impossible." It took me more than a year, reading on the subject and arguing with friends and others, to feel that Mises was essentially right, and another year or two to become completely satisfied. The much-delayed result was my first book, *From Marx to Mises* (1992).

This talk was given at the College of Complexes and is available on YouTube, though I have expounded the basic ideas thousands of times. I have come to feel that preaching this message is my calling or destiny. I see *Jonah* as the all-time classic tale of a man with a calling. Like Jonah, I feel a bit let down that the world now seems to be repenting (from this particular intellectual sin), but unlike Jonah, I won't pout.

10. "The Five Times George Orwell Changed His Mind." This is the bare bones of a talk I have given numerous times, one time preserved on YouTube in 2017, another time at an Austrian Economics Research Conference at the Ludwig von Mises Institute in March 2021. It distils a few essential points from my 2017 book, *Orwell Your Orwell: A Worldview on the Slab*.

11. "Are Critical Rationalists Completely Out of Their Minds?" Jeffrey Huemer posted a piece on his blog seriously contending that we Popperians are all insane.

I first posted this reply to Huemer, on the Libertarian Alliance blog, the London Libertarian, on September 13th 2020. I added the few paragraphs about Duhem on September 25th. Since then I have made a few very slight changes of wording, in the interest of clarity.

12. "The Steele Effect: A New Explanation of the Flynn Effect." This appeared on Ray Percival's Enlightenment Defended Facebook page in September 2022.

I thought of this theory about twenty-five years ago, around the time our four exceptionally intelligent children had been born (in 1990, 1993, 1996, and 1998), all by c-section. I assumed that this idea would be obvious to anyone working in a related field, and would be well-known, at least as a hypothesis, perhaps abandoned for a reason I could not think of. Reading later references to the debate over the Flynn Effect made me realize that the possibility had, apparently, never been considered, or if once considered, had been forgotten. And so, after mulling it over some more, I banged out this little squib. The immodest title is an attempt to falsify Stigler's Law.

13. "Why Do We See Lysenko-Type Mass Delusions in Western Democracies?" How can we account for the collective craziness of the official response to the Covid virus? This piece gives my alternative to the highly popular but somewhat flawed theory of Mattias Desmet. It appeared in *Mattias Desmet: Critical Responses* (2024), edited by Ray Scott Percival.

14. "The Most Evil Man in History." Ayn Rand propounded the theory that all the twentieth century's totalitarian atrocities resulted from the philosophical ideas of Immanuel Kant. This Randist theory has some followers, especially prominent in libertarian circles, and many others have been influenced by it. I have refuted it many times, point by point, and my refutation has gotten better as I've learned more about the wonderful world of Kant. This piece incorporates segments of my previously published articles "Ayn Rand and the Curse of Kant" and "Is Naive Realism the Cure for Postmodernism?" as well as numerous talks I have given over the years.

INDEX